P9-BTO-636

DATE DUE

APR 0 4 2013	
APR 2 0 2015	
APR 1 8 2016	

BRODART, CO.   Cat. No. 23-221

Although she enjoyed only modest success during her lifetime, Kate Chopin is now recognised as a unique voice in American literature. Her seminal novel, *The Awakening*, published in 1899, explored new and startling territory and stunned readers with its frank depiction of the limits of marriage and motherhood. Chopin's aesthetic tastes and cultural influences were drawn from both the European and American traditions, and her manipulation of her 'foreignness' contributed to the composition of a complex voice that was strikingly different to that of her contemporaries. The essays in this Companion treat a wide range of Chopin's stories and novels, drawing her relationship with other writers, genres and literary developments, and pay close attention to the transatlantic dimension of her work. The result is a collection that brings a fresh perspective to Chopin's writing, one that will appeal to researchers and students of American, nineteenth-century and feminist literature.

THE CAMBRIDGE
COMPANION TO
KATE CHOPIN

EDITED BY
JANET BEER

CAMBRIDGE
UNIVERSITY PRESS

CAMBRIDGE UNIVERSITY PRESS

Cambridge, New York, Melbourne, Madrid, Cape Town, Singapore, São Paulo, Delhi

Cambridge University Press
The Edinburgh Building, Cambridge CB2 8RU, UK

Published in the United States of America by Cambridge University Press, New York

www.cambridge.org
Information on this title: www.cambridge.org/9780521709828

© Cambridge University Press 2008

This publication is in copyright. Subject to statutory exception
and to the provisions of relevant collective licensing agreements,
no reproduction of any part may take place without
the written permission of Cambridge University Press.

First published 2008

Printed in the United Kingdom at the University Press, Cambridge

A catalogue record for this publication is available from the British Library

ISBN 978-0-521-88344-3 hardback
ISBN 978-0-521-70982-8 paperback

Cambridge University Press has no responsibility for
the persistence or accuracy of URLs for external or
third-party internet websites referred to in this book,
and does not guarantee that any content on such
websites is, or will remain, accurate or appropriate.

ACC LIBRARY SERVICES AUSTIN, TX

CONTENTS

CONTRIBUTORS

JANET BEER is Vice Chancellor of Oxford Brookes University. She is the author of *Edith Wharton: Traveller in the Land of Letters* (1990), *Kate Chopin, Edith Wharton and Charlotte Perkins Gilman: Studies in Short Fiction* (1997), *Edith Wharton* (2002), and the co-editor of *Special Relationships: Anglo-American Antagonisms and Affinities, 1854–1936* (2002), *American Feminism: Key Source Documents 1848–1920* (2002), *The Awakening: A Sourcebook* (2004), *Lives of Victorian Literary Figures IV: Edith Wharton* (2006), *Edith Wharton's 'The House of Mirth'* (2007). She is currently working with Avril Horner on *Edith Wharton: Sex, Satire and the Older Woman*.

DONNA CAMPBELL is Associate Professor of English at Washington State University. She is the author of *Resisting Regionalism: Gender and Naturalism in American Fiction, 1885–1915* (1997), and her articles have appeared in *Studies in American Fiction*, *Legacy* and *American Literary Realism*. Recent publications include '"Where Are the Ladies?" Edith Wharton, Ellen Glasgow, and American Women Naturalists' (*Studies in American Naturalism*, 2006) and 'Howells's Untrustworthy Realist: Mary E. Wilkins Freeman' (*American Literary Realism*, 2006). Her current project is a study of American women writers of naturalism.

SUSAN CASTILLO is Harriet Beecher Stowe Professor of American Studies at King's College London. Her publications include *Colonial Encounters in New World Writing, 1500–1787: Performing America*; *Notes from the Periphery* (2006), *The Literatures of Colonial America* (2001) and several edited essay collections. She is Editor of the *Journal of American Studies* and is on the Executive Board of the International American Studies Association.

ANN HEILMANN is Professor of English at the University of Hull. The author of *New Woman Fiction* (2000) and *New Woman Strategies: Sarah Grand, Olive Schreiner and Mona Caird* (2004), and the General Editor of Routledge's History of Feminism series, she has published three essay collections, most recently *Metafiction and Metahistory in Contemporary Women's Writing* (2007, with Mark Llewellyn), and has co-edited four anthology sets, including *The Late-Victorian Marriage*

Question (1998). Her most recent publication is a five-volume scholarly edition of *The Collected Short Stories of George Moore* (2007, with Mark Llewellyn), of which she edited three volumes.

AVRIL HORNER is Professor of English at Kingston University, London. Her research interests focus on Gothic fiction and women's writing. She has co-authored many articles and books chapters with Sue Zlosnik, with whom she wrote *Daphne du Maurier: Writing, Identity and the Gothic Imagination* (1998) and *Landscapes of Desire: Metaphors in Modern Women's Fiction* (1990). Her most recent books are an edited collection entitled *European Gothic: A Spirited Exchange, 1760–1960* (2002) and (with Sue Zlosnik) *Gothic and the Comic Turn* (2005). She is currently working with Janet Beer on *Edith Wharton: Sex, Satire and the Older Woman*.

KATHERINE JOSLIN is Professor of English at Western Michigan University, specialising in American writers at the turn of the twentieth century. She has written *Jane Addams, A Writer's Life* (2004) and *Edith Wharton* (1991), and co-edited *Wretched Exotic: Essays on Edith Wharton in Europe* (1993) and *American Feminism: Key Source Documents, 1848–1920* (2002). Her essays consider Kate Chopin, Willa Cather, Theodore Dreiser, Charlotte Perkins Gilman and Edith Wharton, as well as Virginia Woolf and Émile Zola. She is currently completing a book about fashion in literature and is planning, as her next project, a literary biography of Theodore Roosevelt.

PAMELA KNIGHTS lectures in the Department of English Studies at Durham University. Her essay in this volume brings together her interests in American women's writing of the late nineteenth and early twentieth centuries, regional fictions and literature for children. She has published widely in these areas, including editing *The Awakening and Other Stories* (2000), novels by Edith Wharton and R. D. Blackmore's *Lorna Doone*. She is the co-author, with Janet Beer and Elizabeth Nolan, of *Edith Wharton's 'The House of Mirth'* and of the forthcoming *Cambridge Introduction to Edith Wharton*. She is currently Secretary to the Board of the International Research Society in Children's Literature and is editing the inaugural issues of the journal, *International Research in Children's Literature*.

BERNARD KOLOSKI is Emeritus Professor of English at Mansfield University of Pennsylvania. He has published articles about Kate Chopin in *American Literature*, *Studies in American Fiction* and *Louisiana Literature*, and has written several books. He edited the Modern Language Association's *Approaches to Teaching Chopin's 'The Awakening'* (1988), authored the Twayne volume *Kate Chopin: A Study of the Short Fiction* (1996) and edited two editions of Kate Chopin's work: *Bayou Folk* and *A Night in Acadie* (1999) and *At Fault* (2002). He is currently editing a volume about the Kate Chopin revival of the 1970s and 1980s.

ELIZABETH NOLAN lectures in the Department of English at Manchester Metropolitan University. She has co-edited *The Awakening: A Sourcebook* (2004), *The House of Mirth* (2005), the *Lives of Victorian Literary Figures IV: Edith Wharton* (2006) and *Edith Wharton's 'The House of Mirth'* (2007). She also works on women's war writings and women's periodicals of the early twentieth century.

HELEN TAYLOR is Professor of English at the University of Exeter. She is the author of *Gender, Race, and Region in the Writings of Grace King, Ruth McEnery Stuart, and Kate Chopin* (1989), *Scarlett's Women: Gone With the Wind and its Female Fans* (1989) and *Circling Dixie: Contemporary Southern Culture through a Transatlantic Lens* (2001), and is Co-editor of *Dixie Debates: Perspectives on Southern Cultures* (1996) and Editor of *The Daphne du Maurier Companion* (2007). She is writing a book about transatlantic representations of New Orleans' prostitution district, Storyville.

EMILY TOTH is Professor of English and Women's Studies at Louisiana State University and is the author or editor of ten published books, including *Ms. Mentor's Impeccable Advice for Women in Academia* (1997); *Inside Peyton Place: The Life of Grace Metalious* (1981) and five books related to Kate Chopin. These include two biographies – *Kate Chopin* (1990) and *Unveiling Kate Chopin* (1999); two collections of Chopin's private writings – *A Kate Chopin Miscellany* (1979) and *Kate Chopin's Private Papers* (1998) and an edition of her last, unpublished short story collection *A Vocation and a Voice* (1991).

MICHAEL WORTON is Vice-Provost and Fielden Professor of French Language and Literature at University College London. He has written extensively on modern French literature and on issues in critical theory and gender theory. His publications include *Textuality and Sexuality: Reading Theories and Practices*, co-edited with Judith Still (1993), *Michel Tournier* (1995) and *Typical Men* (2001; catalogue of the exhibition *Typical Men: Recent Photography of the Male Body by Men*, co-curated with Judith Still; Nottingham, Colchester and Glasgow, 3 March 2001–27 January 2002), *Women's Writing in Contemporary France: New Writers, New Literatures in the 1990s*, co-edited with Gill Rye (2002), and *National Healths: Gender, Sexuality and Health in a Cross-Cultural Context*, co-edited with Nana Wilson-Tagoe (2004). He is also the author of sixty articles and chapters in books on modern European and American literature.

KATE CHOPIN CHRONOLOGY

1850   Born Catherine O'Flaherty, 8 February in St Louis, Missouri to Thomas O'Flaherty, an Irish immigrant, and Eliza Faris, a French-Creole. Their home is at Eighth Street.

1855   Kate enrols at the Academy of the Sacred Heart. Her father, Thomas O'Flaherty, dies in a railway accident.

1863   Her great-grandmother, Victorie Verdon Charleville, and her half-brother George, a Confederate soldier, both die.

1865   The family moves to 1118 St Ange Avenue. Kate attends the Academy of the Visitation but then re-enrols at the Sacred Heart Academy.

1868   Kate graduates from the Sacred Heart Academy. She enters into St Louis society as a debutante.

1869   She writes the short story 'Emancipation: A Life Fable' (unpublished).

1870   Kate marries Oscar Chopin, a cotton trader and the son of a plantation owner. The Chopins embark on a three-month honeymoon tour of Europe, spending time in Germany, Switzerland and France. They return and set up home in New Orleans.

1871–8 The Chopins have five sons: Jean Baptiste (1871), Oscar Charles (1873), George Francis (1874), Frederick (1876), Felix Andrew (1878).

1873   Kate's brother Thomas dies in a buggy accident.

1879   Following the failure of Oscar's cotton business, the family moves to Cloutierville, a rural area of Louisiana. Kate's daughter, Lélia, is born.

1882   Oscar Chopin dies.

1883–4   Kate Chopin likely to have been in a relationship with Albert Sampite.

1884   Kate Chopin returns to live at St Ange Avenue, St Louis.

1885   Death of mother, Eliza O'Flaherty.

1889   She publishes her first literary work, a poem, 'If It Might Be'. Her first short story, 'A Point at Issue!', is published in the *St Louis Post-Dispatch*. She begins work on her first novel, *At Fault*.

1890   Publication of *At Fault*, at Chopin's own expense.

1894   Publication of *Bayou Folk*, a collection of short stories. *Vogue* publishes 'Dream of an Hour' ('The Story of an Hour').

1895   A collection of Guy de Maupassant translations by Chopin is rejected by the publisher Houghton, Mifflin.

1897   Publication of second collection of stories, *A Night in Acadie*. Kate's grandmother, Athénaise Charleville Faris, dies.

1899   *The Awakening* is published to mixed reviews.

1900   The publisher Herbert S. Stone declines to publish the collection of stories, *A Vocation and a Voice*.

1902   Kate's last published piece of work, a story, 'Polly', appears in *Youth's Companion*.

1904   Kate Chopin dies in St Louis on 22 August.

JANET BEER

Introduction

Kate Chopin (1850–1904) first published a story, 'Wiser than a God', in the *Philadelphia Music Journal* in 1889; her last, 'Polly's Opportunity', appeared in the *Youth's Companion* in 1902. The thirteen years in between marked a hugely productive career as a writer, primarily of short stories, with a novel at the beginning and at the end of the 1890s; an earlier novel, *Young Dr. Gosse*, she seems to have destroyed. Chopin did not work seriously at her fiction until she was a widow and had returned to her birthplace, St Louis, Missouri, to live. During her brief married life (although it was long enough for her to produce six children), she lived in Louisiana, first in New Orleans and then in Cloutierville, and it is in this southern state, in every way more French than American in its heritage and culture, that she set most of her stories and both her novels. Indeed, the publisher's advertisement for her first collection of short stories, *Bayou Folk*, in 1894, drew attention to the fact that Chopin's characters were 'semi-aliens' and featured in narratives 'quite unlike most American tales'.[1]

Chopin's work was published in the leading magazines of her day; she wrote for a variety of different audiences, including children, but she also found ways and exercised the means to place stories which were often daring in terms of their subject matter and expression. She was expert in her manipulation of both form and language so as to position herself to write about issues which she found compelling – issues which were often controversial. Commentators on her work are always sensitive to the level of Chopin's awareness of the editorial and critical reception of her writing in turn-of-the-century America. It is clear that the knowledge she had of the literary marketplace operated alongside a determination to write about difficult subjects. Working, as she did, in a particular sector of the literary world, writing mainly short stories for magazines, she became adept at finding ways to accommodate the tastes and idiosyncrasies of the editors without too much compromise on her part.

When Chopin published her novel, *The Awakening*, however, she came under a different kind of scrutiny. Chopin's biographer, Emily Toth, has dealt effectively with the overstatement of the detrimental effects that the negative reviews of the novel may have had on Chopin,[2] but it seems highly unlikely that Chopin thought that the subject matter of her novel would be uncontentious. Her voice was often a transgressive voice; some of her stories were not deemed fit to print, even by the most liberal of magazine editors, and others she did not attempt to place in the public domain – the most famous of these being the story of joyful adulterous sex, 'The Storm', written in 1898. The majority of her tales, however, did see the light of day and were published in magazines such as *Vogue*, *Harper's*, *Century*, *Atlantic Monthly*, *Two Tales*, *Youth's Companion* and a variety of St Louis and New Orleans periodicals and newspapers, as detailed by Bernard Koloski in his essay here, '*The Awakening*: The First Hundred Years'. Chopin's writing brought her in much-needed income, and she kept detailed records of submissions and money earned. She wrote for a living but, as Pamela Knights has made clear: 'although she often yielded to the compromises required for publication, she would also defend her artistry, and was prepared to resist editorial suggestion'.[3]

One of the features of Kate Chopin's short stories and novels is that family members appear and reappear, the same characters are represented across a variety of different narratives, sometimes taking the main stage, as Tonie Bocaze does in the story 'At Chênière Caminada', written in 1893, and sometimes a small or even offstage part as he does in *The Awakening*, whispering with Robert Lebrun whilst Edna sleeps in his mother's house. Alcée Laballière appears in 'Croque-Mitaine', on his way to a ball; in 'At the 'Cadian Ball' he attends, unsurprisingly, a ball but becomes engaged to a woman who does not dance, and in 'The Storm', he makes passionate, adulterous love to a woman with whom he danced but failed to marry. His brother Alphonse plays a much less well-tempered role in the story, 'In and Out of Old Natchitoches' but also gets the girl in the end.

In this introductory essay to the *Companion*, I would like to discuss briefly the appearances and reappearances of another family, the Santiens, in order to say something about Chopin's narrative strategies, particularly in her short stories, before talking about the essays that feature in this collection. I have already mentioned Chopin's willingness as an artist to engage with difficult issues. One of the ways in which she achieves this is by fracturing what might otherwise be larger narratives and allowing information to seep out from the edges of the stories. For instance, she does not create the conventional family saga she could have written with the Santien family at its heart; instead, she has them play very particular roles in a number of tales, tales in which our attention is diverted by the lives of others: in two cases towards the completion of a conventional romance, and in one to the end of a romance. Chopin makes the building up of information about the family a privilege for the dedicated reader, weaving a range of references and a cast of characters across story and, in the case of the Santiens, story/novel boundaries, creating a momentum that can travel across narratives. There is no doubt that Chopin had a readership that made connections; for instance, the exploits of the Santien brothers had been sufficiently noticed for Houghton, Mifflin, the publishers of Chopin's volume of short stories, *Bayou Folk* (1894) to mention the fact that the collection would 'bring the three "Santien boys" together'[4] as a desirable feature.

The three Santiens, not permitted by Chopin's splintering of their family story to be the heroes of a saga of the vanquished South as displaced plantation owners, feature in a number of narratives but always as agents of change in women's lives. Grégoire liberates an abused wife in the story 'In Sabine' and courts and loses a woman in the novel, *At Fault*; Placide honourably frees his fiancée from her promise to marry him by feigning dishonourable behaviour in 'A No-Account Creole'; and Hector refuses to become involved with Suzanne St Denys Godolph in 'In and Out of Old Natchitoches' and so effectively drives her into the arms of Alphonse Laballière. In all the stories where they appear, Chopin laces an atmosphere of danger around the Santien boys, whether as a result of their violent behaviour – as with Grégoire, who commits murder and Placide, who threatens murder – or their socially unacceptable behaviour – as with the smooth-talking Hector: 'the most notorious gambler in New Orleans'.[5] Whilst the women with whom they are associated all change their lives – either through marriage or an escape from marriage – and the stories ostensibly centre on that change, the Santien men are portrayed in ways that are distinct and different to the women and the men they marry or unmarry. They bob and weave through the landscapes they variously inhabit in Louisiana and Texas, and their reputations – chiefly as hell-raisers – do not so much follow as precede them.

The over-arching narrative of the three short stories in which they appear and *At Fault* can be considered as both a counterpoint to the manner in which Chopin tells women's stories and also as yet another strategy for undermining the conventional. Chopin's work is rightly celebrated for its lambent, compelling portraiture of women: women in crisis, women at moments of disillusion or awakening, women at fault and women exonerated. What is less often discussed is the manner in which she portrays men at moments of destiny, the often subtly structured narratives in which the lives of men are shown in the process of vast and significant change. The Santien narratives are stories of men displaced by war and economic slump, of failed southern aristocrats who are in the process of falling out of the society in which they were born, living by a code which is no longer appropriate or perhaps even legal, galloping down the road to their final destruction. The three brothers are epigones; they are ultimately irrelevant to the economic and social life of the South, they are not heroic, except in small acts of kindness, and are actually interesting to Chopin because they are doomed.

In plot terms, Chopin is able to make very powerful use of the outsider status of the ill-fated brothers: Grégoire is travelling away from his failed relationship with Melicent in *At Fault* towards his pointless death in a drunken confrontation in Cornstalk, Texas when he pauses to liberate 'Tite Reine in the story, 'In Sabine'; and Placide Santien in 'A No-Account Creole' is very clearly the going not the coming man. Chopin begins the latter story with a beautifully judged portrait of Placide's rival, the 'cool and clear'-headed Wallace Offdean. Characterised as 'temperate', 'moderate' and 'healthy' and at a 'turning-point in his life' (81) he is set up in simple opposition to the last remaining Santien on Red River, the 'No-Account Creole' of the title, busy squandering his many talents along with his patrimony but retaining his honour, or at least his own notion of his honour. Chopin treats Offdean throughout in a tone of light irony, gently mocking his intention to 'banish [Euphrasie] from his thoughts' (93) and to 'set about forgetting her' (96) as if it could be a matter of simple determination. Placide, however, is characterised in quite a different manner; stories are told about him, by La Chatte, for instance, but he is communicated largely through his own action or inaction. Chopin describes the manner of his leaving the plantation after supper, justifying the time of departure in some detail:

> He would not wait until morning, for the moon would be rising about midnight, and he knew the road as well by night as by day. He knew just where the best fords were across the bayous, and the safest paths across the hills. He knew for a certainty whose plantations he might traverse, and whose fences he might derail.

She then follows this treatment of his journey plan with a sentence that undoes, with devastating effect, the rational Placide: 'But, for that matter, he would derail what he liked, and cross where he pleased' (88). This method of characterisation or narrative momentum is one of Chopin's most effective techniques: the predictable, reasonable explanation, which might be offered as a justification or a defence, is proffered and then completely undermined by a swift assault on the carefully accumulated evidence, which then communicates an essential truth about the situation. She does this in the short short story 'Doctor Chevalier's Lie' where the extreme economy of language does not preclude the rise and subsequent fall of the expected in the contradictions that follow:

> with a dead girl stretched somewhere, as this one was. And yet it was not the same. Certainly she was dead: there was the hole in the temple where she had

sent the bullet through. Yet it was different. Other such faces had been unfamiliar to him, except in so far as they bore the common stamp of death. This one was not. (147)

Just as this tells us much about Dr Chevalier: that he was used to reacting to the screams that arose in the night from the red-light district, that he was accustomed to clearing up after the suicides of prostitutes, and also that this was a girl he knew, so the apparently incidental explanation of Placide's decision to cut short his visit to Euphrasie tells us of his stubbornness, yes, but also of his deep, intimate knowledge of the landscape, his relationships with his neighbours and, finally, and devastatingly, of his arrogance and his wilfulness.

We are also invited in this story to take note of the fact that Placide has little time for his brother, Hector, and the manner in which this is conveyed is such that it exists in ambiguity in this narrative but can be explained by a reading of 'In and Out of Old Natchitoches': 'Placide was not very well acquainted with the city [. . .] His brother Hector, who lived in some obscure corner of the town, would willingly have made his knowledge a more intimate one; but Placide did not choose to learn the lessons that Hector was ready to teach' (93). We learn in the subsequent story that Hector earns a living from gambling and that his sexuality is something of an enigma, either of which explanation might suffice as a reason why Placide would want to keep Euphrasie away from him; however, it is also perfectly possible to read it as further evidence of Placide's refusal to take advice or, indeed, to learn. Chopin may mock Offdean gently throughout the story, but his thoughts and actions do communicate a sense of process and progress, an engagement with life. In her portrait of Placide, she is telling a determinist tale: in spite of his apparent wilfulness, the majority of his actions are predictable, not necessarily by him but by others who know how his story goes. Euphrasie knows his mind before he does, even Offdean is able to calculate what his reactions will be and so is able to save himself from being shot in the back; the double bluff is in the hands of men educated beyond 'the state of mutiny and revolt' (85) inhabited by the brothers. The narratives of all the Santiens are known in advance: Grégoire, it is widely acknowledged by all in *At Fault*, is heading for a violent death, and that destiny is fulfilled; Hector arouses such moral outrage in the eyes of most who behold him, not least Laballière, that he cannot be long for the world; and Placide, afraid of nothing except learning something, most especially from an outsider, will live an even more itinerant life, failing to earn a steady living or form enduring relationships because of the handicap of being a 'Santien always, with the best blood in the country running in his veins' (84).

In the story 'In and Out of Old Natchitoches', Suzanne St Denys Godolph's childhood intimacy with Hector Santien is quickly shown to be irretrievable because of the new relationship they must form in the public spaces of the city. She is, at first, like Athénaïse, in the story that bears her name, a refugee from the attentions of a decent but rough-speaking country landowner, another woman who must come to the city in order to be shown that her destiny lies in marriage and motherhood in the country. Hector in his guise as Deroustan, an apparently notorious gambler, is recognisably an intimate of the homosocial city; he is an unabashed dandy, evasive and non-committal in the face of Suzanne's affection for him. Suzanne invites him to be her suitor or even her lover by trying to incite him to walk out with her in spite of advice she has received not to be seen with him. He concedes to the accusation that such an outing would be inappropriate but refuses to put into words the reasons why. Chopin, however, gives us a choice of answers. Like his brothers, he is an outsider, but it may not be because of the way in which he earns his living, rather because of his sexuality: 'posed' on the streets of New Orleans, he is 'a fashion-plate' who never looks at 'the women who passed by' (266). Suzanne's attempt to goad him into direct expression of the possible signification of their being seen on the street together receives a physical rebuff with a stripped-down unsexed rose, a flower with which he stains her face, reddening her skin with the blush that would, necessarily, arise if her reputation were to be similarly stained by a public intimacy with him; the sweeping of her face with the rose is a substitute for that which 'a lover might have done with his lips'. His solution to the problem of her feelings for him is to send her away whilst he returns to the decadence of life as a 'bon à rien' (265). As in 'A No-Account Creole', the portrait of the Santien in question is not ironised, unlike Alphonse Laballière, whose hot temper, actions and reactions are mocked. Instead, Hector is spoken of and described as finished, 'his attire was faultless', the maintenance of his person clearly being of more interest to him than the maintenance of the Santien plantation which, as we know from Grégoire in *At Fault*: 'Hec, he took charge the firs' year an' run it in debt' (751).

Grégoire is more in the mould of Placide than Hector, but, still, his own story is done before it begins. There is no family life he cares to retrieve, the discipline of a job has no effect: his 'duty' on his Aunt's plantation 'was comprehended in doing as he was bid, qualified by a propensity for doing as he liked' (742). As with Placide, the stories told about him by the black workers testify to a life of hell-raising, and his reputation is enough to make the drink-sodden Bud Aiken cheer up: 'his face brightened at the prospect before him of enjoying the society of one of the Santien boys' (327). However, that reputation is also enough to make 'Tite Reine believe that she has at last found the means to escape from an abusive marriage. This is the paradox of the Santien narratives: Chopin is at her most naturalistic in the depiction of the brothers, that is, at her most predetermined and least ambiguous in their outcomes as individuals, but she employs them as agents of change in the lives of others and as a means to produce indeterminacy and ambiguity. As Pamela Knights notes in her essay, Chopin threads the appearance and agency of children through her narratives in very particular ways: 'Even where a younger character's story is not the primary strand, thinking about the children can highlight dominant strands of the text – the discourses of race and region, sociology or natural science'. The Santien boys serve something of the same purpose; the over-arching narrative is one of decay and despair, of decadence and superannuation, of the pre-eminent 'blood in the country' now become at best counter-cultural and, at worst, murderous, but the incidents and events – which they trigger – change other lives and draw attention to instances of both social good and social evil. The Santiens move, across the narratives, from *seigneur* to outlaw. They all position themselves against the Zeitgeist, but only Hector is rendered immune to the power of insult, being doubly estranged from the accepted standards – sexual and professional – whereas his brothers are still in the clutches of their own dying notion of honour, a death that Chopin refuses to mourn but nonetheless commemorates.

The essays in this collection range over Chopin's stories and novels and draw her into relationship with other writers, literary developments, genres and critical perspectives and pay particularly serious attention to the transatlantic dimensions of her work. Her aesthetic tastes and influences, her language, her culture, her manipulation of her 'foreignness' for her principally North American audience – all these contribute to the composition of the unique voice that is Chopin's. Of the four critics identified by Emily Toth as foremost in the rebuilding of Kate Chopin's literary reputation after more or less fifty years in the doldrums, three are represented in this collection: Toth herself, Bernard Koloski and Helen Taylor, who, with Per Seyersted, 'resurrected [Chopin's] reputation, and she is now solidly in the American literary canon'.

Toth's biographical essay provides a confident but also playful account of Chopin's history, linking incidents and episodes in Chopin's life with individual stories and life writings. Toth also provokes us with a number of speculations about periods of silence – mainly during the period of Chopin's married life in Louisiana – and brings the writer into new contiguities with other artists, editors and commentators. One of Toth's emphases here is on the importance of Chopin's relationships with women and also the fact that she had had, unlike many women writers, a serious education: whilst the female members of Chopin's extended family were an important influence on her, so were the Sisters of the Sacred Heart. As Toth says: 'The Sacred Heart nuns taught needlework, but cared much more about French, history, and laboratory work in science (extremely rare for young girls). Their minds were to be stretched, and Kate O'Flaherty had over a decade with the Sacred Heart nuns.'

Donna Campbell, in her 'At Fault: A reappraisal of Kate Chopin's other novel', makes a serious case for a reconsideration of the text as a social-problem novel, a sub-set of the nineteenth-century realist tradition, practised most famously by Charles Dickens and Mrs Gaskell in England and in America by Rebecca Harding Davis. Campbell explores the extensive structural doubling in the novel: the relationship between David and Thérèse being echoed by that between Grégoire and Melicent; and domestic issues, notably divorce and alcoholism, being considered alongside social and economic issues, for example, the industrialisation of the South and the concomitant complexities of race and power relations. As she says, 'Like many social-problem novels, At Fault is at heart a story about change and resistance to change, as an idea worked out on the regional and on the individual level.' At the outset of Chopin's writing career, Campbell argues, having At Fault published at her own expense was 'her bid to be considered as a serious writer' who could be compared to novelists like W.D. Howells, the dominant American realist writer of his generation and someone Chopin admired. The multiple plotting, the inclusion of a wide range of issues, settings and characters allows Chopin to crowd the text with controversial issues so that, for instance, the arson plot, as Campbell says: 'equates white violence toward blacks with the social problem novel's cycle of violence and retaliation between industrial workers and managers', and in so doing Chopin provides a distinct and different account of the complex of relationships that lie simmering under any traditionally rendered picture of unthinking African-American fealty and obeisance.

'Kate Chopin and the subject of childhood' by Pamela Knights provokes us to look at children as both audience and subject in Chopin's writing, opening with the salutary reminder that the language used against Chopin in reviews of The Awakening emphasised its unsuitability for the young and also, perhaps, suggested that in writing such a novel Chopin had in some way betrayed her proper audience. Knights provides a detailed context in which to place Chopin's engagement with the literary marketplace (specifically with those periodicals aimed at young persons), her portrayal of children as individuals and her structural use of children in the short stories and in The Awakening. The 'complex and multiple discourses' which were, in the period, competing to inscribe what might constitute childhood are clearly and fully drawn by Knights, as are contiguities and continuities between Chopin's work and that of Louisa May Alcott and Frances Hodgson Burnett. The argument is clearly made that Chopin maintains a delicate balance between a focus on children as readers, children as subjects and children as the means by which to progress a theme in story or novel, such as racial exploitation or male economic domination. Knights discusses the tension between the structural and thematic claims of the child in Chopin's work whilst also providing a substantial picture of the complications of the social construction of the child as audience.

Susan Castillo's essay, 'Race and ethnicity in Kate Chopin's fiction', places Chopin's work in the context of the unique social and linguistic environment that was late-nineteenth-century Louisiana. She traces the history of settlement and provides an illuminating account of the many 'cultures, languages, skin colours, and ethnic affiliations' that went to make up the urban and rural communities in which Chopin set her fictions. Focusing her discussion on the novel *At Fault* and on selected short stories from *Bayou Folk*, Castillo illuminates the conditions of existence and the terms of Chopin's engagement with her subjects, for those living under slavery and for those in post-bellum Louisiana, paying particular attention to the position of black women. Castillo takes Chopin's problematisation of racial categorisation into a discussion of the portrayal of 'free people of colour, who in the ante-bellum period often owned slaves themselves' but who nonetheless occupy segregated space, and also examines the stories which show Chopin rebutting 'the objectification of Cajuns that was characteristic not only of much local colour writing, but also of its reception by the eastern critical establishment'.

'Kate Chopin on fashion in a Darwinian world' is Katherine Joslin's wry look at Chopin's use of fashion to signal not only the exigencies of climate and location but also the subtle and not-so-subtle nuances of class, status, gender, ethnicity and morality. Linking her discussion of the meaning of dress in Chopin's writing with the influence and effect of the social and natural scientists on her fiction, Joslin looks at the points at which flesh meets fabric, at the suggestiveness of the clothed as opposed to the unclothed, moving from the unleashing of a feast of sensual pleasures and personal gratification simply by the donning of 'A Pair of Silk Stockings', to a discussion of the later stories where 'The fashion in these tales is minimal, suggesting the naked animal beneath the social fabric.' Joslin, like Toth, emphasises the fact that Chopin was prepared to engage with complex scientific thinkers, and she makes a detailed analysis of the points of contiguity between the ideas of Edvard Westermarck and Kate Chopin's style and substance, focusing particularly on his deliberations on promiscuity, on the limits of freedom for the individual, on divorce and suicide and on fashion.

In '*The Awakening* and New Woman fiction', Ann Heilmann positions the novel and its protagonist in a complex of relationships: with the Anglo-American fiction of the New Woman; with French literature – in particular,

Guy de Maupassant, Madame de Staël and George Sand; with the male-authored heroines of the European adultery novel as well as with sensation novelists such as Louisa May Alcott, Mary Braddon and Wilkie Collins, who 'created strong-willed, single-minded, and resourceful heroines'. Heilmann explores the manner in which controversial and often unpalatable subjects were treated by the sensation writers, providing an overview of the way in which shocking plot elements were used to explore woman-centred themes such as 'the social construction of gender, the sexual exploitation of women, the perils of marriage'. The essay reveals *The Awakening* to be part of a nexus of thematic concerns across genres, gender and continents, focusing principally on a continuum of cultures where 'married women held no legal rights over their bodies' but where Chopin, exceptionally, 'hazarded openly to explore women's sexual desire'.

Michael Worton's 'Reading Kate Chopin through contemporary French feminist theory' brings a fresh critical perspective to an understanding of her work, shifting our attention to a reader-centred focus that illuminates the fiction through recent French feminist theory. Whilst Worton emphasises the 'kaleidoscopic' capacity of Chopin's writing – her authority in a range of languages, themes, genres, environments – he is clear that she goes beyond the realisation of what constitutes the authentic in the lives of women, to 'foreground the importance of the relational', here privileged in his reading. He discusses, in particular, the intimacies between women that Chopin portrays and the differences between male and female social and homo-social interactions, asserting that 'Her work is less a manifesto of emancipation than a multi-faceted exposition of quests for enduring relationships.'

In her essay '*The Awakening* as literary innovation: Chopin, Maupassant and the evolution of genre', Elizabeth Nolan reorientates the angle of the discussion of Chopin's iconoclastic reputation from the subject matter of her writing into a consideration of the effect her experimentation with genre may have had upon her critical reception. Nolan positions Chopin on the 'cusp' of modernity but also as uniquely placed at an intersection of European and American literary traditions and influences. She re-examines the extent and nature of the debt Chopin owed to Maupassant in particular and reinvigorates the discussion by looking at points of differentiation and innovation in her work. As Nolan says, the debate about Chopin's work is complex and vibrant: 'Now, her writing is quite properly considered in terms of its sophisticated engagements with romanticism, transcendentalism, literary realism, naturalism and New Woman fiction and as anticipating the concerns of feminism and literary modernism.'

Avril Horner, in her 'Kate Chopin, choice and modernism', seizes that challenge, inviting us to examine the 'choice of narratives' Chopin offers. She outlines the range of possible approaches to reading the fiction: from the Darwinian, through the transcendent, the romantic, the Victorian 'angel in the house', the gendered to the economic; arguing that all or none of these are valuable in reading Chopin and that her work 'anticipated the later critical insight that plurality offers a healthy antidote to dominant ideologies'. The complex balance of ambiguity, conflict and uncertainty in Chopin's fiction is, Horner says, proto-modernist in its technique and content; the dialogue between alternative 'grand narratives' is made explicit in stories like 'Two Portraits', and the endings of many of her stories offer no ease or comfort in terms of resolution. Horner concludes that the work of Chopin, particularly in *The Awakening*, asserts its modernity in pluralism, anticipating, through use of 'metafictional devices', the multivalency of twentieth-century writing as practised by Woolf, Joyce, Lawrence and Mansfield in particular.

Helen Taylor's essay '"The perfume of the past": Kate Chopin and post-colonial New Orleans' discusses in detail the nature of Chopin's rendition of the complexities of the French culture of Louisiana. Chopin situates the French-speaking region through, as Taylor says, 'offering multiple perspectives on fin-de-siècle issues of gender, ethnicity and language' in the particular conditions of the post-bellum south. Chopin is shown to be engaged in constructing a series of dialectical relationships – for example, illustrating the continuities and contiguities between Paris and New Orleans as well as the contrast between life in the city and life in the rural community of Red River – whilst complicating her readers' responses even further by her imaginative engagement with the mixture to be found in both country and city and in different social classes of 'Catholic/Protestant, Native American/French/ Spanish/African American/English cultures'. Finally, Taylor suggests that *The Awakening* marks a leap of confidence for Chopin as she moves from the creation of fiction designed to explain French Louisiana culture towards a critique of the insularity and ultimate irrelevance of Creole society.

As Bernard Koloski asserts in his authoritative overview of the critical reception of Kate Chopin in '*The Awakening*: the first 100 years', she has been served well – especially latterly – by her biographers. He is clear about the huge credit that Per Seyersted and Emily Toth are due both for their scholarship and their critical acuity, but he also reminds us of the good and important reasons for reviewing the work of Daniel Rankin. Whilst Rankin's judgements were inevitably circumscribed by the tenets of his faith, he was in no doubt about Chopin's importance as an artist – as long as *The Awakening* was excepted from any positive comment – and had, as Koloski reminds us: 'access to Kate Chopin's children, relatives, friends, and at least one of her publishers'. Rankin provided information and leads that Toth, in particular, was able to follow up in her tireless quest to produce the fullest possible biography of Chopin. Koloski begins his essay with a reminder that there are differences between the critical history of *The Awakening* and that of the short stories which were not only published in a range of prestigious journals in her lifetime but also continued to be anthologised after her death. He amply demonstrates the range and scope of critical approaches to Chopin's work and the many themes and topics which critics have treated, and he is generous in his assessment of the impact, in particular, of Seyersted's work in locating Chopin's fiction in the context of women's writing, European literature and thought, and American contemporary writing, whilst recognising the capacity she had to be a southern writer who had a global view and reach. Koloski also gives an account of the nature and extent of Emily Toth's role in the establishment and promotion of Chopin studies, studies which are vibrant and, as this volume demonstrates, in ceaseless renewal.

NOTES

1. Emily Toth, *Kate Chopin* (London: Century, 1990), 223.
2. Toth, *Kate Chopin*, 368.
3. Kate Chopin, *The Awakening and Other Stories*, ed. Pamela Knights (Oxford: Oxford University Press, 2000), xvi.
4. Letter to Kate Chopin from Houghton, Mifflin Co., 19 December 1893, reprinted in Per Seyersted and Emily Toth (eds.), *A Kate Chopin Miscellany* (Oslo and Natchitoches, La.: Universiteitsforlaget and Northwestern State University Press of Louisiana, 1969), 110.
5. Kate Chopin, *The Complete Works of Kate Chopin*, 2 vols, ed. Per Seyersted (Baton Rouge, La.: Louisiana State University Press, 1969), 267. All references to Chopin's fiction throughout the volume, unless otherwise stated, are to this edition, and the page numbers are given in the body of the text.

I

EMILY TOTH

What we do and don't know about Kate Chopin's life

An anonymous newspaper friend once called Kate Chopin 'a rogue in porcelain, flashing her witty, provocative and advanced opinions right into the face of Philistia'.[1] Others noted Chopin's quiet manner and her gift for saying 'so many good and witty things'.[2] She possessed 'every grace and talent essential to the maintenance of a brilliant social circle'.[3] She was wise and cosmopolitan and did not make moral judgements. Nor did she force her own children, five sons and a daughter, to leave home or get jobs, and only one was married before his mother died at fifty-four. She deliberately kept a condemned book, Thomas Hardy's *Jude the Obscure*, on her parlour table so that young visitors would peruse it out of curiosity and discover that it was 'unpardonably dull; and immoral, chiefly because it is not true' (714).

Real life and mixed emotions were much more interesting to her than Hardy's melancholy story. According to her daughter, Chopin had a 'habit of looking on the amusing side of everything', but also 'rather a sad nature'.[4] She knew that life has both beauty and brutality – and she also knew how to keep secrets.

The facts of Kate O'Flaherty Chopin's life are well known. Although her tombstone lists her birthdate as 1851, her baptismal record shows that she was born on 8 February 1850, in St Louis, Missouri. She was the second child and first daughter of Eliza Faris O'Flaherty, twenty-two, whose husband was Thomas O'Flaherty, forty-five, an Irish immigrant and wealthy businessman who owned four household slaves. Kate had an older brother, an older half-brother and two little sisters who died young, which may be why, at five, she was sent to boarding school at the Sacred Heart Academy.

Two months later, her father was killed in a train accident, Kate was brought home, and her grandmother and great-grandmother moved in – making three generations of women who were widowed young and never remarried. Kate O'Flaherty grew up in a matriarchy, where women handled their own money and made their own decisions, as did the nuns at the Sacred Heart Academy, where she returned two years later. She was sixteen before she ever lived with a married couple again (an aunt and uncle), and so she had little opportunity to form traditional notions about marriage and submissive wives. When she married Oscar Chopin on 9 June 1870, she started off on their European honeymoon with a clean slate and an open mind.

The Chopins settled in New Orleans, where Oscar was a cotton factor (the middle man between growers and buyers). Within nine years, Kate had given birth to six children, the last in Cloutierville ('Cloochy-ville') in north Louisiana, where the family moved when Oscar's business failed. In that small village, Kate Chopin entertained and annoyed local people with her flamboyant fashions and brusque urban manners. Oscar was a local favourite, but when he died of malaria on 10 December 1882, $12,000 in debt, Kate was left without his social protection. She paid off the debts, had a scandalous romance with a local married planter, Albert Sampite ('Sam-pi-TAY'), and quickly moved back to her mother's home in St Louis in 1884 – just a year before her mother died of cancer.

Her doctor, seeing her deep grief, suggested that she try writing, and, by 1890, Chopin had become St Louis' first woman professional writer. Eventually she published two novels (*At Fault* and *The Awakening*) and two collections of short stories (*Bayou Folk* and *A Night in Acadie*), while producing several dozen other pieces, including short stories, essays, poems, translations, one play and one polka.

The Awakening, though, received mixed to hostile reviews, at a time when Chopin's health was deteriorating. Within a few years, she also became the caregiver for her eldest son. His wife had died in childbirth, sending him into a nervous breakdown from which he never fully recovered. Chopin rallied to enjoy the St Louis World's Fair, but on one very hot day she had a cerebral haemorrhage and died on 22 August 1904.

Outside of Louisiana, she was mostly forgotten for half a century, until Per Seyersted, a Norwegian graduate student studying in the USA, rediscovered her and promoted her work. Other dissertation writers and scholars, among them Bernard Koloski, Helen Taylor and Emily Toth, resurrected her reputation, and she is now solidly in the American literary canon. Yet, there are still many mysteries about her life. Chopin's first biographer, Daniel Rankin, completed his work twenty-eight years after her death when many people who had known her were still alive, but he relied too heavily on Chopin's sister-in-law, Fannie Hertzog Chopin, who was, by then, losing her memory. Rankin was also a priest, and people are reluctant to share gossipy titbits with the clergy.[5]

Seyersted interviewed whomever he could find by the mid 1960s and got some recollections of the Chopins' jolly marriage during their New Orleans years (1870–9). But he also could not, or perhaps would not, ask impertinent questions. In the 1960s, publishing, too, was more restricted than it is today. When Seyersted discovered Chopin's 'The Storm' in her 1894 diary and wanted to publish it in the *Missouri Historical Society Bulletin*, he was told he could not do so. It was too erotic, too explicit.[6] Now, of course, it is reprinted everywhere, and Kate Chopin is viewed as a pioneering writer about sex.

But, like Edna in *The Awakening*, Chopin seems to have lived with an 'outward existence which conforms', but with an 'inward life which questions' (893). Her first two biographers concentrated on the men in her life and did not see how deeply Kate Chopin was connected with women, nor how outside the mainstream she truly was. In *The Awakening*, for instance, the most beautiful woman is the bountifully pregnant Madonna figure Adele Ratignolle – even though, in real life, a pregnant woman was not to be seen in public nor mentioned directly in literature. Moreover, few significant American writers of Chopin's day were Catholic. Most were white Protestant men from the north-eastern USA, who controlled what was published and what was suppressed.

But Kate O'Flaherty's intellectual mentors were women. After her father's early death, she was tutored at home for two years by her great-grandmother, Victoire Charleville, who emphasised French and music and tales of rebellious St Louis women. Kate's second mentor was a Sacred Heart nun, Mary O'Meara, 'gifted for composition in verse and prose', who assigned her students to write regularly, to be self-critical, and to become 'valiant women'.[7] The Sacred Heart nuns taught needlework but cared much more about French, history and laboratory work in science (extremely rare for young girls). Their minds were to be stretched, and Kate O'Flaherty had over a decade with the Sacred Heart nuns.

Thanks to Madame O'Meara, Kate began a Commonplace Book, her first surviving writing, in 1867. She copied some pompous historical writings and well-known poems (which she mischievously revised) and also practised her own conversational voice. The Commonplace Book, later her honeymoon diary, shows that she had the writing gift: the ease with words, the surprising turns of phrase and the ironic ability to make fun of herself and others, even during the self-conscious adolescent years. She was generally popular in school, but her special friend was Kitty Garesché, and they read books together, laughing and crying – until the Civil War tore them apart. Not long after the war began in Missouri in 1861, Kate and Kitty's school was abruptly shut down for their safety during 'Mary Month', May, when girls made garlands and celebrations in honour of the Virgin Mary. By 1863, Kitty's family was banished from St Louis because her father had been making munitions for the Confederacy. That year Kate's half-brother

George, a Confederate soldier, died, and so did her great-grandmother and first teacher, Madame Charleville.

Then, after the Union victory at Vicksburg (July 1863), a group of Union soldiers invaded the O'Flahertys' house and forced Kate's mother to hoist a Union flag at the point of a bayonet. We do not know what else they did, but a neighbour called the invasion an 'outrage', a term usually used in the nineteenth century to refer to sexual molestation.[8]

Afterwards, Kate spent a great deal of time alone in the attic, silently reading – the healing withdrawal still recommended for survivors of trauma and abuse. It took the warmth of the Sacred Heart nuns, and their community of women, to restore her spirits.

By the time Kitty returned, the two friends were seventeen, and they took very different paths. Kate became a debutante, Kitty became a Sacred Heart nun, and their two vocations inspired Kate Chopin's 'The Nun and the Wanton', also known as 'Two Portraits'. They remained lifelong friends, and Kate visited Kitty for consolation during sad moments in her own life. On Kitty's birthday in 1900, Kate wrote a special poem: 'To the Friend of My Youth: To Kitty' (735).

But in 1868, Kate O'Flaherty, an honours student, had not been eager to leave the cocoon of school. She took another year of music lessons before finally submitting to her social duty, the debutante whirl that she hated. 'I dance with people I despise', she complained in her Commonplace Book, 'amuse myself with men whose only talent lies in their feet'.[9] We do not know how her courtship was conducted, what was said and whether it was in English or French. Oscar Chopin, born in Louisiana in 1844, had spent his young manhood in France, where he failed his baccalaureate because he was too busy chasing young women. But he was lively and far more sophisticated than any of the St Louis beaus she might have married. She was astute enough to marry a man who did not limit her in conventional ways, and, by the time they returned from their three-month European honeymoon, she was expecting their first child.

In New Orleans, young Madame Chopin took long solitary walks around the city, as Edna does in *The Awakening*. She smoked cigarettes, and Oscar reportedly abetted her talents for mimicking animals, priests and neighbours. But the nine years in which Kate Chopin came of age in New Orleans (1870–9) are a mystery, since no diaries or letters survive. The only nearby family member was Oscar's grouchy father, who – like Edna's father in *The Awakening* – had abused his wife and driven her to an early grave. (At fourteen, Oscar had helped his battered mother escape, but later she went back.) Oscar's widowed father died just two months after the young Chopins arrived and set up their household in the neighbourhood called the Irish

Channel, a symbolic compromise that was neither the French Quarter nor the Garden District (centre of 'the American side'). In New Orleans, English had overtaken French as the language of business. Oscar, almost certainly more fluent in French, was a jovial father who loved to romp and play with their children. Their last New Orleans home, still standing at 1413 Louisiana Avenue, was a lovely double cottage surrounded by gardens; they were living in a lively and unusual city.

Mardi Gras was developing into a grand holiday; horse racing and the French Opera flourished. The young Madame Chopin heard about the slaves' dancing in Congo Square before the war (described later in 'La Belle Zoraïde'), and she learned about the animosities between Creoles and native-born Americans who lived on the 'American side' ('A Matter of Prejudice'). She later wrote about artists and street characters ('Neg Creol', 'Cavanelle') and portrayed a worldly and kind obstetrician, much like her own Dr Charles Jean Faget, in 'Doctor Chevalier's Lie'.

We do not know who was telling Kate Chopin those stories, because we do not know about the women who were her friends. Her closest tie was with her mother, who visited frequently from St Louis and who had outlived all her children except Kate. Most nineteenth-century women writers – among them the Brontës, George Eliot and Harriet Beecher Stowe – had lost their mothers before they were ten years old. But Kate Chopin had her mother as a confidante and supporter until she was thirty-five. That gave her an uncommon sense of security about her own point of view.

Evidently she gossiped with the French painter Edgar Degas, who spent half a year in New Orleans (1872–3) with his uncle, Oscar's Cotton Exchange colleague. Degas's New Orleans neighbours included a pompous husband named Leonce, whose wife did not love him, and Degas's Parisian friends included a painter who gave up her art to marry and move to the provinces, where she was sad and unfulfilled. Her name was Edma Pontillon – and so, twenty-five years before she needed them, Kate Chopin already had the names for *The Awakening*'s Leonce and Edna Pontellier.

Like *The Awakening*'s Robert, Degas left Louisiana suddenly – around the time that Kate Chopin became pregnant with her third son, Oscar Charles. He grew up to be the only artist in the Chopin family, a prize-winning newspaper cartoonist. Three of Kate and Oscar Chopin's children were born in New Orleans: Jean (1871), Frederick (1876) and Felix (1878). Their brothers Oscar (1873) and George (1874) were born in St Louis, and the daughter Lélia in Cloutierville in 1879. The New Orleans years were an immersion in motherhood but also a time for observing, listening and gathering stories. During summers at the Grand Isle resort, Chopin and her children lived in a women's community, with swimming, games and lazy conversation. In the

1870s, Grand Isle was a tropical paradise with lemon groves and acres of chamomile and sonorous sounds from the swamps – but much of it was destroyed in the deadly hurricane of 1893. (*The Awakening*, published in 1899, describes the pre-1893 Grand Isle and Chênière Caminada.)

In south Louisiana, though, Kate Chopin was something of a foreigner. On Grand Isle, she was an American among the Creoles; 'Creole' then meant white people of pure Spanish or French ancestry, but it now means racially mixed. Like Edna in *The Awakening*, Chopin was unfamiliar with the open, affectionate ways and risqué conversations of the Creoles, whose French was also different from hers. At home in New Orleans, during the winter, she was also an outsider. Until 1877, the city remained occupied by Union troops, and to her neighbours Chopin was from 'the North', the hated part of the nation that had conquered and pillaged New Orleans. There was much bitterness, some directed against Oscar because he had not fought in the war. (His French-born father, who hated everything American, had taken his family to France for the war years.) When Oscar joined a branch of the White League, a self-appointed militia opposing the new legal rights of black men, he may have been trying to atone to his white neighbours.

In September 1874, while Kate was in St Louis awaiting the birth of her third child, Oscar and his White League colleagues attacked the metropolitan police on Canal Street in downtown New Orleans. At least twenty-seven people died, and over 100 were wounded. Oscar was listed among the participants. Kate Chopin did not write anything that survives about this 'Battle of Liberty Place', but she must have been fearful and probably angry as well. Oscar was, after all, a family man, although not a good provider: five years later his bad business luck forced them to leave New Orleans for his family property in tiny Cloutierville, 700 inhabitants, nestled in Natchitoches ('Nak-i-tosh') parish in north-west Louisiana. (Louisiana has parishes rather than counties.) For Kate, who loved urban amusements, it was a shocking change; instead of grand opera, for instance, there were travelling circuses. To her neighbours, she seemed brisk and unforgivably original. At least once, she rode Oscar's horse bareback and astride and, on another memorable occasion, she proved to be helpless at milking a cow.

She much preferred her own afternoon promenades on horseback, riding her horse down the middle of Cloutierville's one street, sporting her lavender riding habit and her hat with a plume. Local people stopped and gawked, especially when she smoked cigarettes, which a lady did not do. She was outspoken and aggressive, and when one of her relatives confronted her on the street, she whipped him with her little riding crop. Decades later, a neighbour who'd cared for her children liked to tell everyone that 'Kate Chopin was a *dirty* lady.' She sometimes worked at Oscar's general store, like the one in 'Azelie', and she enjoyed meeting whites and blacks and Indians and people of mysterious mixed ancestry, including some Chinese labourers who'd come from Cuba after the war. She was fascinated by local customs and grew well acquainted with the local priest, Father Jean Marie Beaulieu, whose lack of compassion later appears in her 'Père Antoine' character in *At Fault* and 'Love on the Bon Dieu'. Still, she did not make major enemies until Oscar's death just before Christmas in 1882. Then she became the focus, or the prey, of a wealthy, handsome and very married local planter, whose hobby was consoling widows.

Some of Albert Sampite's land adjoined the Widow Chopin's. Both appreciated horse flesh and the dark nights, and she drew on his French appeal and volatile temper for her alpha male characters named Alcee ('At the 'Cadian Ball', 'The Storm', *The Awakening)*. And when she wrote a story about an ugly female character, one who watches a wildly drunk gambler named 'Sambite', Chopin named the character 'Loka' – the first name of Albert Sampite's wife. Everyone in town knew he was 'sweet on Kate', and that he drank too much and that he beat his wife.

'Kate Chopin broke up my parents' marriage', the Sampites' daughter used to say later, years after Kate Chopin had left Cloutierville for St Louis. Maybe it was mostly conversation and flirtation – but probably not. Albert Sampite was said to be an exceptionally charming man, at least when he was sober, while Kate Chopin was glamorous, passionate, vulnerable. If Kate Chopin had wanted to marry Albert Sampite, he could not have obtained a divorce unless he left the Catholic Church. A civil divorce was possible, though rare, and the divorced partner could not legally marry his or her 'accomplice'. A legal separation would have let him have a long and scandalous romance with Kate Chopin, as he later did with another woman. That was not, apparently, what Kate Chopin wanted, but there are no surviving diaries and letters to tell us what she really thought. All we know is that she spent a little more than a year settling Oscar's estate, which included selling land and furniture and collecting debts. Sampite evidently helped or helped himself: her financial records turned up with his a century later, in his granddaughter's attic.

Meanwhile, Chopin also knew that if she wanted her children to be educated beyond the primary grades, she would have to send them away to boarding school, which would leave her alone among her enemies. But St Louis had one of the best public-school systems in the nation – and her mother was urging her to come home. For the rest of her life, Kate Chopin would be thinking about women's loyalty to women. In *The Awakening*, there is a climactic moment when Edna leaves her lover Robert to be with her mother-woman friend, Madame Ratignolle, and Robert, instead of waiting, flees. In 'Désirée's Baby', the title character is thrown out of the house by her violent husband, but her mother wants her to come home, 'back to your mother who loves you' (243). Kate Chopin, in 1884, chose mother love and her children's futures over a man's uncertain passion – and if she ever regretted that decision, she left no traces.

She did, however, separate herself from the family. After her mother's death, she moved to a newer part of town, where she created the first salon in St Louis. Writers, professors, artists and visiting celebrities attended her 'Thursdays', where the conversation was famous for being vibrant and witty. Kate Chopin had brought the French style and tradition to Missouri.

Her first stories were mostly set there but were based on avant-garde ideas proposed in her salon. In 'Wiser than a God', a young pianist chooses her career over marriage to a society man. In 'A Point at Issue!' two idealistic newly-weds attempt a long-distance marriage and in 'A Shameful Affair', an intellectual young woman finds herself hopelessly and humorously attracted to an impetuous farmhand. Those stories were published in small magazines or newspapers. Chopin knew that serious professional recognition and money would not come from small romantic comedies from Missouri. But there was a national market for local-colour stories showing quaint provincial customs in less-known locales. Local colour was also attractive for revealing unconventional truths; Chopin's favourites Mary E. Wilkins Freeman and Sarah Orne Jewett were writing stories that were carefully regional but featured strong, wise and rebellious women who often rejected marriage and male definitions.

Chopin already knew Louisiana would sell. Grace King, Ruth McEnery Stuart and George W. Cable were all writing Louisiana stories, as Alice Dunbar-Nelson would a few years later. But only Chopin wrote about Natchitoches parish, a world of special meaning for her. Her first Cloutierville story, 'For Marse Chouchoute' (1891), was about children, race and violence, but it followed her first novel, which clearly draws on her own secrets.

At Fault (1890) contrasts grey, cold St Louis with warm, sunny Natchitoches parish. Like Kate Chopin, the central character is a Louisiana widow who has to take charge of her late husband's business affairs. She is also attracted to the wrong man: a divorced northerner, David. Rigidly Catholic, Thérèse insists that he return to his ex-wife, who is one of the first female alcoholics in American fiction. *At Fault* is also one of the first American novels to depict the touchy subject of divorce. Eventually the wife dies, paving the way for Thérèse and David to marry, but the story's livelier subplots contain rich meditations on romance and Louisiana life.

David's sister, for instance, has been engaged on a 'few occasions' (773) – a fact reviewers found shocking – and she breaks the heart of a raw young man who has some of the roughness of Albert Sampite. Meanwhile, a violent and rebellious mixed-race young man breaks his father's heart, and *At Fault* is partly about the universal problem of raising sons to be strong but kind – also a question dear to Kate Chopin's own heart. She satirises some recognisable pompous and silly St Louis characters, including club women – although Chopin herself was a charter member of the scholarly and progressive Wednesday Club; she resigned from the club in 1892 but remained friends with many of the women.

We cannot know if Kate Chopin ever openly discussed her ambitions, but they were very evident in the 1890s. When the first publisher she approached said no, Chopin had *At Fault* printed at her own expense. Its national reviews and her Louisiana short stories won her a contract with the prestigious Boston firm Houghton, Mifflin to publish her first short-story collection, *Bayou Folk* (1894). By 1894, Chopin had also found the editor who would publish her most radical and subversive stories. Josephine Redding, who headed a new magazine called *Vogue*, was an eccentric independent woman who believed that society ladies would appreciate ironic and pithy revelations about women's lives and secret thoughts. *Vogue* not only published Chopin's stories about women who scrimped and saved ('A Pair of Silk Stockings') but also about blind men ('The Blind Man') and about young women who were bored and annoyed with men's fawning over them ('Two Summers and Two Souls', 'Suzette', 'The Kiss'). As the first publisher of such stories as 'La Belle Zoraïde', 'A Lady of Bayou St John' and 'The Story of an Hour', *Vogue* allowed Kate Chopin to be a social critic.

She also created a public image for herself, long before women routinely did that. Her friend Sue V. Moore called Chopin 'the exact opposite of the typical bluestocking', without 'literary affectations', 'fads', or 'serious purpose in life'.[10] Chopin herself claimed to be entirely spontaneous, 'completely at the mercy of unconscious selection' and without much self-discipline.[11] She had no writing studio, she said, and preferred to write in the common living room, her children swarming about her. She portrayed herself as a mother who wrote as an unserious hobby.

But her surviving manuscripts show that Chopin was a meticulous reviser who made many changes before sending a story out. Moreover, she did have her own writing room, with a Morris chair and a naked Venus on the shelf, and her children were young adults, much too large to be swarming rug rats. When *Bayou Folk* appeared, her daughter Lélia was nearly fifteen and her eldest son Jean was twenty-three.

Chopin had quickly become a serious professional, but she did not give up her ties with Louisiana. In the decade of her writing career (the 1890s), Chopin often visited Louisiana relatives, but whether she saw Albert

Sampite is unknown. After several tries, his wife finally got a legal separation in 1891, with a petition saying that Albert isolated her from her family and beat her with a leather strap so badly that she could not work for a year. She did not have everyone's sympathy, and it was a common saying that 'All Frenchmen beat their wives.'[12] Loca Sampite was a plain countrywoman, a battered wife who had been pregnant six times but had only two living children. When she ran from Albert, her mother did take her in, and perhaps Kate Chopin felt some sisterly sympathy.

In her writings, Chopin's sympathies are with women, including black women who deeply love children ('La Belle Zoraïde', 'Beyond the Bayou') and white women who revel in being widows ('A Lady of Bayou St John', 'The Story of an Hour', 'A Sentimental Soul'). Chopin also creates an unlikely, warm and unique bond in 'Odalie Misses Mass', which may be the only American story from the 1890s to show a friendship between an old black woman and an adolescent white girl – crossing racial and generational lines.

Chopin also wrote about worn-down wives. In 'A Visit to Avoyelles', she describes a tired, sad, overwhelmed wife who nevertheless loves her husband and would never leave him. But in 'In Sabine', Chopin makes it clear that the wife, once a young belle who ran off with a handsome stranger, is now abused by her drunken, violent husband. The wife is far more helpless than Loca Sampite: she is illiterate; she has no means to communicate with her family. But Chopin gives her allies: a passing white man and, even more unusual, a local black farmhand. And so she gallops away to her freedom, making 'In Sabine' unique among American women's short stories in the 1890s. According to literary archaeologist Susan Koppelman, it is the only story of its era in which the battered wife escapes and the only one with a happy ending.[13]

Still, the story was not praised as innovative. Magazines rejected it, and it reached print only because Chopin slipped it into *Bayou Folk* at the last moment. Kate Chopin's innovations were rarely recognised in her day, unless – as in *The Awakening* – they challenged the power and prerogatives of wealthy white men, the class who were the gatekeepers in publishing. When she wrote about worlds based on women's values – freedom from fear, unconditional mother love and loving friendships unto death – only women readers appreciated what she was doing.

Chopin was disappointed with the *Bayou Folk* reviews. As she noted in her diary, few showed 'anything like a worthy critical faculty'.[14] Reviewers saw regional charm in her stories but did not recognise how many tales are about women without men – women who are kind and selfless, often in the face of great cruelty (as in 'Désirée's Baby'). One superficial reviewer even wrote that 'In Sabine' is 'full of humor'.[15]

By 1894, Chopin had been widowed for nearly twelve years, and she was sometimes introspective: 'If it were possible for my husband and my mother to come back to earth', she wrote in her 1894 diary,

> I feel that I would unhesitatingly give up every thing that has come into my life since they left it and join my existence again with theirs. To do that, I would have to forget the past ten years of my growth – my real growth. But I would take back a little wisdom with me; it would be the spirit of a perfect acquiescence.[16]

Yet, she also treasured her independence, her coffee, her cigarettes, her card-playing and her own home. She had grown up with contented widows, and she was not interested in marrying any of her admirers. Her salon visitors included journalist Florence Hayward, who called herself 'an independent spinster' and resembles the main character in Chopin's 'Fedora'. There were also some women who wanted to keep their husbands away from Kate Chopin, but that had always been true.

Her literary allegiance was unquestioned. Chopin was an active, working writer whose model was Guy de Maupassant, the racy French author whose erotic and strange tales she translated (but mostly did not attempt to publish). Through the mid 1890s she drew away from the well-structured local-colour stories, with their surprise endings, and moved toward a more dreamlike slice of life. By 1897, when her second short-story collection *A Night in Acadie* was published, Chopin was also drawing away from Louisiana material. Her characters include emotionally stunted young men and grumpy older women, but she also alludes to taboo subjects such as menstruation, pregnancy and a young woman's distaste for sex ('Athénaïse'). Although some of the stories are about mischievous children, they are really for adults, and most could take place anywhere. She was brushing against boundaries.

After she finished writing *The Awakening*, a novel combining Louisiana local colour with acute observations about marriage, Chopin entertained herself by writing 'The Storm', the story of an afternoon delight between two former lovers, now married to others. The man (Alcee) resembles Albert Sampite. The woman resembles Maria Normand, who replaced Kate Chopin in his affections, and their lovemaking is far too explicit to be published in the 1890s. Chopin never attempted to do so.

As the centre of a forward-thinking group of intellectuals who read Continental literature, Chopin read the raciest French novels – and so she was not prepared for reactions to *The Awakening* when it came out in April 1899. Her novel was praised by its first reviewer Lucy Monroe, one of the 'New Women' in Chicago, but then there was a chorus of disapproval for Edna as a wife and mother who strays. Willa Cather, then a twenty-three-year-old in Pittsburgh, criticised Edna as too dependent on love as a purpose in her life. Chopin's friend Charles Deyo explained in the St Louis newspaper that it was a novel for 'seasoned souls' who could understand 'the life behind the mask', but most critics, mostly men, called the novel 'morbid' and 'poison'.[17]

Few noted, or cared, that Edna loves music and is a serious and ambitious artist. Nor did critics note that the smart, insightful conversations in *The Awakening* are between women. Except for Dr Mandelet, the men mostly produce orders or flirtatious banter. Robert, whose sexual orientation seems uncertain to modern readers, resembles more than a few confirmed bachelors whom Kate Chopin knew. But if they recognised themselves, no one said so in print, and in the end of the novel, Edna leaves everyone behind. Later, it was rumoured that *The Awakening* had been banned in St Louis, but no library evidence has ever surfaced to prove that.[18] Chopin's women friends rallied, wrote letters of praise and invited her to speak to 400 people at the Wednesday Club's authors' luncheon. But, by the start of the new century, Chopin had lost heart. The publisher had cancelled the contract for her next story collection, *A Vocation and a Voice*, and her health was declining.

She wrote a few, mostly uninspired stories, and then, just five years after *The Awakening*, she died. Although she had long fallen away from the Catholic Church, there was a Catholic funeral and burial. Some of her children remained devout Catholics – most did not – but they always talked of her with respect and affection. Her grandchildren also played with her manuscripts, and so very few of her papers survive. We will never know what letters she wrote home from Louisiana, nor how she described the joys and griefs and secrets of her life.

Nor are we likely to learn much more about her most interesting women friends. Sue V. Moore, for instance, wrote her cheerful magazine profile of Kate Chopin while recovering from her own husband's desertion. (He was a complainer along the lines of Leonce Pontellier.) Carrie Blackman, a 'woefully unballanced'[19] visitor to Chopin's salon, may have inspired 'Her Letters', the tale of a woman who dies and leaves her loving husband with tormented imaginings. There was also Rosa Sonneschein, a cigar smoker who wore extravagant theatrical costumes and founded *The American Jewess*, the first magazine of its kind. Its first gentile contributor was Kate Chopin with the story 'Cavanelle'. Sonneschein had left her rabbi husband after juicy allegations of adultery and sexual inadequacy – and one wonders just what she and Kate Chopin said about that. No doubt other women also inspired Kate Chopin, as did her memories of Oscar Chopin and Albert Sampite. Love can be 'an animal instinct', Chopin once wrote for a St Louis newspaper, and 'an indefinable current of magnetism' and 'an uncontrollable emotion that allows of no analyzation and no vivisection'.[20] Writing in *The Awakening* about Edna and Madame Ratignolle, Chopin's narrative voice wonders, 'Who can tell what metals the gods use in forging the subtle bond which we call sympathy, which we might as well call love' (894). But the keys to Chopin's writing are not primarily in Oscar (a benevolent husband) or Albert (an arrogant lover), nor are they solely in the women who inspired, befriended and supported her.

Kate Chopin was also animated by ambition – her drive to satisfy her own standards as a writer and to gain professional recognition. Like most women writers, she wanted to share what she knew from years of observation as a student, wife, mother, widow, lover, social leader and social outsider. But what drives a St Louis society belle to have a 'commercial instinct'[21] and to make her fantasies and the fruits of her imagination available to the world?

After more than thirty-five years in her company, I still find Kate Chopin something of an enigma. She was indeed a 'rogue in porcelain' who may have harboured all sorts of wicked and unbidden thoughts. Her friends wondered, for instance, what she meant by such ambiguous lines as this one from 'Athénaïse', in which a newspaperman is said to be 'a liberal-minded fellow' because 'a man or woman lost nothing of his respect by being married' (444). 'Now what may she mean by that?' asked Chopin's friend, then conceded that 'The "rogue" will never tell you.'[22] But that does not stop us from wondering.

NOTES

1. Emily Toth, *Unveiling Kate Chopin* (Jackson, Miss.: University Press of Mississippi, 1999), 197.
2. Toth, *Unveiling*, 162.
3. Toth, *Unveiling*, 182.
4. Daniel Rankin, *Kate Chopin and Her Creole Stories* (Philadelphia, Pa.: University of Pennsylvania, 1932), 35.
5. Personal interviews, 1984–97, with Lucille Carnahan.
6. Per Seyersted, Per Seyersted Collection, Missouri Historical Society.
7. Toth, *Unveiling*, 38–9.
8. Toth, *Unveiling*, 30–1.
9. Emily Toth, Per Seyersted and Cheyenne Bonnell (eds.), *Kate Chopin's Private Papers* (Bloomington, Ind.: Indiana University, 1998), 82.
10. Toth, *Unveiling*, 160.
11. Toth, *Unveiling*, 164–5.
12. Personal interviews, 1984–97, with Lucille Carnahan.
13. Personal interview, 1996, with Susan Koppelman, see also Susan Koppelman, *Women in the Trees: U.S. Women's Short Stories about Battering and Resistance, 1839–1994* (Boston, Mass.: Beacon Press, 1996).
14. Toth et al., *Private Papers*, 187.
15. Toth, *Unveiling*, 149.
16. Toth et al., *Private Papers*, 183.
17. Toth, *Unveiling*, 219–22.

18. Emily Toth, *Kate Chopin: A Life of the Author of 'The Awakening'* (New York: Morrow, 1990), 422–5.
19. Toth, *Kate Chopin*, 251–2.
20. Toth, *Unveiling*, 201.
21. Toth et al., *Private Papers*, 179.
22. Toth, *Unveiling*, 197.

2

DONNA CAMPBELL

At Fault
A reappraisal of Kate Chopin's other novel

The republication of Kate Chopin's *The Awakening* in Per Seyersted's *The Complete Works of Kate Chopin* in 1969 after decades of comparative neglect established *The Awakening* as a major work, one that quickly became canonical in feminist literary studies. The same cannot be said, however, for the other novel in the volume: *At Fault*, Chopin's first novel and the only one besides *The Awakening* that she ever published.[1] Printed in 1890 at Chopin's expense, *At Fault* is the story of a young widow who successfully runs a plantation but rejects the man she loves because of false idealism. Although it received some positive reviews when it first appeared, *At Fault* has inspired less critical comment, and much less favourable treatment, than its more controversial successor. Early critics saw the novel as a tale of social change, as Alice Hall Petry writes in her introduction to *Critical Essays on Kate Chopin*:

> the novel is intended to probe disparate individuals' responses to a world of
> rapid (especially technological) change in the post-Reconstruction era. As the
> machine of the railroad ruptures their garden of a Louisiana forest, everyone in
> the novel is forced to reconsider his or her values regarding economics, social
> class, race, gender, and even marriage.[2]

The emphasis on social change is also prominent in Peggy Skaggs's exploration of women's roles in the novel and in Barbara Ewell's study of its competing claims of individualism and social responsibility.[3] More recent criticism by Pamela Menke, Jane Hotchkiss, Jean Witherow and others has emphasised its feminist themes and relationship to other genres, with Hotchkiss using feminist theory to suggest that Hosmer is 'at fault' and Menke, like Withrow, recasting the novel as a response to realist fiction such as W.D. Howells's divorce novel *A Modern Instance* and to women's regional fiction such as Mary E. Wilkins Freeman's *Pembroke*.[4] Both earlier and later critics, however, have to a greater or lesser extent agreed with Lewis Leary's early assessment that *At Fault*, despite its 'freshness of perception [. . .] the eye for scene, the ear for dialect', suffers from 'superfluous characters', a lack of focus, 'harshly improvised' plot elements and unconvincing motivation for its characters.[5]

But the seemingly disparate elements of the novel serve an important function, according to Winfried Fluck, who argues that they represent Chopin's redefinition of three genres used to influence as well as to record social change: the domestic novel, local colour fiction and the 'New Woman' novel. Chopin's purpose was 'to turn the clash of two deficient civilizations into a new synthesis [. . .] a genre which would be able to link social commitment and individual wish more convincingly than existing generic codes'.[6] However, At Fault borrows from another genre as well, one not mentioned by Fluck: the Anglo-American social-problem novel. First used by Louis Cazamian in 1903 to describe British novels of the 1830s through to the 1850s, the term 'social-problem novel' describes works that dramatised complex social ills and tried to influence public debates over such issues as treatment of the poor, industrial conditions and labour-management disputes.[7] As a genre, they often incorporated the very features that twentieth-century critics have found so problematic: multiple subplots, a profusion of themes, and numerous characters, some seemingly extraneous, that may not advance the protagonist's moral growth but instead serve to illustrate a particular social ill. As Fluck demonstrates, At Fault borrows its regional detail from the local-colour tradition and its courtship plot of self-improvement and redemption from the domestic novel, but it also uses the form of the social-problem novel to address contemporary issues ranging from divorce and the industrialisation of the South to deeper cultural debates over race and realism. It thus represents Chopin's only sustained, fully developed attempt at writing in the influential nineteenth-century genre of the social-problem novel.

At Fault centres on the life of Thérèse Lafirme, the beautiful young widow of a wealthy older man, Jérôme Lafirme, who has left her his plantation, Place-du-Bois, in the Cane River country of north-western Louisiana. Against her neighbours' expectations, Thérèse decides to manage the plantation herself and sells the timber rights to an outsider from St Louis, David Hosmer. In what seems at first a conventional double love plot, Hosmer, a serious-minded businessman who manages the sawmill, falls in love with Thérèse, while at the same time her nephew Grégoire, an irresponsible but charming Creole, falls in love with David's sister, Melicent. When Melicent tells Thérèse that Hosmer has been married and divorced, however, Thérèse, a Roman Catholic, haughtily announces that he must never speak to her of love again, not because her religion forbids divorce but because of her personal moral code, one of the 'prejudices which a woman can't afford to part with' (766). Although Hosmer explains that he and his ex-wife Fanny Larimore had married while knowing little about one another and had divorced when, after the death of their son, Fanny became an alcoholic, Thérèse declares that he has nonetheless failed in his duty to his wife and that the only moral course is to return to St Louis and remarry her. Like everyone else in Thérèse's life, Hosmer complies with her wishes, returning to St Louis where Fanny is contentedly living alone, and apparently sober, in an apartment building near her frivolous but good-hearted friends Lou Dawson and Belle Worthington. By the end of Part I, Thérèse has arranged others' lives and her own, though less happily than she might have wished: she has restored her plantation to good working order, built a new house and ensured financial prosperity by leasing land to the sawmill, but she has also experienced the pain of knowing that she has sent Hosmer back to his ex-wife, thus putting him beyond her reach.

Yet, as Bernard Koloski observes, in Part II, 'Thérèse's world begins to crumble' from order into chaos as her plans to organise others' lives go awry.[8] As Grégoire tells Melicent, 'there is no better woman in the world' than his Aunt Thérèse – as long as 'you do like she wants' (754), and those who had acquiesced to her wishes in Part I chafe at her control in Part II. One piece of mild rebellion is the refusal by Marie Louise, Thérèse's old nurse, to have her cabin moved back from the crumbling banks of the river. Another occurs when Joçint, the mixed-blood Native-American and African-American son of old Morico, rebels against the work Thérèse has found for him in the sawmill and protests the mill's regimentation by burning it to the ground. These events anticipate and set in motion the rest of the novel's disasters: Grégoire's impulsive killing of Joçint, old Morico's death while trying to rescue Joçint's body from the flames, and the death of Grégoire, shot by a stranger after his hot-headed, drunken behaviour in a general store. By this point, Thérèse has learned that the high ideal of indissoluble marriage she forced on Hosmer has led to a miserable existence for him, and she recognises that she is 'at fault' for having caused unhappiness in three lives: hers, Hosmer's and Fanny's. In the novel's climactic episode, Fanny, who has relapsed into alcoholism, crosses the river to Marie Louise's cabin in search of liquor. When Hosmer leaves the cabin after Fanny has refused to return home with him, he is halfway across the roaring river when he sees the riverbank collapse and the cabin slide into the water. Despite his plunge into the water to save her, Fanny drowns, and a 'sick, wounded and broken' (870) Hosmer travels to St Louis with her body. A year later, he returns to Place-du-Bois and is married to Thérèse at last, rendered worthy because of his loyal attempt to save Fanny, his obedience to Thérèse's wishes and, not least, by his new status as a widower. The novel's closing scene unites Hosmer and Thérèse in a future filled with the possibility of equality as well as love, for Hosmer declares that he will leave management of the plantation to Thérèse while he continues to run the sawmill, a recognition that their combined strengths promise hope for the future.

Early reviewers recognised *At Fault* as an ambitious first novel, one that compensated for some awkwardness in structure by its realism and the elegant, lucid style Chopin had gained from her reading in French realists such as Gustave Flaubert and Guy de Maupassant. According to her essay 'Confidences', Chopin 'stumbled upon' Maupassant at about the same time that she began to write *At Fault*, finding in his work 'life, not fiction' (700), a form of realism that could serve as a model for her own writing. Chopin's American contemporaries appreciated realism only up to a certain point, however. For example, the *St Louis Post-Dispatch* praised Chopin's 'artistic skill' and ability as a realist to keep her opinions out of the narrative but 'shuddered' at the vulgarity of Hosmer telling his wife to 'shut up' and the dismaying detail of Melicent's five broken engagements.[9] More serious was the *Nation*'s charge that the characters were an 'array of disagreeables' and its echo of the *Natchitoches Enterprise*'s speculation about who, or what, was 'at fault' since so many characters were flawed.[10] Chopin promptly set the record straight, stating in a letter to the editor of the *Enterprise* that 'Thérèse Lafirme, the heroine of the book[,] is the one who was at fault', adding that Thérèse's 'blind acceptance of an undistinguishing, therefore unintelligent code of righteousness' combined with her willingness to 'constitute herself a mentor' for Hosmer and Fanny condemns her on both counts.[11]

Yet, even reviewers disheartened by Chopin's realism found comfort in her depiction of familiar character types, with the *Natchitoches Enterprise* seeing in Grégoire a 'true to nature' Creole and the *Saint Louis Republic* noting that 'the local-color is excellent'.[12] As if taking note of the reviewers' assessments of her strengths, for she had published only two stories and a poem before *At Fault*, Chopin went on to write local colour short stories such as 'Désirée's Baby' and 'Athénaïse' that established her reputation in her own time, publishing in national outlets such as *The Atlantic Monthly*, the *Century* and *Vogue*, and later collecting her work in *Bayou Folk* (1894) and *A Night in Acadie* (1897).

But the evidence of *At Fault* suggests that Chopin was not satisfied to be considered simply as a writer of local-colour fiction, often considered a minor offshoot of realism. Centring on the carefully described landscape and customs of a remote, often rural, region, featuring slight plots and natives of the region who speak in dialect, local-colour fiction enjoyed considerable popularity during the 1880s and 1890s. In its characteristic form of the short story or sketch, local-colour fiction presented a carefully crafted vision of an authentic, unspoiled America, a picture comforting to city-dwellers beset by problems of modernisation and urban life. Chopin understood the benefits of writing in this genre, as is evident in her praise for the local-colour writer Ruth McEnery Stuart, but she also understood its limitations.[13] After all, the pre-eminent man of letters in the late nineteenth century was not a local colourist but a realist, the critic and novelist William Dean Howells, editor first of the *Atlantic* and then of *Harper's New Monthly Magazine*. As Emily Toth notes, Chopin admired Howells, reading his works aloud to friends and writing a play in imitation of his popular farces. Chopin may thus have had higher hopes for *At Fault* than to have it tossed into the neat but limited box of local-colour fiction, for she had sent a copy of *At Fault* to Howells, who did not review it, though he later praised her story 'Boulôt and Boulotte'.[14] When the *Saint Louis Republic* chided Chopin for using such expressions as 'store' instead of 'shop' and 'depot' instead of station, it was therefore natural for Chopin to respond by citing Howells's interchangeable use of 'depot' and 'station', arguing that following 'so safe a precedent' hardly constituted a flaw in the novel.[15] In fact, Chopin may have been referring to Howells's most recent novel *Annie Kilburn* (1888), which prominently features in its opening chapters a H.H. Richardson-designed train 'station [...] massive and low, with red-tiled, spreading veranda roofs' which is called a 'depot' near the end of the novel.[16] A less controversial realist than Maupassant, Howells treated social issues such as divorce in *A Modern Instance* (1882), business ethics in the Gilded Age in *The Rise of Silas Lapham* (1885) and labour relations in *Annie Kilburn*, thus setting a precedent for Chopin's handling of social issues in *At Fault*.

In writing realism, Chopin strives for the middle ground between what Amanda Claybaugh in *The Novel of Purpose* argues is the difference between Anglo-American and Continental realist practices: 'nearly all continental realists take realism to be an end in itself, while the Anglo-American realists [...] represent the world as it is in order to bring about the world as it should be.'[17] Despite her affinity for French masters such as Maupassant and her insistence on distancing herself, as Helen Taylor argues, from her 'female forebears' sentimental Christian and/or didactic fiction',[18] Chopin follows the Anglo-American practice of attempting to represent the world as it is, but she stops short of dictating how the world should be. As an 1894 essay by William Schuyler put it, 'Mrs. Chopin [...] has great respect for Mrs. Humphry Ward's achievements; but Mrs. Ward is, *au fond*, a reformer, and such tendency in a novelist she considers a crime against good taste – only the genius of a Dickens or a Thackeray can excuse it.'[19] Schuyler's assessment is borne out in Chopin's comments on Émile Zola and Thomas Hardy, both of whom she faults not for immorality, the common charge against their novels of the 1890s, but for letting their purpose get in the way of telling the tale. In 'Emile Zola's *Lourdes*', she ridicules *Lourdes* by noting that when a character

> goes to the barber's to be shaved [. . .] we know that he goes for some other purpose, which soon reveals itself when the intelligent barber tells in round terms what he thinks of certain clerical abuses prevailing at Lourdes, and we are certain that we are hearing what the author himself thinks of those things.
>
> (698)

In 'As You Like It', she finds Hardy's *Jude the Obscure* 'unpardonably dull' because his characters are 'plainly constructed with the intention of illustrating the purposes of the author' and thus miss depicting the 'impression of reality'. Like Howells, who had declared that the chief aim of realism is that it tell the truth, Chopin judges *Jude the Obscure* wanting not because it is 'detestably bad' in its sexual subject matter but because it is 'immoral, chiefly because it is not true' (714). In concluding with the charge of immorality, Chopin turns the customary accusation against Hardy on its head: the book is immoral not because it breaches the contract of conventional morality by depicting a couple living together without being married but because it is dishonest in its representation of that relationship. Too overt an interest in reformist purposes – or, indeed, any sort of proselytising on behalf of a system of belief – tips the novel from the legitimate sphere of the social-problem novel, or the 'novel with a purpose', to the thesis-ridden tract.

What emerges most clearly from Chopin's critical commentary and responses to her reviews is that *At Fault* is her bid to be considered as a serious writer, and, in the 1890s, serious writers were those who, like Howells and Henry James, wrote realist novels, a category that included the social-problem novel. In contrast to the symmetrical plots and rich character development of later realist fiction by James and others, the problem novel seems crowded with characters, plots and themes, but their inclusion is purposeful, not haphazard. Since it provides a detailed panorama of contemporary life and problems, the social-problem novel necessarily includes multiple sub-plots and characters from a range of contrasting classes and generations, each character exemplifying some part of the problem being addressed. Other common features of the problem novel, especially in its industrial form, include the displaced worker who represents others brutalised by the industrial system, the cycle of retaliatory violence – usually in the form of strikes and lockouts, between workers and masters – and the sacrificial victim, typically an innocent for whom efforts at reform come too late. For example, in *Hard Times* (1854), Charles Dickens satirises the excesses of *laissez-faire* capitalism and the cult of the self-made man through the blustering manufacturer Josiah Bounderby of Coketown and criticises the utilitarian, fact-based education of the regimented factory schools of the Lancashire system in his character Thomas Gradgrind. Chopin provides a similar array of representative characters, from Fanny's friends Belle Worthington and Lou Dawson, 'ladies of elegant leisure' and 'professional time-killers' (781) whose uselessness comments on the position of women denied meaningful occupations, to Hosmer's friends, the philosophy-spouting Darwinist Homeyer and his opposite number, the bookish but conventional-minded Mr Worthington, who represent the opposing poles of opinion on Hosmer's dilemma about remarrying Fanny. Figures such as the displaced worker and the sacrificial victim appear in *At Fault* much as they had earlier appeared in novels like Elizabeth Gaskell's *North and South* (1854–5): Gaskell's Higgins, the displaced factory worker who goes on strike when wages are reduced, prefigures the destructive Joçint in Chopin's work, and Sissy Higgins, like Fanny, is a sacrificial victim whose death indicts the flawed system that damaged her. Later social-problem novels, such as Henry James's *The Bostonians* (1886), Mary E. Wilkins Freeman's *Pembroke* (1894) and *The Portion of Labor* (1901), Thomas Hardy's *Tess of the D'Urbervilles* (1891), Frances E.W. Harper's *Iola Leroy* (1892), Edith Wharton's *The Fruit of the Tree* (1907) and Theodore Dreiser's *Jennie Gerhardt* (1911) often tilt towards the objectivity of the realist novel and away from the didactic function of earlier social-problem novels. These works extend the range of narrative practices used by Dickens and Gaskell, relying as much or more on ironic commentary and contrast than on the direct pleas to the reader. They also emphasise the problems that arise when natural facts such as sexual desire and human biology collide with restrictive social norms: the social opprobrium that Tess and Jennie Gerhardt face because of their seduction by more powerful men, for example, or the sexual exploitation and racist behaviour to which Iola Leroy is subjected.

In *At Fault*, Chopin focuses on two issues, divorce in the foreground of the narrative and the industrialisation of the New South in the background, a counterpoint providing the classic 'love and work' plotting of the social-problem novel. The more overt problem, divorce, drives the action of the novel and indirectly allows Chopin to explore issues of realism, while the seemingly secondary problem, the industrialisation of the New South, raises issues of race and power. Like many social-problem novels, *At Fault* is at heart a story about change and resistance to change, as an idea worked out on the regional and on the individual level with the passing of Jérôme Lafirme and the old order and the coming of David Hosmer, representative of the new. According to Donald Ringe, the novel begins in 1881, 'the year the Texas and Pacific Railroad was built in Natchitoches parish', bringing with it access to markets that make Hosmer's sawmill possible and signalling 'the intrusion of modern industry into the agricultural world of the plantation'.[20] As such, the novel presents a historically specific account of growth and disruption, for with the Civil War and Reconstruction already several years in the past, factors such as the extension of the railroad into the Cane River area, the invention of the band saw, which led to more efficient milling operations, and the creation of new industries, shifted the economic base of the region. Although the lush descriptions suggest that Place-du-Bois is a 'latter-day Arcadia', [21] the intrusions of technology – the classic 'machine in the garden' described by Leo Marx – and not the pastoral landscape surround the plantation. Despite her opposition to divorce and her Creole heritage, which position her as a figure of the old order, Thérèse has already accepted the encroachment of industry, simply bidding her forest a 'tearful farewell' (744) once she has made the deal. She literally has a dual perspective: she is first seen surveying her land through an instrument of technology, a field-glass, through which she can see the railroad station, 'a brown and ugly intruder within her fair domain' (742), yet her unaided and more sentimental vision of the place as she sits in the wide hallway presents a pastoral picture of 'a section of the perfect lawn' (743), emblematic of the false vision of serenity attained only by resolutely ignoring the world beyond its boundaries and the African Americans who labour to create that perfect lawn and the other amenities that Thérèse takes for granted.

Like other independent heroines who fancy themselves reformers, Thérèse has much to learn, for although the social-problem novel is not a *Bildungsroman*, it frequently shares that genre's theme of education. In novels such as *The Silent Partner*, *Annie Kilburn* and *North and South*, the plot involves the protagonist's awareness of a social problem, which results in an idealistic programme of reform; when those ideas are tested against the realities of industrial life or social convention, the protagonist recognises that they are inadequate and adopts a more realistic, and more useful, perspective. Perley Kelso of *The Silent Partner*, Margaret Hale of *North and South* and Annie Kilburn share with Thérèse a determination to do right and a certainty that they know how best to accomplish that aim. Perley, the daughter of a mill owner, is shaken out of her ignorant compla-cency by a chance encounter with Sip, a mill girl who cares for her disabled younger sister. Denied the power to effect change in the mills, for, as her patronising fiancé tells her, she can be nothing but a silent partner, Perley abandons her hands-off philanthropy in favour of active involvement in the lives of Sip and the other mill-workers. Margaret Hale of *North and South* likewise must modify her views of class and benevolent paternalism when she moves from Helstone in the agricultural South to Milton in the industrial North, since her Lady Bountiful role assumes a natural class hierarchy that the independent northern workers resist. Like Margaret and Perley, whose beliefs are tested by events that their limited experience has not prepared them to face, Thérèse undergoes an education in the real-world consequences of her idealism when she tries to resolve social disunity in the divorce plot, by reuniting Hosmer and Fanny, and in the industrial plot, by integrating Joçint and Grégoire, representatives of the agrarian South, into the industrial culture that Hosmer brings to the region.

Chopin reinforces this idea of education through the clash of ideals with reality early in Book I during a scene in which Grégoire and Melicent, the secondary set of lovers and foils for Thérèse and Hosmer, glide down the 'dim leafy tunnel' of the bayou. Melicent, restless and emotionally detached where Thérèse is calm and emotionally engaged, is an example of the New Woman who seeks social and intellectual parity with men. She lives by her ideas of freedom as Thérèse lives by her ideas of duty. Grégoire tells Melicent, 'You got to set mighty still in this pirogue' (748), but since it is not Melicent's 'fashion to obey at word of command' (749), she ignores him until she sees the reason for the order: an alligator that Grégoire promptly shoots. A few minutes later, Grégoire issues a similar directive: 'You betta put down yo' veil' (749); declining for the second time to obey without questioning, Melicent is bitten by mosquitoes and, symbolically, by a reality that she refuses to accept. In contrast to Melicent, who, Grégoire says, 'seems' to know everything, Grégoire, with 'eyes black and brilliant as the eyes of an alert and intelligent animal' (749) does know everything, at least about the bayou and his culture. His knowledge is instinctual and experiential for, as he tells her he 'ain't' fraid o' any thing I can see an on'erstan'. I can han'le mos' any thing thet's got a body' (750). The distinction between realities that have a body and those that exist only in the mind cuts to a central conflict in the book between realism and idealism. If Melicent treats love as an intellectual game or Thérèse tries to paper over the realities of human emotions with idealism, as when she pressures Hosmer to remarry Fanny, their ideas necessarily fail when confronted by 'any thing thet's got a body' – in short, anything tangible or real.

In linking the physical self and reality, Chopin adds a new twist to the social-problem novel, for she writes about bodies not merely as vehicles for expressing the oppression and pain of industrialism, as is common in works like Rebecca Harding Davis's 'Life in the Iron Mills' (1861), but as sites of knowledge that contribute to the novel's realism. Bodies constitute a means of measuring the character's grounding in reality: the more substantial the character's body, the better she understands real life. Thus, Thérèse's blonde 'roundness' signals that despite her prejudice against divorce she is more grounded in reality and more able to change than her thin, dark counterpart, Hosmer's sister Melicent. Melicent's thinness, like that of Hosmer, his never-seen friend Homeyer and the intellectual but ineffectual Mr Worthington, signifies a masculine level of idealism at odds with the realism of many of the novel's women. If Melicent's slight build and ceaseless motion place her on one end of the scale whose point of balance is Thérèse, the other end is occupied by Thérèse's former nurse Marie Louise, who is 'so enormously fat that she moved about with evident difficulty' (806) yet possesses an equanimity so vast that she alone can calm the troubled Thérèse. The pattern repeats itself with Thérèse's counterpart and rival, Fanny Larimore. Fanny's figure is indeterminate – '[t]here was no guessing at what her figure might be' (778) – but those of her friends Belle Worthington and Lou Dawson are comic exaggerations of the figures of Marie Louise and Melicent. A bottle blonde with a false hairpiece of blonde curls, Mrs Worthington is 'one hundred and seventy-five points of solid avoirdupois' (780) dressed in flashy clothes, a woman with so little use for books and ideas that she uses her husband's volumes of Schopenhauer and Emerson as bricks to weigh down the washing she has put on the roof to dry. By contrast, Fanny's friend Lou Dawson is thin, dark and attractive to men as is Melicent Hosmer. Through repeated descriptions of bodies and body types, Chopin explores the correlation between physical and emotional attributes, a Darwinian typology of gesture, self-adornment and sexual attraction.

As she was later to do in *The Awakening*, Chopin also provides individual patterns of symbolism and imagery evocative of each character. Thus, Grégoire and Joçint, men at ease in the bayous and woods, are described in terms of animal imagery, whereas Melicent, the restless, modern New Woman, is perpetually in motion, although her movements are usually repetitive and rarely propel her anywhere, as when she swings in a hammock. Similarly, the opening chapters link Hosmer, water and Thérèse's desire in the opening chapters, a pattern that also foreshadows the cataclysmic deaths by drowning that conclude the novel and allow the two lovers to be together.[22] For example, as Thérèse leaves the mill and Hosmer one day, she climbs the stairs to a precarious platform and 'watche[s] with fascinated delight the great logs hauled dripping from the water' (747), an act that leaves her 'giddy'. Barbara Ewell attributes this delight to Thérèse's love of industry and a 'new orderliness', but Chopin's language bears out Pamela Menke's contention that the dripping logs constitute an 'almost phallic vision'.[23] Thérèse's awareness of the physical further reveals itself when she and Hosmer let their horses drink spring water from a hollowed-out cypress log, seeing them '[plunge] their heads deep in the clear water; the proud Beauregard [Thérèse's horse] quivering with satisfaction as [. . .] he waited for his more deliberate companion' (758). '"Doesn't it give one a sympathetic pleasure,"' Thérèse asks Hosmer, '"to see the relish with which they drink?"' (758). The horses' plunging their heads into the water and 'quivering with satisfaction' does not give Hosmer a 'sympathetic pleasure', however: "'I never thought of it,"' he says, using thought rather than feeling to describe his initial response. His frame of reference is intellectual and technological, so his growing attraction to Thérèse is couched in those terms as well. When Thérèse's 'warm, moist palm met his, it acted like a charged electric battery turning its subtle force upon his sensitive nerves' (762), transmitting a current of physical attraction that leads him to confess his love a moment later.

Incidents of violence and death mark both the divorce plot and the industrial plot in the second half of the novel, with the divorce plot reaching a more conventionally satisfying resolution. When Fanny and Hosmer return to Place-du-Bois, Thérèse begins to question her actions in encouraging Hosmer to remarry Fanny, especially after Fanny relapses into alcoholism. Alcoholic characters appear in other social-problem novels, of course, from Stephen Blackpool's wife in *Hard Times* to Ralph Putney in *Annie Kilburn*, yet Chopin makes it clear that Fanny is neither evil nor morally bankrupt but simply a victim of circumstance: she has married the wrong man and is born to live in the city, not the country. Her relapse after just one drink is a realistic detail that portrays alcoholism as a physical craving and not a failure of will. Like the deaf-mute Catty in *The Silent Partner* or the lung-damaged Sissy Higgins in *North and South*, Fanny has been deformed, psychologically rather than physically, by an urban, industrial culture, and, like Catty, she is washed away in a flood that symbolically cleanses the scene to make way for a new beginning. Her death and Marie Louise's in the flood obliterate Hosmer's and Thérèse's respective pasts, conveniently freeing Hosmer and Thérèse to marry. To bring the novel full circle, Chopin has the two meet again on the train returning to Place-du-Bois, thus reuniting them on the instrument of progress – the railroad – that brought Hosmer and his business to the region in the first place. In accepting the railroad and the mill in the opening chapters, Thérèse made her peace with new technology and industrialism, but her inflexible idealism about divorce kept her moored in the old world. Now that a more realistic view has tempered that idealism, she marries Hosmer, who insists that he does not want to take over the plantation and, as he tells her, 'rob you of your occupation' (874). In having an occupation, unlike any other white woman in the novel, and in keeping her home as well, something few other female characters in the novel can claim, Thérèse has the best of both worlds.

The industrial plot, by contrast, concludes less neatly and raises questions that it does not answer about racism in southern industrial culture. Although Joçint's action in burning down the mill has been criticised as lacking sufficient motivation, it is actually a key to the novel's ambivalent treatment of racial politics in the context of industrialism. Viewed as part of a social-problem novel, the arson plot equates white violence towards blacks with the social-problem novel's cycle of violence and retaliation between industrial workers and managers. Chopin's strategy is to bury the historical fact of racial violence within the novel's obsession with African American loyalty and willingness to work for whites. The idea of loyalty is a key feature of the plantation fiction popular during Reconstruction, when stories like Thomas Nelson Page's 'Marse Chan' and others collected in *In Old Virginia* celebrated a mythical ante-bellum past of happy slaves and kind masters. Like those of plantation fiction, the hierarchies of the southern industrial plot are reinforced through what Janet Beer has called the 'post-colonial relationship of Louisiana to the United States' in which the 'domesticated racism' of Louisiana 'obtains complicity from the black population in order to sustain alterity from the rest of the American nation'.[24] Complicity – or, in the novel's terms, loyalty – is measured in what are meant to be humourous discussions among white characters and authorial asides about African American characters who will or will not work. As a consequence, African American characters in the book are judged in relation to the labour that they perform: either industriously and independently, in the case of Marie Louise and Morico; grudgingly, as when Nathan tells Hosmer that 'dis job's wuf mo' 'an I gets fu' it' (866) or Joçint sabotages the work at the mill by knocking logs off the carriage (757); or not at all, as when no one will stay after dark on Halloween or clean house at any price for Melicent. But the surface humour, which itself rests on racist stereotypes about the work ethic of African Americans, is undercut by the recent history of violence during slavery and Reconstruction. Chopin pointedly evokes this history by having Grégoire and Melicent visit the grave of Mr McFarlane, rumoured to be the prototype for Harriet Beecher Stowe's Simon Legree in *Uncle Tom's Cabin*.[25] The choice of when and how to work, like the activity of unionised strikes that pervades the industrial novel, may be called ingratitude or disloyalty by masters such as John Thornton or David Hosmer, but it is in fact a legitimate expression of resistance to assumptions about the ownership of one's labour.

A more subtle reference to this legacy of labour, ownership and racial abuse is the seemingly minor detail of the reason why no one at Place-du-Bois will work for Melicent. As Ann Laura Stoler observes in 'Intimidations of Empire', 'matters of the intimate are critical sites for the consolidation of colonial power',[26] and a deft use of the politics of touch in *At Fault* helps Thérèse to manage her domain of Point-du-Bois, whether preventing Hosmer from continuing his work by laying 'her hand and arm – bare to the elbow – across his work' (745), 'gently stroking' the 'limp hand' of Fanny in 'mildly sensuous exchanges' (801) that soothe Fanny's fretfulness or permitting

Marie Louise to massage away her headaches through the magic of her 'smooth hands' on Thérèse's forehead and unbound hair (808). The unacknowledged racial divide that separates servant from master makes the touch of black hands on white skin acceptable if a service is being rendered. Ignorant of the delicate power negotiations implicit in these exchanges, however, Melicent impulsively threatens to cut off Mandy's pigtail one day, which results in a boycott of her household. The African American community recognises, as Melicent does not, that her gesture proclaims that the white body may do with the black body whatever it wishes, a colonising gesture that carries with it a remembered legacy of violence. Another episode in the novel's continuing economy of touch also makes this point: Thérèse proposes to visit 'that dear old Morico' and 'comb out that exquisite white hair of his' before taking his picture. Thérèse's nonchalant assumption that Morico will stand for these 'monkeyshines' (805), as Grégoire calls the double appropriation of assuming the right to comb Morico's hair and take his picture, is different in degree from Melicent's action but not in kind, for both take for granted their right to control the body of another. Thérèse is more aware of the 'alien hands' of the African Americans that serve her than Edna Pontellier is, and *At Fault* allows them more of a voice, albeit a stereotypical one; but for all her Lady Bountiful gestures within what she sees as the harmonious community of black and white on Place-du-Bois, Thérèse still participates in what Michele A. Birnbaum has called 'the collective amnesia regarding the abuses and uses of the color line in the postwar south'.[27] Birnbaum argues that Edna Pontellier's pursuit of autonomy participates in a colonial enterprise that erases and dispossesses the characters of colour in *The Awakening*, and although Thérèse is more socially aware and less self-absorbed than Edna, her treatment of Joçint in consolidating her industrial-agricultural fiefdom shares some complicity in this colonial enterprise.

Given this context, the 'unmotivated' gesture of Joçint burning down the mill makes better sense. First of all, Joçint has been multiply displaced: as a figure half African American and half Native American, he belongs nowhere and rejects being 'civilised' by either of the two cultures whose blood he bears, by Creole culture or by the industrial ethos that the mill represents. Neither an independent craftsman like his father Morico nor a socially mobile up-and-coming worker in an increasingly racialised and racist south, Joçint, like Grégoire, has been turned out from the natural world of the piney woods, the only place in which his work has meaning. When his clumsy Luddite action of spilling logs for the sawmill fails, he takes the next step and, 'creeping along with the tread of a stealthy beast' (820), sets the mill on fire. Chopin takes pains to make Joçint a villain as well as a victim: before he sets the fire, he softly calls his faithful dog to him and, as it licks his hand, strangles it to death and hangs it from a tree, a gratuitous detail that deflects the sympathy the reader might otherwise feel for him. Yet, in rebelling against the power of the industrial world that Hosmer represents, he rejects complicity in the post-colonial fiction of racial harmony in Louisiana and reveals its submerged violence with his violent act. When shot dead by Grégoire, Joçint lies 'across a huge beam, with arms outstretched [. . .] staring up into the red sky' (822) in an oddly Christ-like pose. His father Morico brushes aside those who are trying to remove his body from the flames and accuses the crowd of being murderers, dying of exertion in the process of rescuìng Joçint's body. The violence that Joçint initiates leads to a chain of other destructive events, from Melicent's rejection of Grégoire because of the murder, to Grégoire's recklessness and subsequent death at the hands of a stranger. Neither the community imposed by the industrial system nor the community of Place-du-Bois is sufficient to contain and control the inherent violence in the system, once the fabric of its surface civility has been ruptured. Thus, although Thérèse's story ends happily, with marriage and a less rigid worldview, her path is littered with the bodies of those who died during the course of this journey of discovery: Joçint, Morico, Fanny, Grégoire and Marie Louise, who dies in the flood with Fanny but is ignored since, as the *Natchitoches Enterprise* reviewer remarked, 'the authoress forgot to drop a tear over Marie Louise's watery grave.'[28] As Mary Papke notes, 'One of the most disturbing elements of the novel is that Black characters must die, in essence be sacrificed, so that she [Thérèse] may relinquish her sense of totality to the new ideology embodied in David.'[29] Joçint's and Morico's stories stand out from the stereotyped humour with which the novel's other African American characters are treated, such as Aunt Belindy failing to grasp the idea of Purgatory when Belle Worthington's daughter explains it to her. Their deaths are dramatic and disturbing, and, although they occur several chapters before the end of the novel, Morico's cry of 'Murderers!' lingers over the text, remaining unanswered in the white community's acceptance of Grégoire's deed, the charge of murder stoutly denied by those who believe that a man of colour's life is a fair exchange for the destruction of property.

When viewed as a social-problem novel, then, *At Fault* is clearly a more complex work than critics have acknowledged, especially in its treatment of realism through the divorce plot and of race through the industrial plot. Chopin's consistent symbolism of the body and touch provides a useful counterweight to the characters' disembodied theorising, and the use of tropes common to social-problem novels casts a new light on the minor characters and themes that crowd the work. While undeniably a less accomplished work than *The Awakening*, *At Fault*, like some other structurally rough social-problem novels, allows more interpretative insights into such contemporary issues as race and the woman question than the polished surfaces of Chopin's later work, since its gaps and fissures reveal more about the attitudes of 1880s Louisiana that she had to confront when making Joçint's murder seem not only justified but laudable. If *At Fault* 'seems almost to embarrass Chopin scholars',[30] as Alice Hall Petry commented in 1996, perhaps a new look at the novel for its cultural work as a social-problem novel rather than for the ways in which it misses the structural unity and character depth of *The Awakening* is in order. Petry notes that in *Patriotic Gore*, Edmund Wilson contended that '*The Awakening* does not qualify as a "problem novel."'[31] Perhaps Chopin did not design *The Awakening* as a social-problem novel because she knew that, with *At Fault*, she had already written one.

NOTES

1. According to Emily Toth's biography, Chopin also worked on a novel in manuscript, *Young Dr. Gosse*, after *At Fault*, but after it was rejected by publishers, Chopin destroyed it. See *Kate Chopin* (New York: William Morrow, 1990), 189.
2. Alice Hall Petry, 'Introduction', *Critical Essays on Kate Chopin* (New York: Hall, 1996), 19. The essays to which Petry refers are Donald A. Ringe's 'Cane River World: Kate Chopin's *At Fault* and Related Stories', *Studies in American Fiction* 3 (1975): 157–66; Bernard Koloski's 'The Structure of Kate Chopin's *At Fault*', *Studies in American Fiction* 3 (1975): 89–95; and Lewis Leary's 'Kate Chopin's Other Novel', *Southern Literary Journal* 1, 1 (1968): 60–74.
3. Peggy Skaggs, *Kate Chopin* (Boston, Mass.: Twayne Publishers, 1985) and Barbara Ewell, *Kate Chopin* (New York: Ungar, 1986).
4. In 'The Catalyst of Color and Women's Regional Writing: *At Fault*, *Pembroke*, and *The Awakening*', *Southern Quarterly* 37, 3–4 (1999): 9–20, Pamela Menke compares *At Fault* to *Pembroke*, while Jean Witherow finds the origins of Chopin's divorce plot in Atherton's advice against divorce in Howells's *A Modern Instance* in 'Kate Chopin's Dialogic Engagement with W.D. Howells: "What Cannot Love Do?"', *Southern Studies* 13, 3–4 (2006): 101–16. Bernard Koloski also notes the connection with Howells's *A Modern Instance* in his introduction to the Penguin edition of *At Fault* (New York: Penguin, 2002, vii–xxii). Jane Hotchkiss uses Carol Gilligan's theories on male and female ethical constructions to conclude that Hosmer is 'at fault' in 'Confusing the Issue: Who's "at Fault"?', *Louisiana Literature* 11, 1 (1994): 31–43.
5. Lewis Leary, 'Kate Chopin's Other Novel', *Southern Literary Journal* 1, 1 (1968): 60–74, 74.
6. Winfried Fluck, 'Kate Chopin's *At Fault*: The Usefulness of Louisiana French for the Imagination', in Udo J. Hebel and Karl Ortseifen (eds.), *Transatlantic Encounters: Studies in European-American Relations* (Trier: Wissenschaftlicher, 1995), 218–31, 227.
7. A basic overview of the social-problem novel can be found in Louis James's 'The Nineteenth-Century Social Novel in England', in Martin Coyle, et al. (eds.), *The Encyclopedia of Literature and Criticism* (London: Routledge, 1990), 544–53,

and James G. Nelson's 'The Victorian Social Problem Novel', in William Baker and Kenneth Womack (eds.), *A Companion to the Victorian Novel* (Westport, Conn.: Greenwood, 2002), 189–208. See also Raymond Williams, *Culture and Society, 1780–1950* (London: Chatto & Windus, 1958).

8. Koloski, 'The Structure of Kate Chopin's *At Fault*', 90.

9. 'A St Louis Novelist *At Fault*, Mrs. Kate Chopin's New Novel', *St Louis Post-Dispatch*, 5 October 1890, 31. Reprinted in Alice Hall Petry, *Critical Essays on Kate Chopin* (New York: Hall, 1996), 39.

10. 'Recent Fiction', *Nation* 53 (1 October 1891), 264, in Petry, *Critical Essays* 40.

11. Letter to the *Natchitoches Enterprise*, 9 December 1890, reprinted in Emily Toth and Per Seyersted (eds.), *Kate Chopin's Private Papers* (Bloomington, Ind.: Indiana University Press, 1998), 202.

12. 'Review of Kate Chopin, *At Fault*', *Natchitoches Enterprise*, 4 December 1890, reprinted in Suzanne Disheroon Green and David J. Caudel (eds.), *At Fault: Kate Chopin, A Scholarly Edition with Background Readings* (Knoxville, Tenn.: University of Tennessee Press, 2002), 165; and 'Review of Kate Chopin, *At Fault*', in 'Literary News and New Books', *Saint Louis Republic* 18 October 1890, reprinted in Disheroon Green and Caudel, *At Fault*, 168.

13. For Chopin's discussion of Ruth McEnery Stuart, see section III of Chopin's essay 'As You Like It' in *The Complete Works*, 706–20.

14. Toth, *Kate Chopin*, 192.

15. Letter to the *St Louis Republic*, 18 October 1890, reprinted in Toth and Seyersted, *Private Papers*, 201.

16. W.D. Howells, *Annie Kilburn*, in Don L. Cook (ed.), *William Dean Howells: Novels, 1886–1888* (New York: Literary Classics of the United States, 1989), 641–865, 650 and 847.

17. Amanda Claybaugh, *The Novel of Purpose: Literature and Social Reform in the Anglo-American World* (Ithaca, NY: Cornell University Press, 2007), 40.

18. Helen Taylor, *Gender, Race, and Region in the Writings of Grace King, Ruth McEnery Stuart, and Kate Chopin* (Baton Rouge, La.: Louisiana State University Press, 1989), 157.

19. William Schuyler, 'Kate Chopin', *The Writer* 7 (August 1894): 115–17. Reprinted in Alice Hall Petry, *Critical Essays on Kate Chopin* (New York: Hall, 1996), 64.

20. Ringe, 'Cane River World', 160.

21. Robert D. Arner, 'Landscape Symbolism in Kate Chopin's *At Fault*', *Louisiana Studies* 9 (1970), 142–53, 146. Margaret Anderson argues that *At Fault* is an inversion of southern pastoral and its gender roles since 'the female protagonist assumes the traditionally male pastoral role' in 'Unraveling the Southern Pastoral Tradition: A New Look at Kate Chopin's *At Fault*', *Southern Literary Journal* 34, 1 (2001), 1–13, 2.

22. For a further discussion of Chopin's use of Darwin in *At Fault*, see Bert Bender's *The Descent of Love: Darwin and the Theory of Sexual Selection in American Fiction, 1871–1926* (Philadelphia, Pa.: University of Pennsylvania Press, 1996), 199–203.

23. Ewell, *Kate Chopin*, 33 and Menke, 'Chopin's Sensual Sea and Cable's Ravished Land: Sexts, Signs, and Gender Narrative', *Cross Roads: A Journal of Southern Culture*, 3, 1 (1994), 78–102, 92.

24. Janet Beer, *Kate Chopin, Edith Wharton and Charlotte Perkins Gilman: Studies in Short Fiction* (Basingstoke and New York: Macmillan and St Martin's, 1997), 27, 30.
25. The site has its roots in Chopin's life. The grave they visit is that of Robert McAlpin, said to be the prototype for Simon Legree. Chopin's father-in-law, Dr Victor Jean Baptiste Chopin, bought the plantation after McAlpin's death and, since he was notoriously cruel to his wife and slaves, was sometimes confused with McAlpin. Toth, *Kate Chopin*, 122.
26. Ann Laura Stoler, 'Intimidations of Empire: Predicaments of the Tactile and Unseen', in Ann Laura Stoler (ed.), *Haunted by Empire: Geographies of Intimacy in North American History* (Durham, NC and London: Duke University Press, 2006), 1–22, 4.
27. Michele A. Birnbaum, '"Alien Hands": Kate Chopin and the Colonization of Race', *American Literature* 66, 2 (1994): 301–23, 303. In *Hidden Hands: Working-Class Women and Victorian Social-Problem Fiction* (Athens, Ga.: Ohio University Press, 2001), Patricia E. Johnson points to a similar kind of invisible labour in the social-problem novel: the working-class women whose presence in the work force disrupts domestic ideology.
28. 'Review of Kate Chopin, *At Fault*', in Disheroon Green and Caudle, *At Fault*, 165.
29. Mary E. Papke, *Verging on the Abyss: The Social Fiction of Kate Chopin and Edith Wharton* (New York: Greenwood Press, 1990), 51.
30. Petry, *Critical Essays*, 19.
31. Petry, *Critical Essays*, 13.

3

PAMELA KNIGHTS

Kate Chopin and the subject of childhood

[T]he national subject, – the child, the American child. It is possible to 'converse'
with any American on that subject; every one of you has something to say
on it; and every one of you will listen eagerly to what any other person
says on it [. . .] It may be because you do so much for children, in
America. They are always on your mind; they are hardly ever
out of your sight.

Elizabeth McCracken, *The American Child* (1913)

Think of the children, Edna. Oh think of the children! Remember them!

(995)

The parting injunction made by Madame Ratignolle to Edna Pontellier at the
close of *The Awakening* reverberated in the agitated conversations roused by
Kate Chopin's book. Just as reviewers deplored Edna's neglect of her children, so references to the young and vulnerable featured in much of the
lexicon of disapproval. *The Awakening* risked promoting 'unholy imagina-
tions and unclean desires'; even admirers agreed, it was 'not for young people
but for seasoned souls'.[1] Similar allusions appeared again, in the *New York
Times*, in July 1902, in a fresh controversy, roused by the Evanston Library,
Illinois, and pursued by the *Chicago Tribune*. Headed by *Jude the Obscure*,
the Library Board's list of books 'retired' from general circulation (or, in the
words of the *New York Times*'s report, its 'black list', 'relegated' to 'a dusty
attic') included *The Awakening* and a dozen others, ranging from Boccaccio's
Decameron to Gertrude Atherton's epistolary romance, *The Aristocrats*
(1901). As with fears about the possible dangers of the Internet today, the
safety of young people was quoted as of central importance on each side of
the debate. The Library Board declared itself 'compelled to protect the public',
in particular those parents ignorant of modern literature, who might inadvertently allow their son or daughter to encounter an 'indelicate or immoral'
volume. The town's mayor concurred: only 'those of more mature mind' should
have permission to borrow from the list. Others opposed such censorship.

The Professor of English at Northwestern University suggested, 'it would be better to lead children into the right [with 'good books'] than to attempt to drive them from wrong'; and the librarian of the Chicago Public Library went further, avowing that the action of banning any book was 'silly' and that no library was 'justified in having a person stationed at the desk to pass upon the age of persons and their fitness to read certain books'.[2]

That any book by Kate Chopin should have come to feature in such a dispute must have seemed astonishing to many of her first readers. For a wide public in 1899, *The Awakening* seemed an aberration: not only had its heroine betrayed her womanly responsibilities but so had its author. Mrs Chopin, mother of six, had hitherto been respected as one who had gained her name as a contributor to family magazines and was known for her charming domestic narratives and delightful local-colour sketches. In such stories, Kate Chopin had, indeed, been seen to 'think of the children'. Her interest in the young, however, extended more broadly and, in spite of what her detractors implied, did not suddenly cease with *The Awakening*. Throughout her writings, young people feature as subjects in their own right, as metaphor and as the focus for far-reaching reflections on psychological, cultural or historical possibilities; *The Awakening* was no exception. Although there is no record that she added her comments to those of the librarians, professors and town governors in the Evanston debate, she had earlier taken a stance in an essay, published in the St Louis *Criterion*, March 1897. She saw no point, she stated, in prohibiting her own children, or others, from access to books such as *Jude the Obscure*; and she affirmed her faith in the general capacities of the young. The 'investigating spirit' was natural, and to ban a book was counterproductive: it could only provoke interest in a volume that youth might well find dull, or meretricious. Were a young reader actually to finish such a book, congratulations would be due on the achievement. Acknowledging the wider principles involved, she diplomatically passed over them: 'The question of how much or little knowledge of life should be withheld from the youthful mind is one which need only be touched upon here. It is a subject about which there exists a diversity of opinion with the conservative element no doubt, greatly in preponderance' (713). However, as mother, writer and reader, whether herself conservative or liberal, Chopin was caught up in such discussions; and their complications are played out in her work.

This chapter will attempt to draw out and contextualise some strands of her engagement. First, it will sketch some aspects of studies of childhood in the 1890s, to give a general sense of this vast 'diversity of opinion'; and of how it might be seen to enter constructions of children and young people in Chopin's texts. Then looking at *The Awakening*, and examples from across her work (including stories which Chopin targeted at family-oriented magazines), it will take up some specific modes of discourse to suggest what they might bring out about her narratives and the often-conflicting perspectives they inscribe. The conclusion will return, briefly, to the child as reader – the audience for many of her own tales – though as an active, not endangered, subject. In the area of childhood, as in others, Chopin's texts are never univocal but, as we shall see, work with a rich, and often contradictory, range of such materials, taking up concerns of widespread contemporary interest.

Constructions of 'childhood' in the period drew on complex and multiple discourses, where literary tropes coincided or competed with empirical, scientific observations, philosophical theory or socio-political agendas. The figure of 'the child' (or the imagined essence of the child) was the meeting point for a range of cultural projections: from the sentimental (the angel, the flower bud), through the economic (the investment), to the biological (the specimen); and any one set of discourses could overflow and colour another. At the turn into the twentieth century, 'Child-Study' was a relatively new, but lively, discipline, where scientific, anthropological and sociological enquiries, such as W.T. Preyer's *The Mind of the Child* (1881; translated 1888), John Dewey's 'Psychology of Infant Language' (in the first issue of the New York *Psychology Review*, 1894), or J. Sully's *Studies of Childhood* (1896), were stimulating keen attention. The leader of the movement since the 1880s, and pre-eminent as a pioneer investigator of adolescence, Professor G. Stanley Hall had circulated his first questionnaires in child studies at Clark University in 1894 and would offer the first summer-school course on the subject there in 1903. This was an international field, where women's contributions were welcomed: Miss Fanny E. Wolff, of New York, for instance, had recently generated interest with 'A Boy's Dictionary' (published in *Child-Study Monthly*, 1897), a compilation of 215 definitions, completed by a seven-year-old; and the 1911 edition of the *Encyclopaedia Britannica* remarked as 'noteworthy' Miss M. Shinn's *Notes on the Development of a Child* (1893) and Mrs Louise E. Hogan's *Study of a Child* (1898). The individuality and method in these writings, commended by the *Encylopaedia*, might seem equally to characterise Chopin's own observational style. Her sketch of 'little Dorothea', for example, in her 1894 diary, 'Impressions' – possibly, Emily Toth suggests, a fiction – carefully records a child's behaviour over two summers, before and after bereavement, drawing implications with restraint. Although Chopin herself, as an adult, finally oversteps the boundary, attempting (physical and emotional) intervention in Dorothea's narrative, she acknowledges the child's resistance:

> "Will you let me be your mama now, Dorothea?" I asked her, lifting her mignonne face up to mine. She did not answer, but stared at me with that

unruffled, incomprehensible gaze of very little children. Then she wriggled from my clasp, slid down from the bench and pattered across the grass trailing her doll behind her. She sat herself squarely down on Mrs. Banhardt's door step and looked over at me mistrustfully, even a little defiantly, I thought.[3]

In stepping back, her short study accepts a three-year-old's autonomy and leaves open the question with which it started ('What will poor little Dorothea do now, I wonder'). Examples of similar detail and objectivity, and recognition of children's self-resolve and purpose, recur throughout her writings.

This outpouring of studies in the 1890s affirmed that the subject of childhood was key to social development. Conversations, however, buzzed far beyond academia. Then, as now, the nature of the child and the well-being of the child-mind were important to a wide constituency, ranging from parents, hygienists and educators to literary editors, artists and politicians – all concerned, at the arrival of a new century, about the society of the future. As the art critic, Harrison S. Morris, declared, opening his essay, 'American Portraiture of Children' in *Scribner's Magazine* (December 1901): 'The plant finds joy in its buds, the race lives anew in its offspring; and hence childhood, with its helpless little needs, its tiny mimicry, its confidence, and the simple purity of its conceptions, is the supreme human interest.'[4] Charlotte Perkins Gilman made the point, in more clinical, eugenicist terms, introducing her book of the same year, *Concerning Children* (1901). Arguing that humanity still had power to improve the species, she reasoned: 'This brings us to the children. Individuals may improve more or less at any time, though most largely and easily in youth, but race improvement must be made in youth, to be transmitted. The real progress of man is born in him.'[5] Fiction, that of Gilman and Chopin included, contributed to such discussions. While Chopin never shared Gilman's polemical impulses, her texts seem, broadly, to underwrite this kind of faith in children's potential; but they explore models of growth more complex than such mission statements perhaps suggest.

Many of Chopin's fictions follow young people's passage into adulthood and meditate upon the shaping of a self within a society; but, unlike Gilman's upbeat vision of cultural (and racial) advancement above, hint at less straightforward progress. Many of her texts that dwell, for example, on masculinity and femininity in the making, draw into their narratives the kind of larger questions and ambiguities about socialisation and society raised in Chopin's fictions more generally. So, even her briefest sketches can generate debate. 'Boulôt and Boulotte', for instance, published in *Harper's Young People* (1891), might be dismissed as a trifling regional cameo or as a piece of whimsy at the expense of the children – the equivalent of the colonising 'local-colour' fiction that patronised and reinforced the inferiority of quaint and socially less powerful subjects; or, as Janet Beer has read it, it may represent, in miniature, the journey into gender. At the age of twelve, after their hitherto barefoot childhood, the 'little piny-wood twins' will step into their adult shoes: their differentiation into the male and female roles ahead. As Beer argues, for Boulotte, on the threshold of her destiny, her glossy high heels mark an end as well as a beginning: '[her] walk will never again be as free from restraint.'[6] Or, yet again, another turn of perspective might bring out further possibilities: that the young are not confined so easily. Perhaps Boulotte, like Dorothea above, resists the adults' story, here, appropriating pre-given cultural materials, to construct her own identity? '[S]he was not one to be disconcerted or to look sheepish; far from it'; she 'was mistress of the situation' (152).

Other texts, too, offer glimpses of young people demonstrating the competence, judgement and articulacy more usually ascribed to adults. Marie Louise, in the 'The Lilies' (*Wide Awake*, 1893), 'had a keen instinct of right and justice for so young a little maid' (195) and finds fitting actions in recompense. (She shows equal poise and bravery in identifying the flaws in Mr Billy's cuisine.)Babette, in 'Ripe Figs' (*Vogue*, 1893), presents Maman-Nainaine with evidence, in a beautifully appropriate form, that the older woman's stern contract has worked its course. Such moments indirectly hint at the limits of nineteenth-century models of periodisation in human development. There might seem little of these individual children in, for example, Dr Sanford's model of 'The Psychological "Ages"', propounded at Clark University in a lecture, in 1899. Here, Stage 2 (three to fifteen years) is 'The age of social adjustment', when: 'The child begins to see the advantage of paying some attention to the rights of others, is less self-regardful, but reflective thought, persistency and will-quality are still weak.'[7] Publishing her portrait of Marie Louise in *Wide Awake*, a Boston monthly for ten- to eighteen-year-olds, Chopin gives more credit to her intended readers.[8] In her diary, the next year, pondering the fuss about birthdays, she exclaims: 'so meaningless. I have known rusé old ladies of 16 and giddy young girls of 35. I am younger today at 43 than I was at 23. What does it matter. Why this mathematical division of life into years?'[9]

Tales where the protagonist's development is at the centre bring debates about appropriate patterns of 'growth' into particular focus – as, notably, in Chopin's late story, *Charlie*, written in March 1900 and unpublished, after rejection by the *Youth's Companion*. Scenes of child-rearing enter this text in a broad set of references, from formal schoolroom settings and the governess's pronouncements to comments made, often lightly, in passing: 'He was her own child, so she enjoyed the privilege of dealing with him as harshly as the law allowed' (641). Like Louisa May Alcott's *Little Women* (1868–9), a frequent point of critical comparison, Chopin's story presents a spectrum of ways of being female. It offers almost a textbook cross-section for its case study: the seven Laborde daughters, aged six to nineteen (including a set of twins), their various older mentors, the gently bred young ladies at the Seminary and the glimpses of the lives of girls and women of other ethnicities: African American Blossom, 'Cadian Aurendele, or Tinette, whose baby 'died o' the measles' (645). Whether in domestic, educational or social environments, Charlie, one of Jo March's most vigorous descendants, is, like her predecessor, the one who harmonises least in the Laborde family 'bouquet' (665). She challenges her teaching: 'What was the use of learning tasks one week only to forget them the next?'(644); and her character resists easy interpretation. Her father regards her 'with complicated interest' (644), and her development through 'revolution' rather than change renders helpless Julia, her more conventionally 'womanly' sister (656). After the series of experiences, experiments and accidents that sweep away her 'girlish' self and 'left her a woman' (667), for some readers, as in 'Boulôt and Boulotte', Charlie's arrival at maturity is also signalled as a closing down of freedom. After emphasising her energy, creativity and resistance to orthodoxy, the repeated images of mutilation perhaps suggest the daughter's circumscription in her self-sacrifice and devotion to adult responsibilities. But read from another viewpoint, Charlie escapes being brought 'within bounds' (656). Her announcement to her father – 'I've been climbing a high mountain, dad' (667) – rings with a sense of higher destinies. Having seen 'the new moon' (667), she affirms her own vision; and, as often, Chopin's text keeps possibilities open: Charlie, in spite of her status as daughter, and (it is hinted) wife, will be no passive dependent, but an actor on her own stage in the future.[10]

Even where a younger character's story is not the primary strand, thinking about the children can highlight dominant strands of the text – the discourses of race and region, sociology or natural science discussed in other chapters here. *The Awakening*, conspicuously, presents an extended sequence of arguments, explicit and implicit, about the role of the mother, the relationship of child and adult and the most appropriate way of raising the young. From Madame Ratignolle's 'impervious garment' for babies (888), to old Madame Pontellier's fear that her grandsons will become 'wholly "children of the pavement"' (953), the text keeps the subject in view. In the narrative economy, even the briefest glimpses have force. Chopin's dead-pan description of the 'little black girl' who works the treadle of Madame Lebrun's sewing machine and the ironic juxtaposition, 'The Creole woman does not take any chances which may be avoided of imperilling her health' (901), open up, for most modern readers, the unspoken forms of racial exploitation that underpin this society. This image of a working African American child, an individual reduced to instrumentality, returns uneasily as we read of Edna's strivings for freedom and disturbs simple celebratory readings of her quest. (It is this same child, now sweeping the vacation galleries, whom Edna deploys to awaken Robert for the fairytale day on the *Chênière*.) Three pages later, another little girl, in 'black tulle and black silk', her hair 'like fluffy black plumes', appears as a strangely disturbing opposite – the emanation of leisure, not labour. Growing up into the privileged class, which the other girl's toil supports, she, too, raises disquiet, though of a different kind. The gulfs of race, class and wealth that separate them should not be underestimated, but here, again, a child seems an annex of an adult: the mother who watches her dance 'with greedy admiration'. The text allows for a more resistant, child-centred reading as this child, like Boulotte, is 'mistress of the situation' (904) and perhaps controls her own performance. But these two figures also seem to mark two poles of nineteenth-century American childhood, a phenomenon described by the modern sociologist, Viviana A. Rotman Zelizer: the 'useful' child – here, the utilitarian worker represented in extreme form by the African American girl – and 'the economically useless but emotionally price-less' child – as ornament and treasured object, displayed in Chopin's little dancer.[11] In Zelizer's historical analysis, the second child, from the 1870s to the 1930s, gradually displaces the first, across all classes; however, within the racial and ethnic dynamics of Creole society, as *The Awakening* presents them, it is hard to see any transformations for the African American child of the future.

In the gendered social patterns Chopin's texts explore, bifurcation begins in childhood. In contrast with the rendering of the little girls above as living tableaux, the sound of the 'bare, escaping feet' (932) of Edna's small sons, pursued by their 'quadroon' attendant, conveys a freedom, even in earliest boyhood. They can play at work on the plantation or refuse to pose for their mother on discovering 'it was not a game arranged especially for their enter-tainment' (939). Shaking off fussing adults, taking on 'the other mother-tots', with 'doubled fists and uplifted voices', (887), they resemble the youthful protagonists of the 'bad boy' genre, popular in the last decades of the century. As with Mark Twain's Huck Finn and Tom Sawyer, the 'boy book's' most famous exemplars, the character of the mischievous youth is regar-ded fondly in some of Chopin's stories. Even the indolent Polydore in the story of that title (*Youth's Companion*, 1896) generates a kind of comic vitality well before his redemption; so, too, do the Santien boys, in 'A No-Account Creole' (1894) or Mamouche, in 'The Lilies' and in the *Youth's Companion* story (1894) that bears his name. For old Dr John-Luis, who will adopt him, Mamouche seems 'the incarnation of unspoken hopes; the reali-zation of vague and fitful memories of the past' (274). Such projections were typical of the genre, which, as Marcia Jacobson explains, celebrated the 'notion of boyhood savagery' as a 'revitalizing' force, perceived as lacking in the present.[12] Writing in 1889, John T. Trowbridge, meditating upon mothers' and sisters' 'silent, cheerful sacrifices' to the 'headstrong selfishness' of 'the boy in the family', urged readers to rejoice in such energy, as an invigorating national resource:

> There was never any better stuff in the world for the shaping of men than there is in the American boy of to-day [...] With all his failings, which are many and manifest, he has courage, gayety, endurance, readiness of wit and potency of will. Give direction to these forces, deepen his conscience and elevate his point of view, and the future of the American boy, the future of America itself, is secure.[13]

However, for the more critical vision of *The Awakening*, perhaps the novelist Frank Norris's comment on 'the boy' has more force: 'He is the average American business man before he grew up.'[14] In a text full of images of dangerously congealed male adult power, Chopin's narrative carefully tracks Raoul and Etienne's passage into white masculine dominance. Within a single paragraph, for instance, at the start of Chapter IX, at the Grand Isle Saturday-evening gathering, they feature both within the category of 'the children' – 'permitted to sit up beyond their usual bedtime' – and among those exerting command, as they monitor other children's access to their comic papers – 'permitting them to do so, and making their authority felt' (903). Already alert to their culture's various systems of classification, they identify where true strength lies, reinforcing and reproducing traditional hierarchies through their own behaviour throughout the text. They engage in power play with their mother and their nurse, kept nameless in the text, and racially marked as 'the quadroon', rejecting their influence, but, using all their available forms of expression, they fling themselves into their father's consciousness, 'tumbling about, clinging to his legs, imploring that numerous things be brought back to them' (887). Contrary to Trowbridge's vision of 'cheerful sacrifices', Edna struggles in conversations with Madame Ratignolle and Dr Mandelet and in dialogues with herself to define the limits of their entitlement – as children and as individuals. Such passages are among the most turbulent in the text, full of broken sentences, negations and retractions, intensifying with Edna's own journey away from fixed identities: '"Nobody has any right – except children, perhaps – and even then, it seems to me – or it did seem –" She felt that her speech was voicing the incoherency of her thoughts, and stopped abruptly' (995). In the unarticulated sequence of images that impel Edna's walk to the sea, the vision of the children's power looms, memorably, in its most extreme form: they appear as the 'antagonists' who 'sought to drag her into the soul's slavery for the rest of her days' (999).

If sociological discourses on 'childhood' lead into the heart of Chopin's texts, so too do those of natural science, adding further layers to discussion. To take but one set of examples: as most readers note, within the patriarchal families at Grand Isle, the wives and mothers are, themselves, positioned as dependants – children or pets, protected and patronised – a trope central to some of Chopin's sharpest feminist observations. Such images, often interchangeable, recur throughout her texts, from the 'girlish' Kitty, with her 'playful gambols of a graceful kitten', in 'A Point at Issue!' (1889) to the 'perhaps too childlike' Athénaïse, with 'a softness, a prettiness, a dewiness [...] that savored of immaturity' (432). However, it is worth reminding ourselves that what might seem now merely conventionalised metaphors were embedded in an established and scientific discourse of the period: the numerous nineteenth-century investigations, which had posited theories of 'resemblance',[15] to classify humankind.

It would take a monumental volume, such as Alexander Chamberlain's *The Child: A Study in the Evolution of Man* (1900), to offer an overview of these theories, but even the briefest summary recalls the exhaustive array of data that gave them force. Chamberlain laid out for critical scrutiny, in chapter after chapter, parallels such as: 'The Child as Revealer of the Past' (an analogy with early peoples), 'The Child and the Savage' (comparisons with 'primitive' tribes and animals), or 'The Child and the Criminal' (similarities in illiteracy, idleness, moral weakness – Polydore comes to mind). Such theories, which also underpinned many pseudo-scientific endorsements of racial difference, generated an interlocking series of developmental hierarchies, that produced, in common, the white adult male as the evolutionary pinnacle. (Chamberlain cites Havelock Ellis's *Man and Woman* (1894) as the best of the 'many excellent authorities'.) For his own frontispiece, Chamberlain chose a photograph of that standard in the making: 'an American boy [...] the child-type in its most genial expression and form' (a cherubic, blond, ringletted, four-year-old). An illustrative comparative table of human characteristics, in the culminating chapter, 'The Child and the Woman', however, brings out how far the mature man outclasses even the finest lower-order specimens of his own kind. This chart aligns 'the child-type and the female type', highlighting features where they seem 'physically, physiologically, and psychologically' similar. In contrast with man, both types are by implication, frailer, morally backward, of lesser intellectual or vocal capability, histrionic and so closer to 'the primitive' or the animal. Typical terms included, for example: 'Cranial capacity ... Smaller (absolutely)'; 'Larynx ... Less developed'; 'Ligaments ... More delicate'; 'Erect posture ... Less removed from quadrupedal'; 'Muscular force ... Much less'; '"Breaking out" (destructive violence) ... More common'; 'Dreams ... Gluttony ... Pouting' – all 'More common'; 'Emotionality ... Greater'; both 'Ruse' and 'Dissimulation ... More frequent'; 'Acting ... Greater ability more frequently displayed'; 'Individuality ... Less developed'; 'Logic ... Less'.[16] Chopin's narrative teases out the cultural manifestations of such schemes, in particular their impact throughout her writings on those classified in this way. That these seemed, to many, 'natural' and unchangeable phenomena intensifies the degree of Charlie's or Edna's struggles for self-definition; and to encounter such a list with Léonce Pontellier's critical voice in mind rouses many echoes. Whether condescended to, sheltered or the object of his 'genuine consternation' (932), Edna challenges such labelling; and in her awakening, she moves into her own adult sphere, as a sensual, powerful woman, ruling her terrain.

However, in *The Awakening*, as in 'Charlie' and elsewhere, Chopin's text unsettles easy readings, even of the oppositional sort. Embedded in these nineteenth-century scientific descriptions is, clearly, a model of childhood as a deficient, or negative, state. However, the metaphors of a woman's growth, central to many modern readings of Edna's story, can unwittingly perpetuate such a model. To construct her narrative as one of emancipation (gaining autonomy, a voice, status and authority – or any of the other signs that code 'adulthood') suggests that she comes into her fullest being when she leaves behind her 'childlike' or even 'childish' condition. As Edna announces after swimming for the first time: 'Think of the time I have lost splashing about like a baby!' (908) While such a journey remains a major strand of *The Awakening*, its final movement offers the alternative suggestion (a trope rooted in literary Romanticism) that it is childhood which is the superior state: that Edna's most intense experience, her sense of authenticity, lies in the past, in the child she once was. Alone, beside the sea, she glories in feeling 'like some new-born creature' (1000); and, in the final paragraphs, returns to the child's perspective, the endless blue-grass meadow,[17] the scents and sounds of home and family. This image gains strength, as it gathers up Edna's memories from earlier in the text and reinforces previous narratorial comments which offer some of the most explicit (and most quoted) insights into her subjectivity: 'Even as a child she had lived her own small life all within herself. At a very early period she had apprehended instinctively the dual life – that outward existence which conforms, the inward life which questions' (893).

In her vivid evocations of this 'small life', Chopin subtly delivers the kind of effects, the representation of an actual child's viewpoint, that even America's then best-known novelist of childhood had described as elusive. Six years earlier, Frances Hodgson Burnett, the creator of *Little Lord Fauntleroy* (1885), had attempted a memoir, *The One I Knew Best of All: A Memory of the Mind of a Child*, which provides a useful point of comparison. Published first as a serial in *Scribner's Magazine* from January to June

1893, this charted the growing up of a girl, known throughout as 'the Small Person', a literary experiment in which Burnett drew on her own recollections to represent the 'Story of *any* Child with an Imagination'. Like Edna, the Small Person revives for the older reader the child's perspective, the visions of the grass and the sky, 'springing, from little island to little island, across the depths of blue which seemed a sea'.[18] In her preface, Burnett had discussed the difficulties of capturing, while seeing 'from the *outside*', the impressions and experiences of the very young: 'There must be so many thoughts for which child courage and child language have not the exact words.'[19] Her solution was to write, as an adult, in the first person, looking back to the past, to recreate in the third person the perceptions and emotions of the 'little unit' of herself: 'the one child of whom I could write from the inside point of view'. Using free indirect discourse, Chopin creates a similar sense of both immediacy and objectivity, sharpness, along with the inarticulate and unformed: emotions, as Burnett expressed it, which 'her child-thoughts could give no shape to, and which were still feelings which deeply moved her'.[20]

Such a mode, however, can often slide from the attempted reproduction of the child's view back to that of the adult who remembers. This kind of slippage will abruptly terminate any effect of youthful subjectivity and present the reader, instead, with childhood as a spiritualised repository for adult fantasies. Chopin keeps out of her writings any surrender to nostalgia, though it is visible in the effusions over children exhibited by various of her characters. Burnett's entire narrative, however, is permeated with such emotion. An extract from her preface will suffice to mark the contrast:

> The Small Person is gone to that undiscoverable far-away land where other Small Persons have emigrated – the land to whose regretted countries there wandered, some years ago, two little fellows, with picture faces and golden lovelocks, whom I have mourned and longed for ever since, and whose going – with my kisses on their little mouths – has left me forever a sadder woman, as all other mothers are sadder, whatsoever the dearness of the maturer creature left behind to bear the same name and smile with eyes not quite the same.[21]

In Burnett's representation, growing up and death are equivalences; she mourns for both her sons – one, in 1893, an adolescent, the other dead in 1890, at fifteen, of consumption. While her references are autobiographical, her sentimentalisation of childhood exemplifies a wider cultural construction of childhood, countering the scientific developmental models above, as a site of purity, plenitude and innocence, lost and longed for by adults. Such rhetoric, and the equally idealised vision of maternal devotion it produces, presumably contributes to Mr Pontellier's vague feelings that his wife was not one of the 'mother-women' (887–8). To be epitomised in J.M. Barrie's Never

Never Land, in his story of 'Peter Pan', staged first as a play in 1904, this image of the child as the elusive, voiceless object of adult wistfulness dominates much late-nineteenth-century literature. It is in the foreground, too, of influential modern critical discussions, such as Jacqueline Rose's *The Case of Peter Pan or the Impossibility of Children's Fiction* (1984) or James Kincaid's *Child-Loving: The Erotic Child and Victorian Culture* (1992). Edna's keen examination of the Lebrun family photographs, as she seeks Robert the man in the features of the baby, the child and the adolescent (927–8) might strike a reader as essentially similar.

Images of children as existing in a pure space prior to, beyond, or outside the social enter *The Awakening*, but, as with the mythic or fairytale strands of the text, Chopin always keeps other, realist, strands in view. In her diary, recalling, with intensity, the birth of her son Jean twenty-three years before, she emphasises the physical. Even the unique poignancy of first touching him, she felt, 'must be the pure animal sensation; nothing spiritual could be so real'.[22] Edna's own liberatory vision of being new born follows closely on her witnessing the harrowing scene of Madame Ratignolle's confinement, rendered for the reader with the grittiness of Naturalism. The pervasive reminders of family dynamics are there: the often-comic caution against over-romanticising childhood, or regarding adults and young people as distinct groups of beings. At twenty-six, Robert can irritate Edna for speaking 'with as little reflection as we might expect from one of those children down there playing in the sand' (900). In the presence of the parent, grown-up siblings (the Lebrun brothers or Edna and her sisters) fall into old patterns of rivalry or affection; while, faced with the exasperating adults who colonise their territory, even the smallest children can make their influence felt: 'they stood there in a line, gazing upon the intruding lovers, still exchanging their vows and sighs. The lovers got up, with only a silent protest [...] The children possessed themselves of the tent' (899). The presentation of Edna's sons, as we have seen, could not be further from Burnett's evocation of her lost Lionel, or Vivian, the long-suffering, real-life, prototype of the velvet-clad Cedric Fauntleroy.

As the cultural critic David Rudd reminds us, emphases on children as the focus of adult yearnings, the 'precious child', have led (at least in literary criticism) 'to the neglect of the child as a social being, with a voice': the 'constructive' rather than the 'constructed' child.[23] There is little danger when reading any of Chopin's writings that one can forget that children are active individuals, or social beings, with a constructive part to play. Even in *The Awakening* ('A Solitary Soul'), vilified for asserting a mother's search for a separate sphere, the narrative focuses time and again on positive moments of interaction between adult and child: play, storytelling, letters.

Edna takes swimming lessons from the children; she soothes or stirs her sons with bedtime tales; Raoul requests bon-bons and describes the wonder of the little pigs in a 'delicious printed scrawl' (987); Robert and Old Celestine talk patois, the old language of childhood.[24] Similar moments occur throughout her fiction: the children in 'Regret' tutor their temporary foster-mother in the differences between rearing chickens and raising children; five-year-old Bibi in 'The Storm', the one who knows his mother's routine, talks on equal terms with his father; the six-year-old twins in 'Charlie' set down their marks 'with heavy emphasis' on the petition that dissuades their father from remarriage (644); the young siblings in 'Croque-Mitaine' demystify and control their nursemaid's threats of the bogey-man; thirteen-year-old Odalie (in 'Odalie Misses Mass') takes on the role of Paulette, long dead, to support Aunt Pinky's reminiscing. In her own 'Commonplace Book', at sixteen, Kate O'Flaherty interjected her own thoughts into the pages of copied-out, worthy, passages.[25] All these set up models of adult–child communication that suggest strong assumptions about the powers of understanding of even the youngest children. As we have seen, unlike her reviewers, Chopin declared herself against censoring young people's reading; and she never underestimated their capabilities in responding to, re-reading and taking command of fictions.

In the popular stories Chopin published for young audiences, from which many of the examples in this chapter have come, her texts held out to readers a constructive role in the narrative. Largely ignored during Kate Chopin's revival, or dismissed as a market expediency, this once-despised genre is now recognised as important, and writings for children ascribed a key place within nineteenth-century culture. In the then prestigious publications, read by the whole family, the USA made plain those values perceived as crucial to the national future.[26] As one of the longest lasting, the *Youth's Companion* (1827–1929) declaimed, in the words that opened its first issue: 'The human mind is becoming emancipated from the bondage of ignorance and super-stition. Our children are born to higher destinies than their fathers; they will be actors in a far advanced period.'[27] However, in guiding its authors in how to shape these destinies, the *Companion*, as one contributor recalled, explained the principles for success: 'Don't experiment. Don't originate: repeat!'[28] Chopin followed something of this prescription, drawing on famil-iar nineteenth-century tropes – the child as redeemer, or the rhetoric of restoration – but she also engaged readers in the wider questions of her day. As the new century approached, what kinds of cultural identities would American parents offer their young? Madame Carambeau's words, from 'A Matter of Prejudice', published in *Youth's Companion* in 1895, resonated, 'Ah, those Americans! Do they deserve to have children?' (284). Who would those children be and what kind of nation would they inherit? With their ambiguities, and uncertainties, most of Chopin's narratives, even the seemingly most conservative, allow room for discussion. Her texts take up and actualise a common conceit; as Samuel Osgood, in 'Books for Our Children', expressed it at the end of the Civil War: 'not of America-as-Child, but of the Child-as-America'.[29] In Chopin's subtle depictions of race, gender and region, both adult and child reader are given the materials to imagine – and perhaps even to construct – a twentieth century which may include all children, as agents of their own futures. In Chopin's translation, 'How to Make Manikins' (1891), a leaflet on creating paper cut-out figures, the final sentence leaves '[f]urther embellishment of these figures and groups [. . .] to the skill and fancy of the young people who may like to fashion them'.[30] In all her writings, Kate Chopin not only thought of the children but also recognised that they were subjects who could very well think for themselves.

NOTES

1. Reviews from *Providence Sunday Journal* (4 June 1899), 15; and Chopin's hometown newspaper, the *St Louis Post-Dispatch* (20 May 1899), 4; reprinted in Alice Hall Petry (ed.), *Critical Essays on Kate Chopin* (New York: G. K. Hall, 1996), 53–6.
2. 'Western Town Has Literary Census', *New York Times* (July 6 1902), 9.
3. 'Impressions' (1894), 44–7; in Emily Toth and Per Seyersted (eds.), *Kate Chopin's Private Papers* (Bloomington, Ind.: Indiana University Press, 1998), 189–90.
4. Harrison S. Morris, 'American Portraiture of Children', *Scribner's Magazine*, XXX, 6, December 1901, 601.
5. Charlotte Perkins (Stetson) Gilman, *Concerning Children* (Boston, Mass.: Small, Maynard, 1901), 4.
6. Janet Beer, *Kate Chopin, Edith Wharton and Charlotte Perkins Gilman: Studies in Short Fiction* (Basingstoke: Palgrave Macmillan, 2005), 83.
7. Recorded in Alexander Francis Chamberlain, *The Child: A Study in the Evolution of Man* (London: Walter Scott, 1900), 67.
8. Details in R. Gordon Kelly, *Mother Was a Lady: Self and Society in Selected American Periodicals, 1865–1890* (Westport, Conn.: Greenwood, 1974), 25.
9. Chopin, 'Impressions', 186.
10. For such a reading, proposing the likelihood that 'as plantation field manager', Charlie will maintain her power, see Bonnie James Shaker, *Coloring Locals: Racial Formation in Kate Chopin's* Youth's Companion *Stories* (Iowa City, Ia.: University of Iowa Press, 2003), 106.
11. Viviana A. Rotman Zelizer, *Pricing the Priceless Child: The Changing Social Value of Children* (Princeton NJ: Princeton University Press, 1994), 209.
12. Marcia Jacobson, *Being a Boy Again: Autobiography and the American Boy Book* (Tuscaloosa, Ala.: University of Alabama Press, 1994), 14.
13. Jacobson draws attention to this essay: John T. Trowbridge, 'The American Boy', *North American Review* (February 1889), 225.
14. Frank Norris 'Child Stories for Adults' (1902); quoted Jacobson, *Being a Boy Again*, 2.

15. Chamberlain, *The Child*, Chapter 3.
16. These represent only a few items from Chamberlain's extensive list: *The Child*, 418–23.
17. The motif of the child in the grass, pervasive in autobiographical writings, gives its name to Richard N. Coe's discussion of childhood recollection as a distinct literary genre, well established by the end of the eighteenth century: *When the Grass Was Taller: Autobiography and the Experience of Childhood* (New Haven, Conn.: Yale University Press), 1984.
18. Frances Hodgson Burnett, 'The One I Knew Best of All: A Memory of the Mind of a Child', *Scribner's Magazine*, XIII, 1, January 1893, 69.
19. Burnett, 'The One I Knew Best of All', 60.
20. Frances Hodgson Burnett, 'The One I Knew Best of All', *Scribner's Magazine*, XIII, 2, February 1893, 244.
21. Burnett, 'The One I Knew Best of All', 60.
22. Chopin, 'Impressions', *Kate Chopin's Private Papers*, 183.
23. David Rudd, 'Theorising and Theories: The Conditions of Possibility of Children's Literature', in Peter Hunt (ed.), *International Companion Encyclopaedia of Children's Literature*, 2nd edn, Vol. I (London and New York: Routledge 2004), 30.
24. See 'Patois', in Pamela Knights, 'Louisiana Observed' (Appendix), in Pamela Knights (ed.), *Kate Chopin: The Awakening and Other Stories* (Oxford: Oxford World's Classics, 2000), 353–4.
25. See Toth's comments, Toth and Seyersted, *Kate Chopin's Private Papers*, 9–12.
26. For a general overview, see Kelly, *Mother Was a Lady*, and Beverly Lyon Clark, *Kiddie Lit: The Cultural Construction of Children's Literature in America* (Baltimore, Md.: Johns Hopkins University Press, 2003). Knights, *Kate Chopin: The Awakening and Other Stories* reprints original magazine versions of stories more usually reproduced from Chopin's 'adult' collections and offers extensive commentary in the introduction and notes; Shaker, *Coloring Locals*, unfolds Chopin's subtle proselytising on the national scene on behalf of a spectrum of Louisiana's ethnic and social groups. Excellent analyses may also be found in: Barbara C. Ewell, *Kate Chopin* (New York: Ungar, 1986); Emily Toth, *Kate Chopin: A Life of the Author of 'The Awakening'* (London: Century, 1990); Bernard Koloski, *Kate Chopin: A Study of the Short Fiction* (New York: Twayne/Simon & Schuster, 1996); Beer, *Kate Chopin, Edith Wharton and Charlotte Perkins Gilman*.
27. Cited in Jerry Griswold, *Audacious Kids: Coming of Age in American Classic Children's Books* (New York: Oxford University Press, 1992), 21.
28. Ray Stannard Baker, quoted in Kelly, *Mother Was a Lady*, 33.
29. Samuel Osgood, 'Books for Our Children', *Atlantic Monthly*, December 1865, 724.
30. Toth and Seyersted, *Kate Chopin's Private Papers*, 241.

4

SUSAN CASTILLO

'Race' and ethnicity in Kate Chopin's fiction

The individuals at the extremes of divergence in one race of men are as unlike as the wolf to the lapdog. Yet each variety shades down imperceptibly into the next, and you cannot draw the line where a race begins or ends.
Ralph Waldo Emerson, *English Traits*[1]

That's the way with them Cajuns ... ain't got sense enough to know a white man when they see one.
(327)

Kate Chopin came of age as a writer at the end of a century that had brought complex social and linguistic transformations to Louisiana. First settled by the French, then ceded to Spain in 1763 at the end of the Seven Years' War, reclaimed for France by Napoleon and then sold to Thomas Jefferson's USA in 1803, it has always been a space characterised by a volatile confluence of cultures, languages, skin colours and ethnic affiliations. Unequivocally, a key factor in the lasting appeal of Chopin's fiction is the vividness with which she evokes the human diversity of *fin-de-siècle* Louisiana. In what follows, I shall begin by providing a brief overview of recent theorisation on 'race' and ethnicity. I then go on to analyse representations of slaves of African origin, free people of colour, Native Americans and French Creoles and Cajuns in Kate Chopin's fiction, focusing on her first novel *At Fault* and on selected short stories from her collection *Bayou Folk*.

In her landmark study *The Word in Black and White: Reading Race in American Literature, 1638–1867*, Dana Nelson observes that 'race' has been convincingly refuted as a valid scientific category, pointing out that it has never been a fixed or stable concept and that at different points in US history it has stood for cultural, evolutionary, moral, metaphysical and biological difference. She makes a compelling case for considering 'race' not as an essentialist, immutable classification but rather as an apparatus in the Foucauldian sense of the term, a discursive formation responding to an urgent need at a particular historical moment, underpinning political systems and permeating every aspect of our lives. In this perspective, 'race' is not a fixed essence which is part of certain individuals who belong to a particular group but rather a social construct, a fiction. It is a fiction, however, not in the sense that it is unreal (indeed, its material effects are all too apparent throughout human history), but rather as a metaphor that serves to inscribe, naturalise and, occasionally, subvert power relationships.[2]

It is certainly the case that the rigid racial taxonomies and categories emerging from the Enlightenment and finding fullest expression in the racialist theories of Gobineau (among others) are no longer viewed as valid; indeed, for the present-day scholar, some appear as an absurdly Procrustean attempt to force human diversity into a rigid schema. For example, Julien-Joseph Virey's *Histoire naturelle du genre humain*, published in 1801, defines several categories between black and white in fractional increments, labelled mulatto, *terceron saltatras*, *griffe* or *zambo*, quadroon, quadroon *saltatras*, *quinteron*, *quinteron saltatras* and so forth.[3] Clearly, although human beings come in many shades and colours, it is impossible to determine exactly where one 'race' ends and another begins. But it is equally true that these same rigid categories and taxonomies are extraordinarily resilient and have had a very real and direct impact on judicial and legislative systems and, consequently, on the lives of many people and nations.

In recent years, theorisation on ethnic affiliation has been characterised by a move away from a conceptualisation of ethnicity in terms of essential identity or authenticity toward a concept of ethnic identity as a dynamic, kinetic process which is subject to the contingencies of history and of individual choice. This certainly is the case with the term 'Creole', which was originally used to describe the first-generation offspring of European settlers and colonisers born in the New World, later expanding to indicate people of mixed race but then, in the Gilded Age, narrowing down once more to indicate Creoles (and Cajuns, in the lower classes) as 'white'. It is true, however, that the terms 'race' and 'ethnicity' are loaded ones that have often become entangled in critical discourse. Michael Omi and Howard Winant have argued for the need to examine what they call 'visible' and 'cultural' modes of group construction in specific cases but question the notion that the two concepts are mutually exclusive.[4] Indeed, as Werner Sollors has pointed out, within a given 'race' there may be degrees of ethnic differentiation, and he cites the case of Jamaicans and African Americans in the USA.

Kate Chopin was throughout her lifetime exposed to racial and ethnic diversity. Her own family was French and Irish in origin. During her early childhood in St Louis, her family owned six slaves, and a male slave was charged with holding her pony when she rode.[5] Interestingly, according to Chopin's biographer Emily Toth, the three oldest slaves belonging to the

O'Flaherty family were recorded by the census as 'Blacks', while the three younger were classified as 'mulattoes'. The paternity of the latter is not known. On the Charleville side of Chopin's family, there were cases of relationships between male members of the family and women of colour. One fathered two mixed-race offspring with an Osage woman, and another had a mixed-race son, the quadroon Louis Dunois, who (taking his father's name) called himself Louis Charleville; he later went on to become a successful dealer in livestock.[6] Later, in the turmoil of the Civil War, Kate Chopin would gain notoriety, as Emily Toth says, 'as St Louis' "Littlest Rebel"',[7] taking down a Union flag which had been affixed to her family's house and narrowly avoiding arrest. Her brother George, to whom she was devoted, fought for the Confederacy and died of typhoid in 1863. During Reconstruction, Chopin's husband Oscar became embroiled in New Orleans with the racist White League and took part in a conflict which became known as the Battle of Canal Street, in which there were more than two dozen dead and many more injured.[8] It is certainly the case that Kate Chopin's South, and particularly the Louisiana where she spent her decisive years, was not a melting pot but rather a bubbling cauldron of 'races', ethnicities and regional loyalties.

In Chopin's first novel, *At Fault* (1890), most critics focus on Chopin's daring depiction of the love between David Hosmer, a man who is unhappily married to an alcoholic called Fanny, and Thérèse Lafirme, a wealthy Creole widow. However, in this novel one also encounters certain early representations of ethnic and racial diversity that reveal the author's keen powers of observation and trace out plots and motifs that will be developed more fully in her later fiction; in some of the minor characters and subplots of *At Fault*, we can find indications of Chopin's (often contradictory) views on the bewildering variety of ethnic and racial groupings of late-nineteenth-century Louisiana. It is true that some of the novel's African American characters, such as Aunt Belindy and Uncle Hiram, appear initially as rather embarrassing caricatures of the Faithful Retainer stereotype. The mixed-race and Creole characters, however, are deftly drawn and hold distinct interest. For instance, Grégoire, Thérèse's nephew, is presented as the prototype of the dashing young Creole, and Hosmer's sister Melicent is bemused by him:

> The young man whom she so closely scrutinized was slightly undersized, but of close and brawny build. His hands were not so refinedly white as those of certain office bred young men of her acquaintance, yet they were not coarsened by undue toil: it being somewhat an axiom with him to do nothing that an available 'nigger' might do for him [...] Close fitting, high-heeled boots of fine quality incased his feet, in whose shapeliness he felt a pardonable pride; for a young man's excellence was often measured in the circle which he had

frequented, by the possession of such a foot. A peculiar grace in the dance and a talent for bold repartee were further characteristics which had made Grégoire's departure keenly felt among the belles of upper Red River.   (749)

Chopin's description of Grégoire portrays him as an intermediate, liminal figure: he is distanced in terms of both race and class from his African American servants, and yet his hands are not as white as those of the 'office bred' Anglophone young men of the St Louis belle Melicent's acquaintance. Bonnie Shaker astutely comments, 'For Chopin, "coloring locals" meant transforming non-Louisianans' general understanding of the Creole and Cajun as mixed-race people into "purely" white folks.'[9] But with Chopin, as always, things are not quite so simple. Grégoire's liminality is further reinforced by Chopin's characterisation of him as an androgynous, dandified figure. Underneath the surface of the plot of *At Fault* there bubbles a dark history of racial violence and ethnic conflict, as we discover when Grégoire takes Melicent in a pirogue into the oppressive depths of a nearby swamp, reputedly haunted by a man called Old McFarlane:

> Nameless voices – weird sounds that awake in a southern forest at twilight's approach – were crying a sinister welcome to the settling gloom. 'This is a place thet can make a man sad, I tell you,' said Grégoire, resting his oars, and wiping the moisture from his forehead. 'I wouldn't want to be yere alone, not fur any money.'
> 'It is an awful place,' replied Melicent with a little appreciative shudder; adding 'do you consider me a bodily protection?' and feebly smiling into his face.
> 'Oh; I ain't 'fraid o' any thing I can see an on'erstan'. I can han'le mos' any thing thet's got a body. But they do tell some mighty queer tales 'bout this lake an' the pine hills yonda.'   (750)

The following day, in broad daylight, the two visit the grave, and Melicent leaves a blood-red flower, saying that she does not believe in Hell. Grégoire, however, is convinced that McFarlane has gone to a place 'w'ere flowers don't git much waterin', if they got any there' (772).

Clearly, for Kate Chopin this reference to racial violence is not a gratuitous one. According to Emily Toth, this episode is drawn from a Cane River story that Chopin had incorporated into her narrative: the tale that Harriet Beecher Stowe had visited the Cloutierville area in the 1840s and had based the character of Simon Legree, the infamous villain of *Uncle Tom's Cabin*, on a story she heard from a slave woman she met on that occasion.[10] Helen Taylor, in *Gender, Race and Religion in the Writings of Grace King, Ruth McEnery Stuart, and Kate Chopin*, brings the grim reference even closer to home for Chopin: McFarlane is apparently based on Robert McAlpin, the notorious slave-owner from whom Kate Chopin's father-in-law Dr Victor

Chopin (also known for treating his slaves brutally) had bought his large Red River plantation.[11] In any event, this Gothicised landscape is haunted by the ghosts of McAlpin/McFarlane/Legree and their enslaved and tortured victims. Significantly, it is Grégoire – the 'whitened' Creole who is careful to distance himself from his 'nigger' servants – who is most sensitive to this dark legend and to its violent undercurrents, while Melicent – representing the more urban and industrialised Anglophone elites of St Louis – reacts to it as merely an occasion for flirting and voyeuristic tourist titillation.

Another intriguing character is the mixed-race youth Joçint, whose mother is described as Native American. He is portrayed as surly, with 'straight and coarse black hair' that hangs over his 'low retreating forehead, almost meeting the ill-defined line of eyebrow that straggled above small dusky black eyes' (756). Thérèse, however, is sympathetic to his feelings of revolt against the relentless, repetitive work he is expected to perform in the sawmill and his longing to escape to the woods. Ultimately, he comes to a bad end: when he is attempting to set fire to the mill, he is shot dead by Grégoire – the first in a sequence of events that leads, in turn, to Grégoire's violent death in Texas where he is killed in a brawl after taking exception to being called 'Frenchy', which he (correctly) perceives as an ethnic slur.

Another character in *At Fault* who complicates Louisiana's racial and ethnic mix even further is that of Marie-Louise, known as *Grosse tante*. She is described as 'coal black and [...] enormously fat', in accordance with the mammy stereotype, and, indeed, we learn that she had been Thérèse's nurse as a child. However, Chopin states unequivocally: 'Grosse tante, or more properly, Marie-Louise, was a Creole.' As we have seen, she is a Creole of the unwhitened variety, but she is disdainful of what she calls '*ces néges Américains*' (806–7), that is, the African American English-speaking fieldhands who work on other plantations. She lives in a cabin perched over the river on a precarious promontory. As the novel builds to a climax, David Hosmer's alcoholic wife Fanny, after drinking heavily, has crossed over to Marie-Louise's cabin in the midst of a raging storm; like Thérèse, she finds the old woman's presence soothing. Hosmer goes there to bring her home, but, before he can do so, in a topos beloved of southern Gothic writers, the entire promontory collapses into the roiling river, taking the cabin with it. Hosmer manages to recover his wife's dead body, though he himself is injured. Marie-Louise, however, vanishes without a trace. The African Creole has been sacrificed – and very conveniently erased – in order to foster the Reconstruction union between northern industrial capital represented by Hosmer and the white Creole landowning elites, personified by Thérèse.

In Chopin's subsequent short fiction, many of these motifs would be repeated and developed further. Her first short-story collection, *Bayou*

Folk, published in 1892, contains several examples. In 'The Bênitous' Slave', for example, she depicts an elderly former slave, wandering about aimlessly in the turmoil of Reconstruction looking for his former owners and incapable of realising that he is now a free man. Another far more complex story, 'La Belle Zoraïde', also has a slave at the centre of the narrative. Chopin begins the story with a framing device: old Manna-Loulou, a Mammy figure 'black as the night', overhears a Creole song about lost happiness, which reminds her of a sad story. Her pampered (and infantilised) white mistress, Madame Delisle, is accustomed to being put to bed:

> And then this old song, a lovers's lament for the loss of his mistress, floating into her memory, brought with it the story she would tell to Madame, who lay in her sumptuous mahogany bed, waiting to be fanned and put to sleep to the sound of one of Manna-Loulou's stories. The old negress had already bathed her mistress's pretty white feet and kissed them lovingly, one, then the other. She had brushed her mistress's beautiful hair, that was as soft and shining as satin, and was the color of Madame's wedding ring. (303)

To modern-day sensibilities, the image of the African American servant kissing the feet of her golden-haired white mistress is not only cloying but actively offensive. It may be the case, however, that Chopin was aware of the difficulties she would encounter in publishing the story and that this image of servility is calculated to reassure nervous strait-laced editors of the Genteel Tradition that what follows is merely a story of quaint old plantation days. This is clearly not the case, and the tale has many layers of meaning. When Madame Delarivière has Zoraïde's baby taken away to a distant plantation, this does not produce the result she expects; she had anticipated the return of 'her young waiting-maid [...] free, happy, and beautiful as of old' (306). But 'free' is precisely what Zoraïde is not; she is a prisoner not only of slavery but also of the rigid 'one-drop' racial taxonomies which were part of Louisiana legal systems until only a few decades ago. She grieves for her baby and her lost African lover, and she loses her reason. Her mistress, in belated remorse, has the child brought back, but Zoraïde rejects it, clinging to the bundle of rags in fear that her 'child' will be taken away.

'La Belle Zoraïde' is a sad and desperate story. Curiously, however, one detail that usually goes unnoticed by critics is that when Zoraïde's real baby is brought back to her, the child is described as a 'pretty, tiny little "griffe" girl' (307). As we know, a 'griffe' is three-quarters black and one-quarter white. Mézor, as we have seen, is described by Chopin as the colour of ebony. This means that either Zoraïde herself, despite her desperate protestations that she is 'not white', has more white blood than Madame Delarivière wishes to publicly acknowledge and which would explain her mistress's outrage at the notion of her marrying 'that Negro' (305), or alternatively, that her child has a white father. But again, as in *At Fault*, the violence and hints of interracial sexual liaisons are not overt but lurk disturbingly beneath the surface of the story.

Another story in the *Bayou Folk* collection, 'Beyond the Bayou', also features a female slave who is driven insane. The character's name is Jacqueline, but she has been known since childhood as La Folle (the madwoman). We learn that as a child she had been literally frightened out of her wits during the Civil War when her master's son had burst into her cabin, bleeding and covered in black gunpowder, escaping from enemy forces. This grim image in blackface had caused her to lose her reason; although she had continued to work in the fields along with the other slaves, she would never go beyond the bayou that marked the boundary of the plantation. Years later, as an adult, she is described as a 'large, gaunt black woman' (175) who spends much of her time telling stories to her master's daughters of things that had happened beyond the bayou. It is their brother, however, whom La Folle calls Chéri, that she adores. One day, when he is in the woods hunting, an accident occurs and he shoots himself in the leg. La Folle is aware that his life will only be saved if she carries him beyond the boundaries of the plantation, and, despite the fact that she is utterly terrified, that is what she does. When she has carried the child to safety and handed him into his father's arms, she faints, but on regaining consciousness at dawn, she awakens refreshed. Walking out to the edge of the bayou, she looks out at the silent fields of cotton and undergoes a sort of epiphany, seeing the lands beyond the bayou as an Arcadian landscape full of fragrant flowers and birdsong. She then goes on to speak to Chéri's mother and promises to stay close at hand. And on this note the story ends.

Although La Folle and La Belle Zoraïde are both driven mad by the circumstances and events of their lives, their fates are very different. Zoraïde has rebelled against a status quo that would deny her the possibility of choice and free will, and she is brutally crushed: her lover and child are taken away as slaves, and her nascent family is destroyed. La Folle, however, is able to regain her sanity at a terrible cost: she has no family of her own and can only find a happiness of sorts by acting as surrogate mother to Chéri and as servant to his family. The Reconstruction world beyond the bayou is presented as an empty landscape, a paradise of moonlight and magnolias, where slavery no longer exists. What Chopin does not say, but does imply, is that for women of colour in post-bellum Louisiana, motherhood exists under very similar conditions to those of slavery. In both stories, the only possible maternity is of the surrogate variety, to the children of white women, but never to children of their own.

Another story from the *Bayou Folk* collection that puts forth a view of motherhood as an acculturating force that underpins racial hierarchies is

'Loka', the tale of a mixed-race Choctaw girl. She appears one day at the side door of an '"oyster saloon"' in Natchitoches, begging for food, and is contracted to wash dishes. She is presented as plain and maladroit, with 'coarse, black, unkempt hair that framed a swarthy face without a redeeming feature, except eyes that were not bad [...] She was big-boned and clumsy.' She breaks many of the glasses she washes, and her wages are docked by her employer, 'until she began to break them over the heads of his customers' (212). Loka is sent to a respectable Cajun family of sharecroppers, the Padues, where her new mistress is unhappy that the young girl does not speak French, and when Loka says apologetically that she can speak English and a bit of Choctaw, Madame Padue responds, '*Ma foi*, you kin fo'git yo' Choctaw. Soona the better for me. Now if you willin', an' ent too lazy an' sassy, we'll git 'long somehow. *Vrai sauvage ça*"' (213). Loka is willing enough to work, but she is unwilling either to forget her Choctaw language or the fact that she herself is part Choctaw. She remembers

> old Marot, the squaw who drank whiskey and plaited baskets and beat her. There was something in being beaten, if only to scream out and fight back, as at that time in Natchitoches, when she broke a glass on the head of a man who laughed at her and pulled her hair, and called her 'fool names'.   (215)

Here, Chopin depicts the Choctaws as drunken and violent, but perhaps no less so than the customers of the saloon who abuse Loka both physically and with racist slurs.

Loka, however, is basically honest, and she has run away from home because she is unwilling to lie or steal at Marot's behest. But she longs for familiar scents such as camomile and sassafras drying in the shade and remembers with nostalgia the freedom of the woods. The one thing that she really enjoys about her work for the Padue family is caring for their baby Bibine. One day when the Padues go to town, Loka is tempted to return to the Choctaws, and she takes Bibine with her for a walk in the forest. The family returns, and when Loka and the child are nowhere to be found, Madame Padue begins to panic. But then, as night falls, Loka appears with the child in her arms. When her mistress threatens to dismiss her, Loka pleads not to be separated from Bibine, and Monsieur Padue intervenes on her behalf, telling his wife that the presence of the child had saved Loka from turning *canaille* or lawless, and that Bibine had in effect acted as her guardian angel.

In 'Beyond the Bayou', nature is seen as the source of La Folle's epiphany, but it is the tamed nature of the Reconstruction South. For Loka, however, nature is a source of temptation, a seductive version of freedom and anarchy, and the only thing that enables her to overcome this temptation is, as in 'Beyond the Bayou', the notion of being a surrogate mother to a white woman's child. Vicarious motherhood is presented once more as the only force that can tame or assimilate 'races' or ethnic groups that are viewed as inferior, 'natural', uncivilised. As in *At Fault*, where the members of the Creole plantation elite, Thérèse and Grégoire, are positioned in relation to African Americans, the Cajun Padue family, though of a lower social class, is 'whitened' in contrast to Loka. Indeed, the story ends with the complacent words of M. Padue: "'*Non, non, ma femme*,*"* he said, resting his hand gently upon his wife's head. "We got to rememba she ent like you an' me, po' thing; she's one Injun, her"' (218). Their own Cajun ethnic identity, their lower-class identity as sharecroppers and their racial identity as white are constructed in opposition to Loka, the dark, clumsy, Choctaw-speaking '*vrai sauvage*'.

We encounter an additional echo of *At Fault* in another story from *Bayou Folk*, titled 'In Sabine', where Grégoire Santien, the ill-starred young Creole of the novel, has gone to Texas. On the way there, in the lawless Texas-Louisiana border area by the Sabine River, he encounters a thuggish sharecropper called Bud Aiken who seems familiar; on reflection, Grégoire remembers that he had met Aiken before 'Tite Reine, one of the most attractive Cajun girls of his Cane River neighbourhood, had eloped with him. When she comes onto the porch, Grégoire sees that she is still lovely but is worn down by menial farm labour and the rigours of life with her husband. She is painfully thin; her clothes are shabby but clean, but her shoes are in tatters. When she stifles an exclamation on seeing Grégoire, her husband apologises on her behalf, saying, 'That's the way with them Cajuns ... ain't got sense enough to know a white man when they see one.' Here, we encounter the suggestion that Cajuns may not be as 'white' as they might seem, but it is significant that it comes from a character who is presented as a shiftless and indigent 'so-called "Texan"' (326), whose only claim to superiority is derived from his allegedly 'white' identity. Grégoire gallantly decides to save 'Tite Reine from her abusive husband; he gets Bud Aiken drunk, gives her his own horse so that she can return to her family in Natchitoches and flees on Aiken's horse across the river to Texas, where he will meet his death.

Another story about Cajuns, 'A Gentleman of Bayou Têche', shows Chopin at her most mordant and ironic. In it, she deftly skewers the objectification of Cajuns that was characteristic not only of much local-colour writing but also of its reception by the eastern critical establishment. Mr Sublet, a photographer, has come to stay on the Hallet plantation with his young son and wants to photograph Evariste, whom he had seen when the latter came to sell a wild turkey to the housekeeper. Evariste is poor; he and his daughter Martinette live in a two-room cabin which is described as 'not quite so comfortable as Mr. Hallet's negro quarters', and he is delighted when Sublet gives him two dollars and tells him he wants to put his photograph in a magazine. But when Martinette tells him he must get a haircut and put on his best clothing, he tells her that Sublet has other ideas:

> 'It's w'at I say,' chimed in Evariste. 'I tell dat gent'man I'm going make myse'f fine. He say, "no, no", like he ent please'. He want' me like I come out de swamp. So much betta if my pant'loon' an' coat is tore, he say, an "color" like de mud.'   (319)

The Cajun that Sublet wants to photograph is ragged, metonymically mud-coloured and the embodiment of exoticised Louisiana nature. Evariste and Martinette are perplexed, but Sublet's money is very welcome; but when Martinette speaks to Aunt Dicey, one of Hallet's African American servants, they hear a different interpretation:

> 'jis like you says, day gwine put yo' pa's picture yonda in the picture paper. An' you know w'at readin' dey gwine sot down on'neaf dat picture?' Martinette was intensely attentive. 'Dey gwine sot down on'neaf: "Dis heah is one dem low-down 'Cajuns o' Bayeh Têche!"'
> (319–20)

Dicey adds that Sublet's little boy had asked to photograph her while she was ironing and that she had brandished her flat iron, refusing his request in no uncertain terms. Martinette therefore tells her father he must not have his picture taken, because it would bear the label 'This is one '*Cajun* of Bayou Têche', editing 'low-down' out of Aunt Dicey's prediction. After Evariste has saved Sublet's son from drowning, however, the photographer tells him that his picture will be captioned, 'A Hero of Bayou Têche'. They finally agree that Evariste will choose his own caption, to appear underneath a photograph of him in his best clothes that finally reads: 'A Gentleman of Bayou Têche' (324).

Here once more we encounter an instance of Kate Chopin's capacity to write tales which were not only subtle and sophisticated treatments of complex themes but also enabled her to appeal to the sensibilities of editors who were probably unaware of what is happening underneath the wealth of sentiment and picturesque local detail. Chopin was all too aware of the inclination of magazine editors who published local-colour fiction toward material that treated Creole and Cajun characters as exotic exemplars of a different species, or as Chopin's biographer Nancy Walker comments, 'as anthropological specimens rather than as citizens of the United States in the 1890s'.[12] A singularly obtuse reviewer of *Bayou Folk*, writing in the *New York Times*, describes Chopin's Cajun characters as 'barbarians softened by Catholicism', characterised by 'a pagan primitiveness'.[13] But in 'A Gentleman of Bayou Têche', Chopin has lampooned the patronising, objectifying tendencies of some local-colour writers, photographers, editors and critics with sophistication and subtlety and suggests that Cajuns are no less entitled to define the terms of their own representation.

One group about which Chopin and her fellow Louisianans reveal certain ambivalence and uneasiness is that of free people of colour, who in the ante-bellum period often owned slaves themselves. In her story 'In and Out of Old Natchitoches', Chopin describes the actions of Alphonse Laballière, a member of the Creole aristocracy who has recently arrived in Natchitoches to take over a cotton plantation. There, he encounters a family of free people of colour, the Giestins, and begins to take his meals with them in their cabin. This causes rumours to circulate about him, and his fellow citizens allege that he is 'entirely too much at home with the free mulattoes'; one comments that 'Laballière had more use for a free mulatto than he had for a white man' (256). He encounters a pretty schoolteacher, Suzanne St Denys Godolph, who inexplicably snubs him. Finally, the mixed-race Giestin tells him that there are rumours circulating about him and his association with free mulattoes and suggests that it would be better for Laballière to avoid his company. Laballière reacts with wrath:

> 'Oh ho! So I'm not to associate with whom I please in Natchitoches parish. We'll see about that. Draw up your chair, Giestin. Call your wife and your grand-mother and the rest of the tribe, and we'll breakfast together. By thunder! if I want to hobnob with mulattoes, or negroes or Choctaw Indians or South Sea savages, whose business is it but my own?' (257)

Laballière then storms down to the schoolhouse with one of the Giestin children and tells Suzanne that he has come to enrol the child in her school. She reacts with priggish outrage, telling him that her school is not one conducted for people of colour, but Laballière leaves the child with her; the young Giestin vanishes immediately thereafter, and his family decamps to the area known as the Isle des Mulâtres. Suzanne speaks to her Cajun pupils of the insult offered both to her and to them and resigns in dudgeon, leaving for New Orleans. Laballière, however, has fallen in love with her. He follows her to New Orleans, where she is involved in a flirtation with Hector Santien, a member of an old Natchitoches family. Finally, Laballière (after gaining her mother's support) goes to bring Suzanne home, and we learn that Hector Santien has a parallel existence as a notorious gambler. And on that note the story ends.

This is a disturbing little story in that it reveals that free people of colour simply do not fit into any easy classification in Louisiana society, and, indeed, they represent a challenge to the notions of whiteness among Cajuns like the pupils in Suzanne's segregated school and also among the Creole elites represented by Alphonse and Suzanne. The only possible resolution for free people of colour is to be exiled to, and territorially contained by, the Isle des Mulâtres. The quite radical reaction of indignation to racial constraints on individual freedom exhibited by Alphonse is neutralised and erased by the conventions of romantic sentiment by Chopin so that he is rendered incapable of future actions on the Giestins' behalf and the story apparently glides by without the status quo being challenged.

In a fragment dating from 1892 unearthed by Per Seyersted, one of Chopin's biographers, titled 'A Little Free-Mulatto', Chopin creates a character called 'M'sié Jean-Ba', and describes him in the following terms:

> M'sié Jean-Ba' – that was Aurélia's father – was so especially fine and imposing when he went down to the city, with his glossy beard, his elegant clothes, and gold watch-chain, that he could easily have ridden in the car 'For Whites.' No one would ever have known the difference. But M'sié Jean-Ba was too proud to do that. (202)

The reference to railways and segregated carriages in a text written in the same year that Homer Plessy was denied access to the 'white' car on a Louisiana train, resulting in the historic *Plessy* vs. *Ferguson* decision in 1896 that legitimised racial segregation and the separate-but-equal concept in race relations, is surely significant. But M'sié Jean-Ba', unlike Plessy, is 'too proud' to challenge the rules of segregation, and his pride renders his daughter Aurélia's life a misery: she is lonely and has no playmates. Finally, M'sié Jean-Ba' packs up his family and, like the Giestins, departs for the Isle des Mulâtres, which Aurélia perceives as a paradise of children just like herself.

Like so much of Chopin's fiction, this fragment leaves the reader in doubt as to her own opinions: she clearly realises the absurdity of certain racial classifications and feels compassion for the child who is caught in the middle of them. However, the situation of free people of colour in her fiction is once again resolved by spatial containment and racial apartheid. Whether life on the Isle des Mulâtres was as paradisiacal as is suggested, however, is something else again.

The most often-anthologised story from *Bayou Folk*, 'Désirée's Baby', is extraordinarily well crafted. Although most readers are taken by surprise at the denouement, Chopin plants clues throughout the story. Early on, there is a reference to Armand's 'dark, handsome face' (242). We are told that Armand's mother died in Paris and, in many cases, the mixed-race sons of the plantation classes were sent to France and educated there. Later, there is Désirée's desperate plea for mercy when she compares the skin of her hand and that of her husband, telling Armand that her skin is whiter than his. Even more intriguingly, the child's nurse Zandrine is described as 'yellow', and

Désirée only becomes aware that her own child is of mixed race when she realises his resemblance to the child of a slave, ironically named La Blanche. Previously, Désirée had mentioned to her adoptive mother, Madame Valmondé, that her own child had cried so lustily that Armand had heard him as far away as La Blanche's cabin, though precisely what Armand was doing there is not stated. It is unclear whether Désirée's shock is due to the fact that her child has Negroid features or to the possibility that his resemblance to La Blanche's baby may mean that the two children share the same father. What is strongly insinuated, though, is the reality of mixed-race relationships on the Aubigny plantation and of the sexual exploitation of female slaves by their owners. As always with Chopin, the violence of interracial sexual relations simmers beneath the surface of the story. Perhaps the story's most intriguing facet, however, is how readily most readers are duped into jumping to the conclusion that it is Désirée who is of African descent, rather than Armand, the 'whitened' Creole landowner. For Chopin, the daughter of slave-owners and the widow of the White Leaguer Felix Chopin, to have written a story implying that Louisiana's plantation elites are perhaps not quite so lily-white as they seem was an act of exceptional daring and courage; to have managed to publish it in 1892 is an extraordinary achievement by any standard.

As we have seen, Kate Chopin's fiction strains against the straitjacket of absurd racial classifications that existed in *fin-de-siècle* Louisiana. Rather than portraying a society made up of racial and ethnic groups existing side by side in airtight compartments, she dared and defied prevailing norms in order to evoke a place and time characterised by conflicts and convergences, by intricate negotiations and shifts of power and disempowerment: a dazzling, kinetic kaleidoscope of human beings.

NOTES

1. Ralph Waldo Emerson, *Emerson: Essays and Lectures* (New York: Library of America, 1983), 790.
2. Dana Nelson, *The Word in Black and White: Reading Race in American Literature, 1638–1867* (New York and Oxford: Oxford University Press, 1992), viii–ix.
3. Léon-François Hoffman, *Le Nègre romantique: personnage littéraire et obsession collective* (Paris: Payot, 1973), 27.
4. Michael Omi and Howard Winant, *Racial Formation in the United States: From the Sixties to the Eighties* (London: Routledge, 1986), 21–3.
5. Emily Toth, *Kate Chopin* (New York: William Morrow, 1990), 30.
6. Toth, *Kate Chopin*, 39.
7. Toth, *Kate Chopin*, 64.
8. Nancy A. Walker, *Kate Chopin: A Literary Life* (Basingstoke: Palgrave, 2001), 42.

9. Bonnie James Shaker, *Coloring Locals: Racial Formation in Kate Chopin's Youth's Companion Stories* (Iowa City, Ia.: University of Iowa Press, 2003), xii.

10. Toth, *Kate Chopin*, 188.

11. Helen Taylor, *Gender, Race and Region in the Writings of Grace King, Ruth McEnery Stuart, and Kate Chopin* (Baton Rouge, La.: Louisiana State University Press, 1989), 142.

12. Walker, *A Literary Life*, 79.

13. Toth, *Kate Chopin*, 226.

5

Kate Chopin on fashion
in a Darwinian world

'How good was the touch of the raw silk to her flesh!' Mrs Sommers senses in 'A Pair of Silk Stockings' (502). The mature mother, full of the fastidious demands of culture, responds with natural animal joy to the leisure and luxury that fifteen dollars can buy, purchasing along with the sleek stockings a pair of 'polished, pointed-tipped boots' and a symmetrical pair of soft kid gloves. The visceral comfort of silk and leather against skin stimulates a craving for 'a nice and tasty bite' of food and entering a restaurant, amid the damask and crystal, she orders 'a half dozen blue-points, a plump chop with cress, a something sweet – a crème-frappée' with a glass of Rhine wine and a cup of black coffee (503). Utterly contented, she wiggles her toes in the silk stockings.

Chopin's naturalist story, published in *Vogue* in 1897, depicts fashion as the border between culture and nature. Beyond the mundane necessities of dress demanded by climate and geography, fashion signals gender, social class and economic status and marks supposed civilisation and intellectual range, as well as ethnicity and the subtle nuances of ideology, morality, idealism and aesthetics. Fashion theorists Alexandra Warwick and Dani Cavallaro in their study *Fashioning the Frame: Boundaries, Dress and the Body* trace the complex and often conflicting semiotics of sartorial meaning.[1] Dress functions as hieroglyph, its material presence drapes the body, revealing and concealing in intricate patterns easily read by members of a society and clearly setting limits on who is included and who excluded from its web of meaning. On a more playful psychological level, fashion is the site of the drama between fabric and flesh, especially for a woman who announces her availability and receptivity to the gaze of others and sets limits on the possibilities of approach and interaction. How much of a woman's body will she reveal and to whom are questions that theorists and critics interpret and debate.

Kate Chopin's story 'A Pair of Silk Stockings' reminds us that garments, too, press real flesh, rubbing texture against skin, a stimulating sign of our physical being. Dress is tactile, after all, a set of sensations experienced by the body. Chopin's story depicts dress as cultural and social marker – damask, crystal and blue points all signal leisure-class refinements – and, also at times, as sexual play: silk stockings, after all, both reveal and conceal the leg which ends in the pointed, tipped boot. And Chopin is especially sensitive to fashion as a sensual experience – the wiggling of the toes in sheer animal delight.

Fashion with its many layers of meaning serves as a provocative focal point for a consideration of Chopin's use of the social and scientific thought of her day. Over the decade of her writing career, she moved from satirical depictions of garments toward a serious consideration of dress as an expression of literary naturalism. Fashion functions in Chopin's fiction as a marker between the rawness of animal nature and the fabric of human culture in such stories as 'A Point at Issue' (1889), 'The Maid of Saint Phillippe' (1892), 'Athénaïse' (1896), 'A Pair of Silk Stockings' (1897), 'Fedora' (1897) and 'The Storm' (1969), as well as in the novels, *At Fault* (1890) and *The Awakening* (1899).

Biographer Emily Toth describes Kate Chopin as a woman who enjoyed tight-fitting clothes, chic hats and the colour lavender. She loved to ride on horseback and had, as her favourite garment, 'a fantastic affair – a close-fitting riding habit of blue cloth, the train fastened up at the side to disclose an embroidered skirt, and the little feet encased in pretty boots with high heels. A jaunty little jockey hat and feather, and buff gloves rendered her charming.'[2] She ordered clothes from New Orleans through her husband Oscar's store and had the reputation of not always worrying about the bills. We know, too, that she relished smoking cigars. She was the sort of woman everyone remembered, flamboyant, with a French sense of style.

When Chopin came to write, she wanted to be stylish in a French way as well. George Eliot had admonished young women writers in 'Silly Novels by Lady Novelists' to avoid fatuity in producing novels of what she labelled the '*mind-and-millinery*' genre. In such female romances, the heroine is 'the ideal woman in feelings, faculties, and flounces', Eliot quips.[3] One line from Eliot's essay struck Chopin and other women of her generation who hoped to be taken seriously: 'To judge from their writings, there are certain ladies who think that an amazing ignorance, both of science and of life, is the best possible qualification for forming an opinion on the knottiest moral and speculative questions.' Such knowledge is too often arrived at, Eliot scolds, by stuffing a woman's head with smattering of philosophy and literature. 'Great writers', she cautions, 'have modestly contented themselves with putting their experience into fiction, and have thought it quite a sufficient task to exhibit men and things as they are.'[4] That call to realism resonated with Kate Chopin. The question for her as a reader and would-be writer was how to establish a complex understanding of science and of life without being thought silly. How might she bring both mind and millinery together?

Women of Chopin's generation who had read Darwin's *The Descent of Man* understood him to believe that man had greater mental power than woman as proven by 'man's attaining to a higher eminence, in whatever he takes up, than can woman – whether requiring deep thought, reason, or imagination, or merely the use of the senses and hands.'[5] He listed poetry, painting, sculpture, music, history, science and philosophy as areas of clear male eminence.

Not surprisingly, women yearned to be associated with male scientists because such reading signalled the intellectual grasp of the female mind. As she graduated at the head of her class at Rockford Female Seminary in 1881, the future settlement house founder and Nobel Peace Prize laureate Jane Addams spoke for the first generation of college-educated women in the USA in her senior essay, 'Cassandra'.[6] She proclaimed that, like the Greek heroine, women were intuitively intelligent but lacked a language that men would listen to and heed. 'I would call this a feminine trait of mind', she chided, 'an accurate perception of Truth and Justice which rests contented in itself, and will make no effort to conform itself, or to organize through existing knowledge.' If they hoped to be understood by men, she counselled, young women would have to study at least one branch of physical science. By synthesising female intuition and male reason, a woman's subtle force might be expressed as creative genius. Edith Wharton, of the same generation but privately educated, faced the same dilemma. Writing to her close epistolary friend, Sara Norton, she stressed the joy in reading scientific books, claiming that 'Taine was one of the formative influences of my youth – the greatest after Darwin, Spencer & Lecky.'[7] Intellectually savvy women believed they might affect a male voice through the study of science.

Kate Chopin trusted that in a post-Darwinian age an American writer might be as candid as modern French writers, her biographer and editor Per Seyersted argues.[8] He credits Dr Frederick Kolbenheyer as the mentor who encouraged her to study scientific writing as early as 1886.[9] We know that she read science in journals and that reading them made her '"a little blown and dizzy"'.[10] In his influential essay 'The Experimental Novel', Zola (1880) had called on post-Darwinian writers to adopt the mode and methods of a scientist in a laboratory. Literary naturalism, as he defined the genre, places characters with inherited tendencies under economic and social pressures and then records how heredity and environment determine individual fate. In a review of Zola's novel *Lourdes*, Chopin acknowledges his brilliance as a writer yet judges the novel 'a mistake' because of his tendency to play the scientist. The merest narrative thread lies 'swamped beneath a mass of prosaic data, offensive and nauseous description and rampant sentimentality' (697). She tells a story of her attempts to write like Zola in the essay 'In the Confidence of a Story-Writer'. Lying awake one night, she plotted a tale that would make her a serious writer and set about building the story through elaborate research, poring over 'folios depicting costumes and household utensils then in use, determined to avoid inaccuracy' (704). Her notes bulged in her pockets, making her feel as though she was wearing Zola's coat. After picking through the mass of detail, with an eye to colour and to artistic effect, she created a tale at much pain to herself and with no appeal at all to editors.

The pressure for Kate Chopin and women of her generation was to prove their ability to read science and, at the same time, to distance themselves from such knowledge, avoiding mere display of knowledge – to be able, that is to say, to think like a man and write like a woman. How to bring, as Eliot sardonically put it, the mind-and-millinery genre into the ranks of respected realism or even forbidden naturalism?

Scholars and critics over the years have combed her fiction to find traces of scientific thought and language. Chafing from the naturalism of *The Awakening*, the reviewer from the Providence *Sunday Journal* became, perhaps, the first critic to turn Zola into a verb. Chopin's realism 'fairly out Zolas Zola', he charged, and sexuality becomes in the novel 'merely animal instinct'.[11] Chopin is often coupled with Darwin and read closely as a realist and, at times, a naturalist. Bert Bender provides a close comparative reading of Chopin and Darwin, making the claim that 'all of Chopin's courtship plots' in the 1890s are 'studies in natural history according to the logic of sexual selection'.[12] For Bender, as for the *Sunday Journal* reviewer, Chopin's heroine Edna Pontellier 'is a post-Darwinian woman-animal'.[13] Donald Pizer argues that the 'plain meaning' of *The Awakening* comes from its literary naturalism: Edna fails because 'she is a woman living within the limitations placed on the conditions of motherhood and marriage in which she exists'.[14]

Reading Darwin is a very different experience from reading Darwinists. Chopin, no doubt, read Herbert Spencer's *The Principles of Ethics* when it was published in 1892 and agreed with him that 'the survival of the fittest' makes laissez-faire liberalism a good idea because it offers individuals a sense of purpose. Seyersted claims that Chopin accepted Spencer's political argument for laissez-faire economics as well as his gospel of selfishness. Her embrace of Spencer explains for him Chopin's irritation with moral reformers. It is likely, too, that Chopin read Thomas Huxley's *Ethics and Evolution* in 1894 and puzzled over his assertion that ethical behaviour demands more than a mere struggle for existence.

In place of ruthless self-assertion it demands self-restraint; in place of thrusting aside, or treading down, all competitors, it requires that the individual shall not merely respect, but shall help his fellows; its influence is directed, not so much to the survival of the fittest, as to the fitting of as many as possible to survive.[15]

That ethical argument may well have been in Kate Chopin's mind – not the survival of the fittest but the fitting of many to survive – as she created Edna Pontellier's last thoughts about her children before her suicide.

Margo Culley and other scholars have scrutinised similarities between Chopin's fiction and the contemporaneous sociological work of Charlotte Perkins Gilman in *Women and Economics* and Thorstein Veblen in *Theory of the Leisure Class*, published, respectively, in 1898 and 1899. Gilman argues that 'the moral nature of woman, as maintained in this rudimentary stage by her economic dependence, is a continual check to the progress of the human soul'.[16] Veblen, too, discusses a woman's economic dependence as proof that she is not a free agent because 'the habitual rendering of vicarious leisure and consumption is the abiding mark of the unfree servant'.[17] Theories of conspicuous consumption detail fashion, the garments that define social rank, leisure, privilege and, in so doing, mark a wife as chattel because she is expected to carry male ceremonial goods literally on her back.

Scholars seem to have overlooked Edvard Westermarck's *The History of Human Marriage* that first appeared in 1891 and may well have been part of Chopin's reading. Westermarck was educated at the Swedish lyceum and then at the University of Helsinki and spent his teaching career as Professor of Sociology at the London School of Economics and Political Science. Influenced by Darwin, he added to his supposedly objective study his own opinions, and his later work would build on his belief that there is no absolute standard in morality. In *Christianity and Morals* (1939), he would characterise homosexuality, his own orientation, as psychical and not moral.

Westermarck draws several conclusions about marriage that might well have caught Kate Chopin's eye. Certainly, his ideas are similar to the ones she was using in crafting fiction in the 1890s. On the subject of promiscuity, for example, Westermarck deduces that such behaviour is 'not found among the very lowest races, but among more advanced people'.[18] Darwin and his followers looked for proof of human evolution by amassing data on various cultures in the nineteenth century together with earlier studies of human behaviour in a synthetic and comparative method of analysis. Studying what they considered to be 'primitive' cultures in their own time, they believed also that they were looking backward into time, gathering information about earlier stages of evolutionary human development. Westermarck reports that he had found no 'savage people nowadays' who practised promiscuity.

Chopin's fiction portrays promiscuity as a feature of her social class and milieu, an acknowledgement that would trouble the reviewers and readers of her day.

Chopin would also have agreed with Westermarck that the late nineteenth century favoured the ethic of unfettered individual freedom advocated by the Darwinists. The assertion of individuality as a right and even a duty seemed to him characteristic of the late nineteenth century. He quotes Lord James Bryce on the dominant pressure of the age, '"the desire of each person to do what he or she pleases, to gratify his or her tastes, likings, caprices, to lead a life which shall be uncontrolled by another's will"'.[19] Over the decade of her writing career, from the character Paula Von Stoltz in 'Wiser than a God' (1889), who chooses a career as a pianist over marriage, to Edna Pontellier, who moves away from her family to live alone and paint, Chopin's heroines experiment with the limits of individual freedom to gratify ambitions, tastes, likings, even caprices.

What Westermarck discovers from his research and Chopin depicts in her fiction is the seemingly counter-intuitive notion that freedom breeds discontent, especially in marriage. He notes a strong correlation between divorce and suicide, the high expression of discontent. The problem seems to him more acute among Protestants than Catholics, Teutons more than Celts, and in cities more than in the countryside. He cites W.F. Willcox, who concludes in *The Divorce Problem* (1891) that 'the proportion of suicides among divorced persons is abnormally large'.[20] The emancipation of women, especially of women able to earn a living, seemed to increase the instability of marriages. In the USA, two thirds of divorces at the end of the nineteenth century were demanded by the wife. Edna Pontellier, a Protestant woman who awakens to a world of promiscuity, separation and possible divorce, depression and, finally, suicide, would have seemed a plausible heroine to Westermarck.

On fashion, Westermarck has much to say that Chopin would have found useful as she dresses and undresses her heroines. Among tribes he calls 'primitive', he notes married women cover themselves and unmarried ones remain entirely naked. A husband might insist on his wife's garment as a sign of 'moral and physical protection against any attack on his property'.[21] Westermarck puzzles over the recorded fact that, for many people, being naked carries no sense of shame and quotes Jean de Lery's observation during a voyage to Brazil in 1585 that 'the nudity of their women proved to be much less exciting than our women's clothing'. And Westermarck marvels at contemporary reports among modern-day painters and sculptors that nude female models do not sexually arouse male artists: 'Venus herself, as she drops her garments and steps on to the model-throne, leaves behind her on the floor every weapon in her armory by which she can pierce to the grosser passions of men.'[22] No image comes closer to Edna Pontellier's exit in *The Awakening*.

Modesty, Westermarck concludes, can hardly be seen as the 'mother of clothing'. Rather, fashion arises from the desire to embellish through ornamentation, even as a 'sexual lure'. He quotes Michel de Montaigne on the irony: '"Why do people cover with so many hindrances, one over another, the parts where our desires and their own have their principal seat?"'.[23] The less flesh one sees, the more the imagination plays with the image, adding piquancy to desire. What he finds ironic is that clothing, although initially designed as a lure, has become among supposedly civilised society a requirement of decency.

As she came to write fiction, Chopin mulled scientific ideas over, thinking hard about the aesthetic question of how much natural science a writer ought to use. She had an eye, too, on the purity movement that demanded the bowdlerisation of questionable manuscripts, especially the writings of literary naturalists. How much realism and its scientific subset naturalism would the American reading public tolerate? Chopin would find that out as she experimented with sketches of female life, crafting increasingly naturalistic fiction.

Fashion lies at the boundary between the naturally appearing animal and the socially constructed lady. Raiment presents the absolute divide between the supposedly civilised cultures of France, Spain and England and the 'primitive' culture of the Cherokees in 'The Maid of Saint Phillippe', a sardonic tale of cross-dress. The heroine Marianne Laronce in her worn buckskin trappings looks 'like a handsome boy rather than like the French girl of seventeen that she was' (116). Her stride and poise are 'stag-like' while she wears the hunting clothes. At home, she adorns herself in her mother's garments: 'a short camlet skirt of sober hue; a green laced bodice whose scantiness was redeemed by a muslin kerchief laid in deep folds across the bosom; and upon her head was the white cap of the French working-woman' (119). After her father's death, two men court her, one offering her Louisiana and other the refinements of Paris. She rejects both men and, especially, 'civilised' culture, choosing unfettered Darwinian individualism. '"Freedom is left to me!"' she shouts, '"Marianne goes to the Cherokees!"'(122). Donning her buckskin jerkin and slinging her gun over her shoulder, she faces 'the rising sun'. The would-be feminism of the story is undercut by the satiric, even flatly funny, ending.

It would be tempting to say that Kate Chopin was a fashion reformer, desiring freedom from the insistent pressure of a corset and the hobbling restrictions of bustle and skirt. Her favourite outfit, after all, was a riding habit that was short enough to show the ankle of her stylish boot. Feminist fashion reformers throughout the nineteenth century advocated less restrict-ing garments and warned against the dangers of corset and bustle. Amelia Bloomer famously designed the gathered pants that bore her name, and, although feminists abandoned the much-lampooned bloomers, the fashion influenced the sort of clothing women wore while engaged in athletics. In leisurely resorts like Grand Isle, the setting of *The Awakening*, women wore tea gowns that required loose corseting and split skirts that allowed a woman to bicycle, ride horseback and play tennis, and bathing suits that made swimming possible. What seemed odd to people who lived in the town of Cloutierville is that Kate Chopin preferred a riding habit for leisurely walks around town.

Her stories, however, satirise a woman's attempt to dress like a man. 'A Point at Issue' features Eleanor Faraday who goes to Paris after her marriage to live alone and learn French. Husband Charles, a university professor, socialises with the family of a colleague who has two daughters: Margaret Beaton, a Woman's Suffragist, timidly pulls on 'garments of mysterious shape, which, while stamping their wearer with the distinction of a quasi-emancipation, defeated the ultimate purpose of their construction by inflicting a personal discomfort that extended beyond the powers of long endurance' (52–3). Margaret's bloomers signal, for Chopin, the ironies of fashion and social reform. Emancipation may be tricky and hard to endure. Her sister Kitty comes dressed as a gambolling kitten with 'a Napoleonic grip' on her rights and a capricious command of the household (53). Her animal nature stirs Charles's passions and, after describing Kitty to his wife, likewise stirs her jealousy. The edges of Chopin's naturalism are softened, here too, by irony.

A later quasi-feminist tale, 'Athénaïse', published in the *Atlantic Monthly*, moves between satiric humour and naturalist seriousness. The heroine, who desires unfettered personal freedom, escapes from her husband, settling in New Orleans into a 'big, cool, clean back room on Dauphine street' (442). She might have gone to the convent, Chopin adds with a tease, except for the vow of obedience. She teases, too, that the first act of Athénaïse's independence as a woman is to go shopping: 'The imperative thing to be done at present, however, was to go out in search of material for an inexpensive gown or two; for she found herself in the painful predicament of a young woman having almost literally nothing to wear' (442). One dress is to be pure white and the other, more enticingly, 'a sprigged muslin', a style that would have been cut in the Empire style, a light design that would free her from the restrictions of a corset. Athénaïse is clearly, as George Eliot put it, the ideal woman in 'feel-ings, faculties, and flounces'. A would-be suitor named Gouvernail 'sounded her literary tastes and strongly suspected she had none' (446). Her sprigged muslin, with its hint of freedom, stimulates his thinking: 'He knew that she would undress and get into her *peignoir* and lie upon her bed' (447). The image of her nearly naked brings him to the very brink of free thinking: 'When the time came that she wanted him, – as he hoped and believed it would come, – he felt he would have a right to her. So long as she did not want him, he had no right to her, – no more than her husband had' (450). Having come as far as any character in Chopin to understanding a woman's right to her body, he loses her not to her husband directly but to pregnancy. As she discovers her condition, she turns animal-like in her attachment to her husband, the baby's father: 'Her whole passionate nature was aroused as if by a miracle' (451). In the female animal, Chopin assures her readers, procreation trumps promiscuity.

As these stories demonstrate, Chopin cushioned naturalism with satiric irony early in her writing career. She plays with details of fashion and Darwinian notions of individual desire, focusing most often on female experience. *At Fault*, a self-published first novel, begins on the periphery of society in Place-du-Bois, where Thérèse Lafirme has lost her husband and gained his 4,000-acre plantation stretched along the Cane River, 'rich in its exhaustless powers of reproduction' (742), as she may prove to be herself. The thirty-year-old widow dresses in 'a frill of soft lace' at the border of an amply rounded body. She has taken up her husband's work, and the plainness of her dress reflects her dread of 'intruders forcing themselves upon her privacy' (742). She is the very picture of Kate Chopin in warm whiteness of skin and coil of waving blonde hair; she shares, perhaps, the author's anxiety about weight, 'suggesting a future of excessive fullness if not judiciously guarded' (743). Later, as she goes for a leisurely horse ride, Thérèse dresses, as her author does, in a 'dark close fitting habit' that 'lent brilliancy to her soft blonde coloring' (754).

At Fault has the makings of the mind-and-millinery school of fiction. What intervenes in the courtship is the appearance of Hosmer's first wife, Fanny Larimore, who was, when he first met her, a 'pretty little thing, not more than twenty, all pink and white and merry blue eyes and stylish clothes' (766). Chopin adds two elements to the conventional female romance that would have pleased Zola: divorce and alcoholism. Thérèse insists that her suitor ought to remarry his divorced wife, although she is an alcoholic, and work within the marriage to reform himself and to redeem her. Chopin is enough of a realist – perhaps truly a Darwinist – to deny Fanny a happy dependency on her husband or a redemptive cure for her dependence on alcohol and to bring about her early death.

Fashion is the key to understanding Chopin's satiric tone in the novel. In the background strut a flamboyant parade of ladies. Melicent, Hosmer's bizarre sister, gazes at herself in the mirror, sorry not to be plump but pleased with 'the great ostrich plume that nodded over her wide-brimmed hat' and 'the pointed toe of the patent leather boot that peeped from under her gown – a filmy gauzy thing' (770–1). In St Louis, the Exposition is in progress, and the streets are full of female shoppers in 'gowns of ultra fashionable' designs. Belle Worthington, for example, comes 'draped, or better, seemingly supported, by an abundance of stiffly starched white petticoats that rustled audibly' and with dyed blonde hair reinforced with false blonde curls (779). It is Belle's husband who discovers and appreciates Hosmer's library that includes French writers, works by Balzac, Racine, Molière, along with Shakespeare.

The gaudy and the imitative tendencies of American fashion are set against Hosmer's library of French books and Thérèse's travel to France for culture and, as it turns out, for shopping. She returns triumphant from her trip to Paris in the penultimate chapter, 'To Him Who Waits'. As she looks ruefully at the smirch on her Parisian gloves, we see: 'This flavor of Paris was well about her; in the folds of her graceful wrap that set to her fine shoulders. It was plainly a part of the little black velvet toque that rested on her blonde hair. Even the umbrella and one small valise which she had just laid on the seat opposite her had Paris written plain upon them' (869). Chopin treats Paris fashion with reverence.

However, Chopin closes the novel by satirising both fashion and natural science. Melicent has taken up with Mrs Griesmann, 'one of those highly gifted women who know everything' (875). The two women are off on a natural-history tour of Yosemite in the magnificent American West with, as Melicent details the fashion, 'those delicious little tin boxes strapped over our shoulders to hold specimens' (875). A hint of lesbianism comes here, as in other Chopin stories, with a specific fashion detail, eyeglasses: 'Mrs. Griesmann thinks I ought to wear glasses during the trip. Says we often require them without knowing it ourselves – that they are so restful' (875).

Chopin's later stories depict sexual, even predatory desire, in more naturalistic form. The fashion in these tales is minimal, suggesting the naked animal beneath the social fabric. The lesbian 'Fedora' wears only 'eye-glasses and a severe expression' as she finds herself sexually attracted to Malthers, a boy who had noticeably grown into a man. Picking up his sister at the train station, however, Fedora gazes into the young woman's face and sees 'the blue, earnest eyes; there, above all, was the firm, full curve of the lips; the same setting of the white, even teeth' (469). Fedora 'pressed a long, penetrating kiss upon her mouth' that leaves the young woman and the reader alike breathlessly stunned.

An often-discussed naturalist story that likewise has the power to stun is 'The Storm', a brief sexual encounter between Alcée and Calixta. The heroine, 'sewing furiously on a sewing machine', perspires from her labour in the hot humidity of the approaching storm and unfastens 'her white sacque at the throat' (592). A dress sacque is a long jacket, often ornamented with hand-embroidered designs and feminine frills, that a woman would wear in the morning before dressing or even, for the sake of modesty, might wear while she is dressing. The loosening of such a private garment signals the loosening of restraint as she succumbs to Alcée's arrival and arousal. 'Her firm, elastic flesh that was knowing for the first time its birth-right, was like a creamy lily' (595): Chopin describes the white body freed even from the delicate sacque. Her passion is utterly natural, 'without guile or trickery', and, as she climaxes, Chopin depicts the two of them 'at the very borderland of life's mystery' (595).

Fashion, too, signals the literary naturalism of her last novel *The Awakening*. At times, Chopin cannot resist caricature as when Miss Mayblunt, a lady suspected of being an intellectual who writes 'under a *nom de guerre*', arrives at Edna's dinner party on the arm of Gouvernail and carrying lorgnettes (970). Other women in the novel appear without a hint of satire. Aline Lebrun wears a white gown with a starched skirt and elbow sleeves and often works at her sewing machine, a mechanical sound that clatters throughout the novel. Adèle Ratignolle, pregnant through the nine months of the novel, dresses in gauzy veils and dogskin gloves with gauntlets over her wrists and in pure white dresses 'with a fluffiness of ruffles that became her' (895). She, too, sews throughout the novel but delicately with her hands. Mademoiselle Reisz would seem to be the sort of character that Chopin would satirise: 'She had absolutely no taste in dress, and wore a batch of rusty black lace with a bunch of artificial violets pinned to the side of her hair' (905). However, she is a subtly accomplished pianist, playing short, plaintive pieces that excite the imagination. Mariequita, a young Mexican woman, perhaps especially signals the naturalism of the novel. She comes clad only in 'ugly brown toes' and 'pretty black eyes' and 'a round, sly, piquant face' (914–15). Readers may be tempted to see her as evidence of a more 'primitive' stage of human evolution, except that Chopin makes clear that she is no more given to promiscuity than is Edna Pontellier.

Edna's fashion is likewise realistically drawn. The resort on Grand Isle is the sort of place a lady might loosen and even remove clothing without the notice and censure of her tribe. A woman would wear a tea gown, requiring a loose corset and no bustle at all. She might swim in a woven woollen suit that requires no stays. Edna's shedding of clothes is the element of the novel that critics have found most striking. As biographer Emily Toth puts it, the novel is about clothing, parasols, hats and veils that disappear one by one in the novel: 'Edna sheds more and more veils, physically and spiritually, until at the end, she is naked.'[24] The reason for taking her clothes off, read against social scientific theory of the 1890s, is that American economic culture has forced her into an ornamental role and only by shedding her clothes can she rid herself of that socially constructed fiction.

Actually, for much of the novel, Edna Pontellier is fabulously clothed. Her body is long, clean and symmetrical at twenty-eight, and she carries herself in 'splendid poses' without being artificial as was 'the trim, stereotyped fashion-plate' of her day (886). On Grand Isle, Edna's clothes are light in fabric and loose in structure. In the mornings, she dresses in a cool muslin gown, 'white, with a waving vertical line of brown running through it; also a white linen collar and the big straw hat' (894). On the beach in the heat of the morning, she removes the stiff collar and opens the dress at her throat. She travels with Robert across the bay to *Chênière Caminada* in a day dress and retreats to 'loosen[ed] her clothes, removing the greater part of them', (917) bathes her neck and arms and takes off her shoes and stockings, an afternoon ritual common to women of her social class. She goes to dinner in 'a dainty white gown' (922) and, after learning that Robert Lebrun intends to go to Mexico, she returns home and changes into 'a more comfortable and commodious wrapper', declining to change from the *peignoir* back into her dress or even, as Madame Ratignolle suggests, to belt it for a final visit with the Lebruns: '"You needn't dress; you look all right; fasten a belt around your waist. Just look at me!"' (924–5). Both women appear often in *peignoirs*, flowing garments of soft, sleek silk and lace requiring no corset or bustle.

In New Orleans, Edna breaks the rules of the city by adopting the comforts of resort fashion. She exchanges her 'usual Tuesday reception gown' for an 'ordinary house dress' (932). Outside the house, she appears 'handsome and distinguished in her street gown', but the unconventional freckles on her face are a sign she has been in the sun. As she cleans what she calls her pigeon house, she puts a 'dust-cap' on her lover Alcée Arobin, rolls up the sleeves of an 'old blue gown' and knots a red silk handkerchief in her hair (968), a hybrid fashion that Carolyn L. Mathews reads as a merging of social class and even ethnicity.[25] At her last dinner party as Léonce Pontellier's 'valuable piece of personal property', Edna wears her most sumptuous gown of golden shimmering satin with a 'soft fall of lace encircling her shoulders' and a bustled satin train heavy enough so that Arobin holds it up in order to free her of its weight (975).

The novel casts away gown and bustle, depicting Edna Pontellier in her return to Grand Isle and on the ocean shore as pure Darwinian animal. She changes into 'her old bathing suit still hanging, faded' and, as her skin chafes at the sensation of the dry scratchy wool, she casts 'the unpleasant, prickling garments' from her, much as any creature might. Her delight in being naked echoes that of Mrs Sommers wiggling her toes in the silk stockings. Edna senses, 'How strange and awful it seemed to stand naked under the sky!' (1000). Chopin details the suicide as a sensuous act of skin against air and water, until the Darwinian mechanism breaks down into sound and smell.

Chopin's straightforward naturalist tale of modern marriage, promiscuity, discontent, divorce and suicide surpasses her early experiments with realism as she abandons the safety of satire. The result was immediate and catastrophic for her as a writer. Even Willa Cather, under the pen name Sibert, accused her of writing 'a trite and sordid tale'.[26] Naturalism, the innovative literary movement of the 1890s, was risky for male novelists but far more perilous for females. Shedding the bustle in a Darwinian world proved fatal both to the heroine and her author.

NOTES

1. Alexandra Warwick and Dani Cavallaro, *Fashioning the Frame: Boundaries, Dress and the Body* (Oxford: Berg, 1998).
2. Emily Toth, *Unveiling Kate Chopin* (Jackson, Miss.: University of Mississippi Press, 1999), 87.
3. George Eliot, 'Silly Novels by Lady Novelists', *Essays of George Eliot*, ed. Thomas Pinney (New York: Columbia University Press, 1963), 300–24, 301–02.
4. Pinney, *Essays*, 310.
5. Charles Darwin, *The Origin of Species and the Descent of Man*, Library of America Edition (New York: Modern Library), 873.
6. Jane Addams, 'Cassandra', *The Selected Papers of Jane Addams, Volume I, Preparing to Lead, 1860–81*, ed. Mary Lynn McCree Bryan, Barbara Bair and Maree De Angury (Urbana, Ill.: University of Illinois Press, 2003), 428–30. See Katherine Joslin, *Jane Addams, A Writer's Life* (Urbana, Ill.: University of Illinois Press, 2004), 58–9.
7. Edith Wharton, *The Letters of Edith Wharton*, ed. R.W.B. Lewis and Nancy Lewis (New York: Scribners, 1988), 136.
8. Per Seyersted, *Kate Chopin: A Critical Biography* (Baton Rouge, La.: Louisiana State University, 1969), 90.
9. Seyersted, *Chopin*, 49.
10. Seyersted, *Chopin*, 86.
11. Providence *Sunday Journal*, 'Books of the Week', (4 June 1899), 15. In *The Awakening*, Norton Critical Edition, ed. Margaret Culley (New York: W.W. Norton & Company, 1976), 149.
12. Bert Bender in 'The Teeth of Desire: *The Awakening* and *The Descent of Man*', *American Literature*, 63, 3 (September 1991), 459–73, 460.
13. Bender, 'The Teeth of Desire', 465.
14. Donald Pizer, 'A Note on Kate Chopin's *The Awakening* as Naturalist Fiction', *The Southern Literary Journal*, 33, 2 (spring 2001), 5–13.

15. Thomas Huxley, *Evolution and Ethics and Other Essays* (New York: D. Appleton and Company, 1916), 82.
16. Margo Culley (ed.), *The Awakening*, Norton Critical Edition (New York: W.W. Norton & Company, 1976), 136.
17. Culley, *The Awakening*, 140.
18. Edvard Westermarck, *The History of Human Marriage*, 3 Vols. (London: Macmillan, 1925), Vol. I, 124.
19. Westermarck, *Human Marriage*, Vol. III, 372.
20. Westermarck, *Human Marriage*, Vol. III, 372.
21. Westermarck, *Human Marriage*, Vol. I, 538.
22. Westermarck, *Human Marriage*, Vol. I, 547–8.
23. Westermarck, *Human Marriage*, Vol. I, 553–4.
24. Toth, *Unveiling Kate Chopin*, 219.
25. Carolyn L. Mathews, 'Fashioning the Hybrid Woman in Kate Chopin's *The Awakening*', *Mosaic: A Journal for the Interdisciplinary Study of Literature* 35, 3 (September 2002).
26. Culley, *The Awakening*, 153.

6

ANN HEILMANN

The Awakening and New Woman fiction

that night she was like a little tottering, stumbling, clutching child, who of a
sudden realizes its power and walks for the first time alone ... She could
have shouted for joy. She did shout for joy, as ... she lifted her body
to the surface of the water.
A feeling of exultation overtook her, as if some power of significant import
had been given her to control the working of her body and her soul.
She grew daring and reckless, overestimating her strength. She
wanted to swim far out, where no woman had swum before.

(908)

Edna Pontellier's euphoria at learning to swim pinpoints the conceptual, and
feminist, dimensions of Chopin's complex metaphor of a turn-of-the-century
woman's 'awakening' to her ability to 'control the working of her body and
soul'. Compared as it is to a toddler's first independent walk – a first step in the
development towards adulthood – Edna's midnight swim is much more than
a victory of physical coordination. It establishes her sense of self-ownership,
physical, mental and spiritual, which in turn triggers two fundamental
insights that determine her progression from disengaged wife to autonomous
subject: in control of her body, she becomes aware of its potential for pleasure
and learns to claim her right to self-determination. The novel begins with
Mr Pontellier's assertion of his ownership rights: his act of 'looking at his wife
as one looks at a valuable piece of personal property' poignantly reminds her
of the wedding ring she gave into his safe-keeping when she went for her sea-
bath (882). It ends with the newly born New Woman Edna's declaration of
economic and sexual independence: 'I am no longer one of Mr. Pontellier's
possessions to dispose of or not. I give myself where I choose' (992). Edna's
proclamation of rights is the equivalent of Chopin's claim to independence in
her choice of subject matter, as is the desire to venture 'where no woman had
swum before'. This essay argues that in its quest for female self-determination,
The Awakening aligns itself with nineteenth-century female traditions of
writing, in particular the Anglo-American fiction of the New Woman.

Chopin's frank treatment of female sexuality broke new ground at a time when married women held no legal rights over their bodies[1] and when few other female or feminist writers hazarded openly to explore women's sexual desire. Unsurprisingly, therefore, many contemporary reviewers considered the author to have violated the dominant codes of moral propriety no less than had her heroine.

The storm of moral outrage at Chopin's 'unutterable crimes against polite society'[2] quickly overshadowed appreciation of her 'flawless art'.[3] Though acknowledged as a 'brilliant piece of writing',[4] this was 'not a pleasant story'[5] nor a 'healthy'[6] or 'wholesome'[7] book, critics warned, condemning *The Awakening* as 'essentially vulgar',[8] 'morbid',[9] 'repellent',[10] even 'nauseating' and 'gilded dirt'[11] that left one 'sick of human nature'[12] (a sentiment echoed as late as 1932 by Chopin's first biographer).[13] Even Willa Cather, soon to embark on her own exploration of female independence in *The Song of the Lark* (1915), deplored that Chopin had 'devoted so exquisite and sensitive, well-governed a style to so trite and sordid a theme'.[14] To many critics, the local colourist had strayed perilously close to reprehensible European movements in art and literature: the 'yellow' English decadence of an Aubrey Beardsley[15] or the French naturalism of an Émile Zola.[16] Notwithstanding her dismissal of Zola's 1894 *Lourdes* as inartistic and over-didactic (697–9) and her no more flattering pronouncements on Thomas Hardy's 1895 *Jude the Obscure* (714), Chopin, influenced as she was by European literature and dismissive of censorship codes, appeared 'one more clever author gone wrong'.[17]

The influence of European and, in particular, French literature on Chopin cannot be underestimated: an admirer of the strong-minded heroines of Madame de Staël's and George Sand's early nineteenth-century novels, she named her daughter after the latter's *Lélia* and between 1894 and 1898 translated eight of Guy de Maupassant's *fin-de-siècle* stories; two of these, 'Solitude' and 'Suicide', bear direct relation to themes she explored in *The Awakening*, originally entitled 'A Solitary Soul'.[18] Anglo-European literature, rather than the 'Provincialism' (691) of the Western Association of Writers, was the intellectual and cultural context in which she located her ideal 'group of readers who understand, who are in sympathy with [her] thoughts or impressions' (705) and in which *The Awakening* is often placed. Dubbed a 'Creole Bovary',[19] Edna has been compared to the protagonist of Gustave Flaubert's *Madame Bovary*, a novel tried, and acquitted, of obscenity charges in 1857. A disenchanted wife with expensive tastes who takes two lovers and, threatened with bankruptcy, swallows arsenic, Emma Bovary bears only superficial resemblance to Edna Pontellier and never attains her level of self-awareness and inner independence. *The Awakening* could be seen as a late-century feminist response to Flaubert, just as Mary Braddon's

The Doctor's Wife (1864) was its mid-Victorian equivalent in the genre of female sensation fiction. Other male-authored heroines of the European adultery novel did not fare much better than Emma Bovary: Leo Tolstoy's Anna Karenina (1877) completes her journey from unhappy wife to mistress and social outcast by throwing herself under a train, her re-enactment of the suicide she witnessed at the outset of the novel indicating her lack of any choice even in death; and Theodor Fontane's Effie Briest (1895) succumbs to depression and a wasting disease. Edna's suicide, by contrast, is a passionate assertion of her new-found identity and unconditional refusal to accept compromise: a rejection not of herself but of a social world that imposes moral imperatives on human desire, a celebration of this desire within a natural context that knows neither boundaries nor limits.

So, influenced by, yet resistant to, the male-authored novel of adultery, *The Awakening* is closely affiliated to a female and feminist tradition of women's writing. The 'revolution in female manners',[20] demanded by Mary Wollstonecraft in 1792 and practised in the new century by Madame de Staël, George Sand and Margaret Fuller, was adopted as a literary paradigm by the Brontë sisters in the mid nineteenth century and the female sensation writers in the 1860s, before becoming the trademark of the 1890s New Woman movement. The 'most alarming revolution of modern times', Margaret Oliphant lamented in 1855, was the emergence of a new type of heroine in women's writing; in the wake of Charlotte Brontë's *Jane Eyre* (1847), passion, sensuality and aggressive self-assertiveness had replaced the more angelic and forbearing qualities of the protagonists of previous times: 'No one would understand that this furious love-making was but a wild declaration of the "Rights of Woman" in a new aspect.'[21] At the height of the Anglo-American New Woman debates of the 1890s, critics still acknowledged Charlotte Brontë as the founder mother of contemporary heroines' individuality, 'unusual experiences and singular temperaments',[22] but were rather more condemnatory of the modern 'erotic-sensational novel' and the 'Tommyrotics' of female sex-writers who in their eyes 'deserve[d] unqualified anger and disgust'.[23] This response was in part due to the association of the New Woman novel with the earlier genre of sensation fiction. New Woman writers frequently employed sensational plot elements (cross-dressing, prostitution, syphilis, madness) in exploring feminist themes (the social construction of gender, the sexual exploitation of women, the perils of marriage). Less explicit in their feminist intentions, sensation writers like Louisa May Alcott, Mary Braddon and Wilkie Collins nevertheless created strong-willed, single-minded and resourceful heroines who, like the later New Woman characters, chafed against the restrictions imposed on their lives but, unlike them, sought to address inequities covertly, through cunning and imposture, plotting adultery, bigamy and murder in the heart of the family. Predominantly female-authored, both genres caused major literary sensations with their bold exploration of unconventional gender identities and the explosive questions they raised about the (im)morality of marriage, motherhood and sexuality, and both spoke to a popular readership primarily composed of women on whom they were thought to have a corrupting influence.[24] Female authors and heroines alike were charged, often simultaneously, with sex antagonism (hostility towards men) and sexual intemperance; with having both too much sexual knowledge and too little sexual tolerance.

It is in the context of what one contemporary reviewer called the 'overworked field of sex fiction'[25] that much of the adverse reception of Chopin's novel needs to be placed. Its 'disfiguring leer of sensuality'[26] proved too much for some readers: 'would it have been better', the *New York Times* pondered, 'had Mrs. Kate Chopin's heroine slept on forever and had never had an awakening?'[27] Advanced thinkers who admired the 'delicacy of touch' and '[c]omplete mastery'[28] of the author's 'subtle and brilliant',[29] sensitive, indeed 'unique'[30] treatment of a woman's 'full awakening of the entire human nature'[31] pointed out that the book was 'for seasoned souls […] who have lived'. As such, it was never intended for a young readership (the moral watermark for literature at the time), 'not because the young person would be harmed by reading it, but because the young person would not understand it'.[32] This is implied by the novel itself with its married mother of two who reaches the age of twenty-eight before her intense physical response to a man who is 'absolutely nothing to her' in emotional terms (960) awakens her to a realisation of her own sexually passionate nature, prompting the insight that love and sex do not necessarily coincide in the same object of desire. An experienced womaniser, Alcée Arobin excites and imparts a sexual pleasure which years of marriage have been unable to arouse: his 'was the first kiss of her life to which her nature had really responded. It was a flaming torch that kindled desire' (967). The novel was 'remarkable', one critic stressed, for its consciousness-raising qualities: 'in studying the nature of one woman [it] reveals something which brings her in touch with all women – something larger than herself.'[33]

There is no doubt that Chopin captured a moment of transition in the cultural and medical conceptualisation of female sexuality. Established medical opinion differentiated sharply between male *sexual* and female *reproductive* desire: 'a modest woman', the leading British physician William Acton declared in 1875, 'seldom desires any sexual gratification for herself. She submits to her husband's embraces, but principally to gratify him; and, were it not for the desire of maternity, would far rather be relieved from his attentions.'[34] Child-bearing and rearing provided plenty of sexual gratification for women: this medical stereotype is reflected in Madame Ratignolle's ecstatic family planning but, importantly, Chopin also offers glimpses of a physically fulfilled marriage (938), suggesting a sensual satisfaction that is entirely absent from Edna's marital life. With the rise of sexology in the 1890s, the old doctrine of the inherent absence in women of sexual desire was being challenged. Thus, Edward Carpenter wrote in 1896 that sex-passion was 'a matter of universal experience' and that to 'find the place of these desires, their utterance, their control, their personal import, their social import' was 'a tremendous problem to every youth and girl, man and woman'.[35] While Edna grapples with the conflict between her romantic and sexual impulses, both urging her towards adultery, her husband appears blissfully unaware that she might have any such desires. *The Awakening* issues an implicit warning to male readers to gain an understanding of and become attentive to their wives' sexual needs. It is Alcée, not Léonce, who 'detected [Edna's] latent sensuality, which unfolded under his delicate sense of her nature's requirements like a torpid, torrid, sensitive bloom' (988–9). Dr Mandelet, who has a good grasp of the situation, counsels Léonce to leave Edna alone for the time being; but as a contemporary reader, posing as a doctor, pointed out, Léonce would have needed to be enlightened about his wife's 'passional being' in order to learn how to relate to her sexually and emotionally.[36]

This is a lesson which Chopin's British counterpart George Egerton (Mary Chavelita Dunne) incorporated into her sexually explicit short fiction. Egerton's *Keynotes* (1893) and *Discords* (1894) scandalised critics for their 'neurotic'[37] subject matter and captured the *fin-de-siècle* mood of decadent New Womanhood. A reviewer, mistaking Egerton for a man, advised the author to tone down his 'appeals to the sexual sense' in order to avert the potentially injurious effects on young and excitable male readers.[38] In 'A Cross Line', Egerton's most notorious story, satirised in *Punch* as 'She-Notes' by 'Borgia Smudgiton',[39] the heroine entertains an adulterous affair with a stranger met at a riverside but dispatches him when she discovers that she is pregnant (a scenario explored differently in Chopin's 'Athénaïse' in 1896). Her husband, while erotically more knowledgeable than the clueless Mr Pontellier, is blinded to 'the problems of [woman's] complex nature' by the 'conservative devotion to the female idea he has created': few men, the heroine muses, have had 'the insight to find out the key to our seeming contradictions. [...] They have all overlooked the eternal wildness, the untamed primitive savage temperament that lurks in the mildest, best woman.'[40] As in Chopin's 'The Storm', the woman's adulterous affair eases the tension in, thus helping to consolidate, the marital relationship. Egerton offers a good point of comparison with Chopin.[41] Both had a keen interest in exploring women's inner lives, emerging consciousness and awakening sensuality, in language and imagery that prefigured modernist techniques; both used music as a structuring device; and both had a conflicted relationship with contemporary feminism. Though considered the quintessential New Woman (a *Punch* cartoon of the New Woman as 'Donna Quixote' in April 1894 even carried her facial features), Egerton took pains to distance herself from social and political feminism and emphasised her writerly preoccupation with the truthful representation of femininity.[42] Chopin occupied a similarly ambiguous position.

If the transatlantic New Woman movement is conceived as the cultural and literary arm of first-wave feminist activism, with the underlying objective of many writers being the use of literature as a political tool for social change, Chopin was certainly not a straightforward New Woman. Unlike Charlotte Perkins Gilman, Olive Schreiner, Mona Caird, Sarah Grand, Elizabeth Robins and other British and American New Woman writers, she never assumed an active role in any feminist organisation.[43] As a writer, she was strongly opposed to didacticism: 'Thou shalt not preach' was her eleventh commandment, she wrote in an autobiographical piece of the 1890s;[44] the propagandist tone of much of New Woman fiction would not have appealed to her. The protagonist of her first novel, *At Fault* (1890), learns only after the object of her misplaced moral reformism has died that 'constant interference in the concerns of other people [might] be carried too far at times' (807). Female social-purity fervour in particular was apt to become the target of Chopin's satire: in a diary entry of 1894 she mocked the smug pretentiousness of an acquaintance who 'wants to work to make life purer, sweeter, better' but whose good intentions always amounted to nothing,[45] and her 1897 story 'Miss McEnders' attacks the moral priggishness and hypocrisy of female philanthropists. Nor did she express any appreciation of 'the present craze for the hysterical morbid and false pictures of life which certain English women have brought into vogue';[46] a reference probably to social-purity novels like Sarah Grand's best-selling *The Heavenly Twins* (1893) or Emma Frances Brooke's *A Superfluous Woman* (1894), which castigated army officers and aristocrats as carriers of venereal disease and advised women to investigate the sexual health of prospective husbands before committing themselves and future generations to an uncertain fate. Chopin had read Grand's novel and rather cryptically commented on a friend's conviction that it was 'a book calculated to do incalculable good in the world: by helping young girls to a fuller comprehension of truth in the marriage relation! Truth is certainly concealed in a well for most of us.'[47]

However much she looked askance at social-purity feminism, in other respects Chopin shared many features of the New Woman: she liked smoking and enjoyed going for solitary urban walks; on her honeymoon she assured one of the Claflin sisters (possibly the later Victoria Woodhull: women's rights activist, stockbroker and proponent of 'free love') that she would not 'fall into the useless degrading life of most married ladies'.[48] In her short stories she frequently engaged with the themes of New Woman fiction: the importance of female independence, tomboyish heroines who refuse to be feminised, women's conflict between art and love, unconventional marital arrangements, marital oppression, prostitution and congenital syphilis.

The Awakening revolves around the key concerns of New Woman fiction – marriage, motherhood, women's desire for a separate identity and bodily autonomy – and reconceptualises these through the metaphors of gestation, awakening and sensual-spiritual epiphany. 'The Woman Question is the Marriage Question', Sarah Grand proclaimed in *The North American Review* in 1894;[49] the woman question was indeed inextricably tied up with marriage at a time when wives held limited rights to their children, property, income and bodies. 'In discussing the right of woman', Elizabeth Cady Stanton declared in 1892, 'we are to consider, first, what belongs to her as an individual'.[50] The answer was, not much: in 1890s Louisiana, a married woman, while entitled to any inheritances received before marriage, could not legally control any possessions or earnings acquired during marriage without her spouse's consent. She was legally bound to reside with her husband, who was the guardian of the children, and could not initiate a lawsuit or appear in court. Divorce, though more readily available than in other states, was highly disreputable in a predominantly Catholic environment.[51] Was it any wonder Charlotte Perkins Gilman asked in *Women and Economics* if, 'in reaction from this unlovely yoke [...] women choose not to marry, preferring what they call "their independence," – a new-born, hard-won, dear-bought independence'?[52]

Filled with a sense of 'indescribable oppression' (886) at the outset of the novel, Edna undertakes progressive steps to establish this independence. One of the reasons for Edna's great attraction to the sea is surely its limitless expanse, which offers welcome release from her feeling of domestic confinement. When she is not outdoors, Edna is at pains to create her own private space, a 'room of her own',[53] like her attic studio, where she can experiment with identities other than that of wife and mother. Her quest for independence, culminating in her move to a small house of her own rented with the proceeds gained from betting and the sale of her paintings, is at best precarious, however, given that her husband is legally entitled to intervene at any point. He does intervene when Edna moves out of the marital home, albeit – in line with Dr Mandelet's advice to humour her – as a face-saving rather than disciplinary measure: by instructing an architect to undertake building work and advertising the planned alterations and the Pontelliers' prospective summer vacation abroad in the local papers, he firmly reinstates himself, at least outwardly, as the controlling force in the household.

The few rights the law does grant Edna, such as access to her mother's estate, are dependent on the goodwill of male guardians; it is 'by driblets' that her father makes available the money which is legally hers (963). Small wonder perhaps that she does not wait for a written answer from Léonce before finalising the arrangements for her removal (967), and that she refers to the dinner party which will seal her independence at her husband's expense as a *'coup d'état'* (969), a political act of insurrection involving the overthrow of a government. This insurrection is couched in feminist terms – 'she had resolved never again to belong to another than herself' (963) – and the form it takes represents a feminist adjustment of the law that dispossessed women of their most basic rights: 'whatever was her own in the house, everything which she had acquired aside from her husband's bounty, she caused to be transported to the other house' (968). Edna is laying claim to her possessions even though in strictly legal terms they are still under her husband's control.

This also and particularly applies to her repossession of her body. The right to self-ownership, in sexual and reproductive terms, was a key demand of the nineteenth-century women's movement. A wife had no legal entitlement to refuse sex to her husband; nor, in the absence of legalised contraception, could she determine if, when and how many times she became a mother. The feminist claim to sexual self-ownership therefore came to be closely associated with 'voluntary motherhood', the right to birth control.[54] With their two sons aged four and five to the Ratignolles' four children in fewer than seven years, the Pontelliers appear to practise contraception. In other respects, however, Edna's desire for self-ownership and privacy is a constant source of friction. Exercised about her 'inattention' and 'neglect' (885), Léonce devises strategies to reaffirm his control: when, half-asleep, she displays a lack of interest in his conversation, he makes her get up on the pretext of one of their son's imaginary illness, and when on another occasion she refuses to come to bed, he insists on joining her outside. In the early stages of the novel, Edna engages in passive resistance, evading and side-tracking Léonce where she can, but not making her flight from his physical presence explicit. In Chapter XI, after her spiritual and physical arousal to music and swimming, she becomes, for the first time, overtly defiant of her husband's demands: 'her will had blazed up, stubborn and resistant. She [...] denied and resisted' (912). In the course of her feminist awakening, her challenge to Léonce's power becomes progressively more determined and outspoken. After an ineffective fit of temper, when his objection to her unorthodox handling of her reception day prompts her to stamp on her wedding ring, 'striving to crush' but entirely failing to 'make an indenture' (934) on the authority of a husband who is not even present to witness her anger, she embraces open rebellion: 'she began to do as she liked and to feel as she liked [...] When Mr. Pontellier became rude, Edna grew insolent. She had resolved never to take another step backward' (938–9). She starts withholding herself from him sexually, claiming her right to self-determination; as Léonce complains to Dr Mandelet, 'She's got some sort of notion in her head concerning the eternal rights of women; and – you understand – we meet in the morning at the breakfast table' (948). Her staunch refusal to attend her sister's wedding completes this process of externalised feminist rebellion, for it calls into question not simply her own marriage but the very principle of marriage. A wedding, Edna asserts, 'is one of the most lamentable spectacles on earth' (948): a statement evocative of the grim series of grotesque weddings that dissuade Sue and Jude from legalising their union in Hardy's *Jude the Obscure* and resonant also with Mona Caird's *The Daughters of Danaus* (1894) where a bride is compared to a sacrificial lamb.[55] Chopin's novel thus traces Edna's progressive development from dissatisfaction and depression, through mental and then sexual resistance, to physical withdrawal to a house, life and sexual-ownership rights of her own.

The carnivalesque feast with which Edna celebrates her freedom on her twenty-ninth birthday stages a symbolic over-enactment of the anarchic spirit that distinguishes the 'free woman' from the wife. Edna presents her guests with a carefully arranged spectacle of *fin-de-siècle* decadent splendour: the dinner table is decorated with a 'cover of pale yellow satin', candles in brass candelabras and 'yellow silk shades', 'full, fragrant roses, yellow and red'; a play of colours reflected in her own pale yellow attire, the 'golden shimmer of the satin gown', which is offset by a lace shawl 'the colour of her skin' (970–2). The visual and culinary delights of the feast are further intensified by aural and olfactory effects, the 'splash of a fountain' and the 'heavy odor of jessamine' drifting in from the garden (972). The quasi-Dionysian crowning of Robert's younger brother Victor with a garland of roses, performed to a recital of Charles Algernon Swinburne's 'A Cameo', completes the association with the 'New Woman', 'decadent' and 'androgyne' (with her 'long, clean and symmetrical lines' [894] Edna is as androgynous in appearance as Victor). Exuding an air of boyish degeneracy, Victor evokes Aubrey Beardsley, to whose decadent style the novel was compared.[56] In contemporary debates, the New Woman was often coupled with that other 'Literary Degenerate' and 'sexual anarchist', the decadent aesthete: in their challenge to marriage, their blurring of gender boundaries and their unorthodox sexual identities and politics, New Woman and decadent man were in equal measure perceived to pose a threat to bourgeois society.[57] The promise of an alliance of sexual anarchists, however, fails to be realised when Edna, provoked by

Victor's choice of song (a reminder of Robert), aligns herself with romantic sentimentality rather than decadence. The garlanded gauntlet flung across the room signals the end of the potential coalition between New Woman and decadent man and confirms Edna in her solitary quest for identity.

Although Edna divests herself of her old self, consolidating her break with the past with her affair with Arobin, she has no new identity that would constructively enable her to strike out on an independent life effectively and permanently. Instead, she experiments with two contrasting female roles exemplified by Madame Ratignolle and Mademoiselle Reisz – the passionate mother and the artist – but ultimately rejects both. The two women are catalysts of her sensual awakening: Adèle with the splendour and charisma of a 'sensuous Madonna' – an image Edna vainly attempts to capture on canvas (891–2) – and Mademoiselle Reisz with her inspirational renditions of Chopin. Both act as surrogate mothers to Edna, whose own mother died in her childhood. Edna is instantly captivated by Adèle, electrified by the frankness with which daring French books and bodily functions are discussed by the Creole community she heads (an experience that enables her to open herself up to Adèle in her turn) and is mystified by her maternal exaltation and 'kittenish display' of femininity in the company of men (951). Edna herself is at best an unenthusiastic mother; with not altogether adverse effects on her sons, who have learnt to be self-sufficient from an early age (887). The over-solicitous care of stereotypical 'ministering angels' (888), Chopin suggests, may not be in the best interests of the child (a point also made by Gilman).[58] But Edna is more than a semi-detached mother. Her emotional volatility is reflected in the unpredictability with which she treats her sons with indifference or affection, the latter usually coinciding with moments of sensual excitement (as when she cuddles Étienne on her return from the Chênière in Chapter XIV: there is a sense in which her maternal effusiveness acts as a displacement of her romantic feelings for Robert). Her relief at her children's periodical absences (899) indicates a reluctant, 'compulsory' motherhood, the very opposite of Madame Ratignolle's radiant maternity. That Edna does not, in speech or thought, address her sons by name until halfway through the novel, in Chapter XXIV (it is Léonce who first names Raoul in Chapter II, and it is Adèle from whom the reader learns Étienne's name in Chapter XIV) may hint at her difficulty in conceiving of them as individuals; rather, they appear a collectivity representing a duty. In the course of her self-liberation, however, Edna starts relating to Etienne and Raoul in individual and affective terms. The change is most marked after her move. As the narrator explains, 'Every step which she took toward relieving herself from obligations added to her strength and expansion as an individual' (978), enabling her to perceive others in an individual light too. Clearly, the absence of moral injunctions encourages 'voluntary motherhood', an affection no longer dictated by custom but imparted freely and willingly. In the process of reclaiming herself as an individual, Edna finds genuine pleasure in the thought of her children and, for the first time in the novel, seeks out their company: 'How glad she was to see the children! She wept for very pleasure [...] she lived with them a whole week long, giving them all herself, and gathering and filling herself with their young existence' (978). In conversation with Adèle in Chapter XVI, Edna had declared that she 'would give up the unessential' for her children – her money, even her life – but 'I wouldn't give myself' (929); here, for a brief period, she does give herself, precisely because it is a voluntary – and also, of course, temporary – arrangement.

The juxtaposition of 'compulsory' and 'voluntary' motherhood in Chopin's novel has affinities with other New Woman texts. In Caird's *Daughters of Danaus*, Hadria pointedly ignores her two (unnamed) sons, the product of an unhappy marriage, but, to make a point about 'free' motherhood, adopts an illegitimate girl, Martha, whom she takes with her when she abandons her family to set out on a pianist's and composer's career in Paris. Caird and Chopin both draw analogies between the imposition of motherhood, social expectations of maternal self-sacrifice and the conventional demands made on women's time and energy. One of the most serious arguments in the Pontellier household arises over Edna's reception day. Irritated by its futility she starts to ignore it, but even after her move, female acquaintances keep calling for brief visits (980). Similarly, Hadria finds her working life in Paris disrupted by well-meaning friends: 'Even here, where she seemed so free, the peculiar claims that are made [...] on a woman's time and strength began to weave their tiny cords around her.'[59] Derived from women's maternal role, these claims, and motherhood itself, Hadria declares, are a strategic device to ensure women's subjection to a lifetime of domestic confinement; children thus become

> the unfailing means of bringing women into line with tradition. Who could stand against them? [...] An appeal to the maternal instinct had quenched the hardiest spirit of revolt. No wonder the instinct had been so trumpeted and exalted! Women might harbour dreams and plan insurrections; but their children – little ambassadors of the established and expected – were argument enough to convince the most hardened sceptics. Their helplessness was more powerful to suppress revolt than regiments of armed soldiers.[60]

Indeed, it could be argued that Adèle's passionate plea that Edna '[t]hink of the children' (995) ends any dreams Edna might harbour even before she finds Robert's farewell note: 'She meant to think of them; that determination had driven into her soul like a death wound – but not to-night' (997). This night is to bring romantic fulfilment, but the reference to death suggests that Edna is already considering a suicide made to look like an accident as a means of remaining true to herself while not harming her children through public scandal. The next day, as she prepares for her final swim, '[t]he children appeared before her like antagonists who had overcome her; who had over-powered and sought to drag her into the soul's slavery for the rest of her days. But she knew a way to elude them' (999).

If Madame Ratignolle has a profound impact on Edna, so does Mademoiselle Reisz. It is the latter's musical genius that prompts an over-whelming experience of sensual and spiritual epiphany in Edna: 'The very first chords [...] sent a keen tremor down Mrs. Pontellier's spinal column [...] the very passions themselves were arranged within her soul, swaying it, lashing it, as the waves daily beat upon her splendid body, she trembled, she was choking, and the tears blinded her' (906). Associated with the elemental force of the sea, Mademoiselle Reisz's piano performance renders Edna speechless while making her body come into its own. It is as a direct result of hearing her play that Edna, who 'all summer' had felt an 'ungovern-able dread' of the water, is now ready to abandon herself to it and learns to swim (908). Edna is so overcome by her body's awakening that she mistakes its 'first-felt throbbings of desire' (911) for romantic love, interpreting her intense attraction to Robert as a stronger, more powerful version of her childhood and adolescent passions for a cavalry officer (a memory so strong that it resurfaces on her final swim), a neighbour's fiancé and an actor. In New Orleans, her visits to Mademoiselle Reisz serve the purpose of feeding her sensual passion with the double stimulant of Chopin and Robert's letters (946). Under the influence of Mademoiselle Reisz, Edna begins to take her own artistic endeavour, previously conceptualised as 'dabbling' (891), more seriously and draws strength for her personal liberation from the maxim that the true artist must 'possess the courageous soul [...] the soul that dares and defies' (946, 1000). But Edna is not so much an artist proper as drawn to the physical work for its sensual potential: 'being devoid of ambition, and striving not toward accomplishment, she drew satisfaction from the work itself' (956). While she is pleased to find her painting a source of income, a profes-sional artistic career in the footsteps of Mademoiselle Reisz is no viable alternative for her. Indeed, while punning on her own authorial persona in her choice of composer,[61] Chopin makes the figure of the woman artist singularly unappealing. Introduced to the reader as 'a disagreeable little woman, no longer young, who had quarrelled with almost everyone, owing to a temper which was self-assertive and a disposition to trample upon the rights of others' (905), Mademoiselle Reisz is a caricature of the 'ugly spin-ster' with more than a hint of the lesbian predator to her – 'She raved much over Edna's appearance in a bathing suit' (931). The 'appearance of deformity' (946) created by her undersized body seems to hint at her perversity of mind. A Svengali-like character,[62] she exerts mesmeric power over Edna and is continually 'creeping up behind' her (927) intent on prying into, probing and whipping up her emotions. If Edna visits her to indulge in daydreams about Robert, Mademoiselle Reisz gains her own voyeuristic gratification from these occasions: 'I should like to know how it affects her' (945) she muses as she prepares to perform Chopin's 'Impromptu'. Edna's object of desire, Robert, promptly materialises the next time Edna drops by at Mademoiselle Reisz's flat.

Neither the romantic lover (who turns out to be another conventionally minded male shocked at female sexual self-governance) nor Mademoiselle Reisz's and Madame Ratignolle's female communities of sinister artists and coquettish mother-women offer Edna an adequate model for an alternative existence. And so she (re)turns to the maternal embrace of the sea, whose 'everlasting', seductive voice has been calling her from the beginning (886). The 'feminine' element of the sea, with its sensual touch and cyclical periodicity, both inscribed into the novel's highly patterned, lyrical use of language and rhythmic structure, acts as the pivotal metaphor of Edna's awakening to her sexuality. Chopin's text here resonates with *fin-de-siècle* invocations of female desire in New Woman fiction. While male writing of the turn of the century and beyond often drew on the image of the untamed, heaving garden or other nature scenery to explore characters' libidinal drives (as in Hardy's *Tess of the d'Urbervilles* or D.H. Lawrence's *The Rainbow*), women writers developed a multifaceted feminine imagery of seascapes which operated as a complex set of metaphors encoding the female psyche, the feminine body and women's sexual desire.

The sea as an emblem of female passion was figured in ambiguous terms in women's fiction, as a site of sensual fulfilment but also as an elemental force driving women towards self-destruction. George Eliot's mid-Victorian *Mill on the Floss* (1860) combines both elements in Maggie's reunion, in death, with her estranged brother. In Elizabeth Stuart Phelps's artist novel *The Story of Avis* (1877), the sea represents a treacherous domain, the burial ground of women's dreams of artistic achievement. In a series of symbolic encounters with the sea, involving a near-death experience in which the protagonist is rescued by the man she loves, while the bird she was attempting to salvage dies in his protection, Avis's determination never to marry in order to concentrate on her artistic career is eroded. Her failure to realise her professional aspirations, sacrificed to marriage and motherhood, is associated with drowning: 'sometimes, sitting burdened with the child upon her arms, she looked out and off upon the summer sky with a strangling desolation like that of the forgotten diver, who sees the clouds flit, from the bottom of the sea.'[63]

Phelps's mournful diver is evocative of Chopin's naked 'figure of a man standing beside a desolate rock on the seashore' in an attitude of 'hopeless resignation as he looked toward a distant bird winging in flight away from him' (906). This, arguably, is an image prompted by Madame Ratignolle's piano performance: viewed from Adèle's perspective, the outcome of Edna's trajectory can only be tragic.

Gloom and despondency are also the keynotes of Mona Caird's *Wing of Azrael* (1889). Trapped from childhood in an oppressive environment, Viola is forced to marry a man she loathes, and, with the tide, she rushes to her doom. The sea here represents the inexorable power of patriarchal society as well as the heroine's resignation in the face of her condition: 'Her intense love of the sea [left] an indelible mark upon her character. Her instinctive fatalism might have been the lesson of unresting tides, of the waves, for ever advancing and retreating, blindly obedient, in spite of their resistless power and their vast dominion.' Provoked beyond endurance, she kills her violent husband and is last seen on the moonlit cliffs, presumably about to throw herself into the sea. The sea is her only refuge and an element with which she has felt the greatest kinship all her life: 'If only she could reach the sea she would not be lonely any more.'[64] In its promise of release and a return to the oceanic mother, the ambiguous ending has affinities with *The Awakening*.

A further point of contact with Chopin's sea metaphor arises from Sarah Grand's writings: here the sea – rather unexpectedly for a writer notorious for her social purity stance – encodes spiritual transcendence combined with sensual arousal and sexual fulfilment. In *Ideala* (1889), the protagonist tells two versions of the same story about the forbidden love of a married woman and a monk (a variant of Edna's own wish-fulfilment story of two lovers in Chapter XXIII): in one version they part on the seashore and are engulfed by the incoming tide; in the other the waves orchestrate their passionate embrace. In both cases, death by drowning represents an erotic consumma-tion of desire. This is also invoked in *The Beth Book* (1897), when the teenage heroine and her young lover narrowly escape drowning at their first meeting on the beach. Beth is a creature of the sea who draws erotic and social energy from her experience; thus, a sea bath with other girls leads to her being elected the leader of a quasi-feminist society. Most importantly, the sea is the site of spiritual and auto-erotic epiphany:

> The tide was coming in. The water [...] was [...] bright dark sapphire blue, with crisp white crests to the waves [...] [I]ts voice called to play, rather than to that prayer of the whole being which comes of the contemplation of its calmness; it exhilarated [...] and made her joyous [...] The sweet sea-breeze sang in her ears, and braced her with its freshness, while the continuous sound of wind and water went from her consciousness and came again with the ebb and flow of her

thoughts. But the strength and swirl of the water, its tireless force, its incessant voices [...] invited her, fascinated her, filled her with longing – longing to trust herself to the waves, to lie still and let them rock her, to be borne out by them a little way and brought back again, passive yet in ecstatic enjoyment of the dreamy motion.[65]

In Grand, as in Chopin, the sea is a source of orgasmic fulfilment, a fulfilment that threatens the dissolution of self. Beth almost proceeds to her death when '[t]he longing became an impulse. She put her hand to her throat to undo her dress – but she did not undo it – she never knew why. Had she yielded to the attraction, she must have been drowned.'[66] Unlike Edna, Beth is facing no domestic or romantic crisis; it is desire, not desperation, that attracts her to the water. The appeal of the sea is irresistible, and irresistibly erotic. In her exploration of Edna's oceanic desire, Chopin was drawing on a vibrant metaphor in New Woman fiction:

> The voice of the sea is seductive; never ceasing, whispering, clamouring, mur-muring, inviting the soul to wander for a spell in abysses of solitude; to lose itself in mazes of inward contemplation.
>   The voice of the sea speaks to the sea. The touch of the sea is sensuous, enfolding the body in its soft, close embrace.   (893; also 999–1000)

That Edna's walk to the beach is accompanied by a 'bird with a broken wing' (999) might suggest her defeat in conventional terms; but, once she has stripped herself of her clothes (her old identity), her resurrection as a Venus[67] (997) invokes a Phoenix-like transformation: 'She felt like a new-born creature, opening its eyes in a familiar world that it had never known' (1000). In a realistic sense, of course, Edna is about to swim to her death; symbolically, however, she triumphs over her condition the way Gilman's narrator does at the end of 'The Yellow Wallpaper': having broken free from the patriarchal structures of marriage, both women have 'got out at last' and, whatever might happen to their physical entities, in spiritual terms they 'can't [be] put [...] back'.[68] Like the eternal self-renewal of the sea, Edna's rebirth marks a return: to childhood, to the 'blue-grass meadow' with 'no beginning and no end' from which she had gained so much pleasure as a young girl, to the 'oceanic maternal space' of the womb.[69] Edna's suicide, if that is what it is, is a homecoming.

NOTES

1. It was not until 1978 (in UK law 1991) that rape in marriage was made a criminal offence in a US state (New York).
2. Review in the *St Louis Republic*, 20 May 1899, quoted in Linda Huf, *A Portrait of the Artist as A Young Woman* (New York: Frederick Ungar, 1983), 59.

3. C.L. Deyo, 'The Newest Books', *St Louis Post-Dispatch*, 20 May 1899, in Janet Beer and Elizabeth Nolan (eds.), *Kate Chopin's The Awakening* (London: Routledge, 2004), 56.
4. 'Literature', *Congregationalist*, 24 August 1899, in Margo Culley (ed.), *Kate Chopin: The Awakening*, Norton Critical Edition (New York: Norton, 1994), 173.
5. 'Books of the Day', *Chicago Times-Herald*, 1 June 1899, in Culley, *Kate Chopin*, 166.
6. 'Notes from Bookland', *St Louis Daily Globe-Democrat*, 13 May 1899, in Culley, *Kate Chopin*, 163.
7. William Morton Payne, 'Recent Fiction', *Dial* 37, 1 August 1899, in Culley, *Kate Chopin*, 172; see also 'Literature', *Congregationalist*, 173.
8. 'Fiction', *Literature* 4, 23 June 1899, in Culley, *Kate Chopin*, 168.
9. 'Notes from Bookland', *St Louis Daily Globe – Democrat*, 163.
10. 'Novels and Tales', *Outlook*, 3 June 1899, in Beer and Nolan, *The Awakening*, 58.
11. 'Books of the Week', *Providence Sunday Journal*, 4 June 1899, in Beer and Nolan, *The Awakening*, 58.
12. Frances Porcher, 'Kate Chopin's Novel', *Mirror* 9, 4 May 1899, in Culley, *Kate Chopin*, 163.
13. Daniel S. Rankin, *Kate Chopin and Her Creole Stories* (Philadelphia, Pa.: University of Pennsylvania Press, 1932), in Culley, *Kate Chopin*, 184.
14. 'Silbert' [Willa Cather], 'Books and Magazines', *Pittsburgh Leader*, 8 July 1899, in Beer and Nolan, *The Awakening*, 59.
15. 'Fresh Literature', *Los Angeles Sunday Times*, 25 June 1899, in Culley, *Kate Chopin*, 169.
16. 'Books of the Week', *Providence Sunday Journal*, 58.
17. 'Recent Novels', *Nation* 69, 3 August 1899, in Culley, *Kate Chopin*, 173.
18. Per Seyersted, *Kate Chopin* (Baton Rouge, La.: Louisiana State University Press, 1979), 147. For Chopin's translations see Thomas Bonner, Jr., *The Kate Chopin Companion* (New York: Greenwood Press, 1988).
19. 'Sibert', 'Books and Magazines', *Pittsburgh Leader*, 59.
20. Mary Wollstonecraft, *Vindication of the Rights of Woman* (Harmondsworth: Penguin, 1985), 132.
21. Margaret Oliphant, '*Modern Novelists*' (1855), in Harriet Devine Jump (ed.), *Women's Writing of the Victorian Period 1837–1901* (Edinburgh: Edinburgh University Press, 1999), 90–5, 93.
22. 'The New Heroines of Fiction', *Harper's Bazaar*, 1 January 1898, in Beer and Nolan, *The Awakening*, 23.
23. Amelia E. Barr, 'The Modern Novel', *North American Review* 159 (November 1894), in Beer and Nolan, *The Awakening*, 20; Hugh E.M. Stutfield, 'Tommyrotics', *Blackwood's Edinburgh Magazine* 157 (1895), 833–45.
24. Lyn Pykett, *The 'Improper' Feminine* (London: Routledge, 1992); Elaine Showalter, *A Literature of Their Own* (London: Virago, 1984), 153–215.
25. 'Books of the Day', *Chicago Times – Herald*, 166.
26. 'Fresh Literature', *Los Angeles Sunday Times*, 169.
27. '100 Books for Summer Reading', *New York Times*, 24 June 1899, in Culley, *Kate Chopin*, 169.
28. Deyo, 'The Newest Books', *St Louis Post-Dispatch*, 56.

29. Lucy Monroe, 'Chicago's New Books', *Book News* (March 1899), in Culley, *Kate Chopin*, 161.

30. Deyo, 'The Newest Books', *St Louis Post-Dispatch*, 58.

31. 'Books and Authors', *Boston Beacon*, 24 June 1899, 4, quoted in Toth, *Kate Chopin*, 348.

32. Deyo, 'The Newest Books', *St Louis Post-Dispatch*, 56.

33. Monroe, 'Chicago's New Books', *Book News*, 161.

34. William Acton, *The Functions and Disorders of the Reproductive Organs* (1875), in Sheila Jeffreys (ed.), *The Sexuality Debates* (New York: Routledge & Kegan Paul, 1987), 57–73, 62.

35. Edward Carpenter, *Love's Coming of Age* (London: Methuen, 1914), 2.

36. 'Dr Dunrobin Thomson' to 'Lady Janet Scammon Young', 5 October 1899, in Culley, *Kate Chopin*, 177–8. For details see Toth, *Kate Chopin*, 358–360.

37. Stutfield, 'Tommyrotics', 835.

38. T.P. Gill to 'Ardrath', 10 March 1893, in Terence de Vere White (ed.), *A Leaf from the Yellow Book: The Correspondence of George Egerton* (London: Richards Press, 1958), 24.

39. 'She-Notes', *Punch* 106 (1894), 109, 129.

40. George Egerton, 'A Cross Line', *Keynotes* (1893), in Sally Ledger (ed.), *Keynotes and Discords* (Birmingham: Birmingham University Press, 2003), 9.

41. See Charlotte Rich, 'Reconsidering *The Awakening*: The Literary Sisterhood of Kate Chopin and George Egerton', *Southern Quarterly* 41, 3 (2003), 121–36.

42. George Egerton, 'A Keynote to *Keynotes*', in John Gawsworth (ed.), *Ten Contemporaries* (London: Ernest Benn 1932), 57–60, reprinted in Ann Heilmann (ed.), *The Late-Victorian Marriage Question* (London: Routledge Thoemmes, 1998), Vol. V.

43. Chopin briefly (1890–2) was a member of the St Louis's Wednesday Club, where she met local feminists and women's suffrage activists (Toth, *Kate Chopin*, 207–10).

44. Chopin, 'Confidences', 702; redrafted as 'In the Confidence of A Story-Writer', 703, and published anonymously in 1899 (Toth, *Kate Chopin*, 295).

45. Chopin, '"Impressions": Kate Chopin's 1894 Diary', 2 June, in Emily Toth and Per Seyersted (eds.), *Kate Chopin's Private Papers* (Bloomington, Ind.: Indiana University Press, 1998), 185–6.

46. Chopin, 'Impressions', 12 May 1894, 181.

47. Chopin, 'Impressions', 2 June 1894, 185.

48. Chopin, 'Diaries', 13 June 1870, in Per Seyersted, with Emily Toth (eds.), *A Kate Chopin Miscellany* (Natchitoches, La.: Northwestern State University Press, 1979), 69. For the Claflin sisters see Toth, *Kate Chopin*, 102–3.

49. Sarah Grand, 'The New Aspect of the Woman Question', *North American Review* 158 (1894), 270–6, 276.

50. Elizabeth Cady Stanton, 'The Solitude of Self' (1892), in Miriam Schneir (ed.), *The Vintage Book of Historical Feminism* (London: Vintage, 1996), 157.

51. Margo Culley, 'Editor's Note: Contexts of *The Awakening*', in Culley, *Kate Chopin*, 120; Jessie J. Cassidy, 'The Legal Status of Women', *Political Science Study Series*, 2, 4, (March 1897), in Beer and Nolan, *The Awakening*, 42.

52. Charlotte Perkins Gilman, *Women and Economics* (1898, Amherst, New York: Prometheus Books, 1994), 91.

53. See Virginia Woolf, *A Room of One's Own* (London: Hogarth, 1929).
54. Margit Stange, 'Female Property: Exchange Value and the Female Self in *The Awakening*', in Nancy A. Walker (ed.), *Kate Chopin: The Awakening* (Boston, Mass.: Bedford Books, 1993), 201–17, 203.
55. See Mona Caird, *The Daughters of Danaus* (New York: The Feminist Press, 1989), 249.
56. 'Fresh Literature', *Los Angeles Sunday Times*, 169.
57. Janet E. Hogarth, 'Literary Degenerates', *Fortnightly Review* 57 ns (1895), 586–92; Elaine Showalter, *Sexual Anarchy: Gender and Culture at the Fin de Siècle* (London: Bloomsbury, 1991), 169; Sally Ledger, *The New Woman: Fiction and Feminism at the Fin de Siècle* (Manchester: Manchester University Press, 1997), 94–100.
58. Gilman, *Women and Economics*, 85.
59. Caird, *Daughters of Danaus*, 322.
60. Caird, *Daughters of Danaus*, 65.
61. See Elaine Showalter, *Sister's Choice: Tradition and Change in American Women's Writing* (Oxford: Clarendon, 1991), 76.
62. In George Du Maurier's bestselling novel *Trilby* (1894), the Jewish musician Svengali takes hypnotic possession of an artist's model, turning her into an internationally celebrated opera singer.
63. Elizabeth Stuart Phelps, *The Story of Avis* (London: George Routledge and Sons, 1877), 194.
64. Mona Caird, *The Wing of Azrael*, 3 vols. (London: Trübner, 1889), Vol. I, 5; for previous reference, see Vol. III, 156.
65. Sarah Grand, *The Beth Book* (London: William Heinemann, 1898), 324–5.
66. Grand, *The Beth Book*, 325.
67. See Sandra Gilbert, 'The Second Coming of Aphrodite', Introduction to *The Awakening and Selected Stories* by Kate Chopin (Harmondsworth: Penguin, 1986), 31.
68. Charlotte Perkins Gilman, *The Yellow Wallpaper* (1892, London: Virago, 1981), 36.
69. Elizabeth Fox-Genovese, 'Kate Chopin's Awakening', *Southern Studies* 18 (1979), 276.

7

MICHAEL WORTON

Reading Kate Chopin through contemporary French feminist theory

Much critical work on Kate Chopin has focused on the historical, geographical and personal contexts to her writings, illuminating her work by reference to social practices in Louisiana, the world of the Creoles, the myths of the Bayou and her own upbringing and adult experiences. Of particular interest to critics has been the issue of literary influence, with much attention being paid to French writers. Contemporary reviewers compared her unfavourably with such minor French writers as Paul Bourget,[1] and Willa Cather's labelling of *The Awakening* as 'a Creole Bovary'[2] continues to dominate much critical thinking, even though Edna Pontellier has little in common with Emma Bovary and Chopin's use of descriptive language and of direct and indirect speech is very different from that of Flaubert. More recently, Per Seyersted asserts that Chopin was influenced by 'the 'feminism of Madame de Staël and George Sand and by the realism of Flaubert and Maupassant' (32), and Eliane Jasenas emphasises the importance of Flaubert and Maupassant and asserts Baudelaire as an important influence.[3] Chopin herself includes references to French writers, with the result that suppositions are made about their influence on her. However, the fact that, for instance, she refers in *The Awakening* to a novel by Daudet (890) is in itself not directly meaningful, since it could be either one of his charming stories of southern France, a Zolaesque novel such as *Fromont Jeune et Risler aîné*, or *Sapho*, which anatomises bohemian French society.

This essay represents a shift from a focus on the author's readings and influences to a reader-centred approach, wherein Chopin's work is read through the prism of contemporary French feminist theory. While this may seem wilfully anachronistic, readings that centre on 'influences' all too often privilege the critic's rather than the writer's readings (for which there is little precise evidence) and therefore are spuriously speculative, however plausible they may initially seem. What interests me in Chopin's work is the fluidity of her thinking and the kaleidoscopic nature of her presentations of life, be it that of urbane Creole society, or of the Bayou folk. My metaphors of 'fluidity' and 'the kaleidoscopic' may seem too harsh a juxtaposition, too radical a mixing of metaphors. However, for me, Chopin's work is characterised by both, in that she writes in sensuous prose and foregrounds thematics of birdsong and seas, whilst also swinging between standard American English and jagged representations of the language of the Cajuns, Creoles and Acadians in her portrayals of domestic life in different classes and cultures.

Underpinning all her work is a concern with the authenticity of woman's existence and the importance – and the possibility – of choices. She is much more than the author of *The Awakening*, just as she is much more than the author of short stories such as 'Charlie' or those collected in *Bayou Folk*. Her work is less a manifesto of emancipation than a multifaceted exposition of quests for enduring relationships. Reflecting the tensions and the temptations between insiders and outsiders, between the individual and society, Chopin anatomises relationships in order to foreground the importance of the relational. Indeed, I would argue that in her work what I call 'relationality' is even more important than the independence, sexuality or even authenticity of women.

Culturally, women are associated with the home, defining it but, crucially, not owning it, as is seen notably in *The Awakening*, where Edna is classified essentially by her relationship with the home and its upkeep and by the raising of children; she is 'a valuable piece of personal property' (882) for her husband Léonce. In 'A Family Affair', Madame Solisainte maintains her despotic authority over her household by keeping the keys to the cupboards, and her niece Bosey liberates the household and creates her own future by taking over the keys and, thus, the management of the house. In 'Regret', Mamzelle Aurélie, an old maid of fifty, discovers the joys of (surrogate) motherhood after her cook tells her brusquely that she must learn how to 'manage' her neighbour's children while fostering them temporarily. She learns the joy of caring and, later, the pain of loss when the children go back to their parents, leaving her crying: 'Not softly, as women do. She cried like a man, with sobs that seemed to tear her very soul' (378).

In most cultures, even today, the home is conceived as the locus not only of stability but also of a unifying identity, and at the heart of the home is the woman, and, *a fortiori*, the mother. Manager of the house but not head of the household (that role is reserved for the husband and/or father), a woman has no space of her own, in the sense that she has no time for her own thinking, her own growing, her own inwardness and, above all, her own selfness.

Simone de Beauvoir famously argued in *The Second Sex* that domestic work is a form of exploitation and of oppression. She asserted that the obligation to undertake or oversee household tasks leads women to constant activity that does not actually produce anything. For her, domestic work simply perpetuates the status quo and imprisons women in immanence. On the other hand, men are free to live in movement, in progress, in becoming. In other words, they have transcendence in that they can express and live out their individual subjectivity.[4] Building on, whilst also critiquing, Beauvoir's work, Irigaray has argued that a woman puts the home at the disposition of the man without actually disposing of it herself, since her role is to manage it but not decide what happens to it: men want women to *be* the place of home without enabling or allowing them fully to inhabit or possess it.[5] Thus, while the man sets up the family home and the woman runs it, her real task is to reflect the man's identity back to him, maintaining and strengthening the development of his subjectivity at the expense of her own. This is clearly seen in the case of *The Awakening*, where Mr Pontellier, 'the best husband in the world' (887), cannot understand why Edna does not want simply to behave as all wives do, notably her friend Madame Adèle Ratignolle, whose 'domestic harmony' is, however, for Edna, no more than 'colorless existence' (938). Where Beauvoir is blinkered, and this is not wholly surprising given her own historical context, is in her identification of housework only with immanence. This means that she is – or chooses to be – blind to the household work of maintenance and preservation, which is richly creative and socially cohesive. Indeed, in his seminal 1951 essay 'Building Dwelling Thinking', Martin Heidegger argued powerfully and poetically that to be a human being is to dwell, and that dwelling is that which defines humanity. For Heidegger, it is through building that Man builds a place for himself in the world, an identity, a history. In other words, building is essential for the creation of subjectivity. He identifies two key aspects of building and dwelling: construction and preservation. While Heidegger's essay has been read as privileging construction, I would refute suggestions that building is exclusively male and patriarchal, whereas preservation is or can be female and matriarchal: Heidegger's argument about dwelling is more complex and less narrowly binarist than this. Some feminists define the very idea of house and home as totalising, imperialistic and patriarchal,[6] and the home can undoubtedly be the site of repetitive drudgery, with socially determined gender roles often a prison-house for women. On the other hand, the home is also the locus of the preservation of the family, and a place of security, privacy – and potentially of individuation and growth. It is also, in all cultures, a real and symbolic place of safety.

In her ongoing creative engagement with, and critique of, Heidegger, Irigaray emphasises that man's need to construct and build is a means of creating himself and the possibility of his own subjectivity – as well as creating for himself the comfort of another maternal home to replace the one he has lost. However, in a radical turn, Irigaray leads us to rethink the temporal relationship between construction and preservation: while the building of the house must come before the preservation of it, woman must precede (and make possible) building and, ultimately, male subjectivity.[7] The real question is not who or what precedes whom or what, but why precedence matters so much in the determination of social, societal and individual roles.

For Heidegger himself, building is also an act of gathering, of bringing together disparate objects and surroundings which have no centre or relationship until they are gathered in and around the building. Contemporary French feminism increasingly recognises the complexity of women's relationship with the home, emphasising that homemaking is much more than constructing walls and a roof: it is about furnishing it and personalising it with objects that have, or acquire, meaning. And here the role of the woman, and especially of the mother, is crucial: it is she who creates the nurturing space that her husband and children shall cherish as the primal and symbolically eternal home.[8] So, Woman can be positioned as Mother and as incarnation of the home or protectiveness and also as the focus of nostalgia and lost oneness. She has a vital role in the imaginary and symbolic lives of men, yet there is always the danger that whilst fulfilling this role, she nonetheless remains an object of men's fantasies. Edna may be 'the sole object of his [Mr Pontellier's] existence', but he nonetheless finds it 'very discouraging' that she 'evinced so little interest in things which concerned him, and valued so little his conversation' (885). In other words, a woman will be the central focus of a man's thoughts and fantasies only in so far as she is an object of his fantasies and devotes her energies to maintaining and bolstering his subjectivity.

What is interesting in much of Chopin's fiction is the fact that she creates female protagonists who are much more than simple rebels against either materialism or patriarchal oppression. For instance, Edna 'liked money as well as most women' (887), and little Mrs Sommers in 'A Pair of Silk Stockings' 'knew the value of bargains' (501). What is important in many of the tales is not so much the success or failure of individual women to achieve autonomy, either emotional or financial, but that they start on a journey towards a greater sense of selfness. When Mrs Sommers spends her windfall money on herself and goes to the theatre, she is seized on her way home by 'a powerful longing that the cable car would never stop anywhere, but go on and on with her forever' (504). She is returning home but she has also begun to realise that the house belongs to her husband and children and not to her. She has colluded in being the 'spirit of the home' and will undoubtedly continue to play that role, but the seeds of selfness have been sown. Marianne Laronce in 'The Maid of Saint Phillippe' is one of Chopin's most dramatic heroines. Named after the symbol of France and its Revolution, she is ablaze with a fierce sense of independence. Yet, the story foregrounds duality and ambiguity, as when, after the death of her father, Marianne is presented as simultaneously alone and not alone, with solitude and sociability interminging. When Captain Vaudry offers to take her to France and luxury, she replies, 'I have sometimes thought I should like to know what it is that men call luxury; and sometimes have felt that I should like to live in sweet and gentle intercourse with men and women. Yet these have been but fleeting wishes' (122). Like so many of Chopin's women, she is interested in material things as well as in emotions and instincts; more significantly even, she has been drawn to the prospect of dialogue with others. While her final decision is a melodramatic commitment to freedom with the Cherokees, the encounter with Vaudry has opened her to greater understanding of difference: this is a victory almost as important as her decision to cling to a romanticised freedom.

Indeed, it is the small triumphs of opening to selfness and otherness that make Chopin's work so important today, rather than the 'momentous' choices, such as Edna's forced suicide, or Marianne's theatrical 'death rather than bondage' (122). Indeed, one could see Chopin's stories as charting in a variety of ways the coming to terms with complexity, which is the beginning of a recognition – and assumption – of selfness that is never unitary but always fluid and shifting. In 'Athénaïse', the eponymous heroine rebels against marriage not because she hates her husband: 'It's jus' being married that I detes' an' despise. I hate being Mrs Cazeau, an' would want to be Athénaïse Miché again' (431). A strong Chopin heroine, she seeks to rebel against the 'social and sacred institution' of marriage (432), even though she realises that it is futile. Her first alternative to her marriage arises from a memory of 'a blessed life at the convent, at peace' (431). Similarly, Adrienne in 'Lilacs' returns to 'the haven of peace, where her soul was wont to come a refresh itself' in the company of 'pure and simple souls' (355–6). For the wife Athénaïse and the courtesan Adrienne, the convent is a fantasy of peace; it is also a fantasy of sorority, where women can choose enclosure and escape the tyranny of patriarchy and men's projections. However, the convent is never a solution in Chopin's world, because her women do not have the essential ingredient: a true religious vocation. The convent is a fantasy offering the prospect of safety, but a safety from otherness – and the fantasy is essentially one of regression to childhood. Athénaïse and Adrienne need in different ways to 'grow up' and accept the choices they have made and must learn to work at living in complexity – which is not necessarily compromise or defeat.

After running away from home to New Orleans, Athénaïse learns to think seriously about her choice of life, recognising that while she may have been ready to embrace the vows of poverty and chastity, the vow of obedience was well nigh impossible for her (442). She finally realises that she loves Cazeau and wants to go back to him of her own volition. When she returns home, it is to begin a true marriage in which she and her husband are happy to be together and to have chosen each other. Athénaïse has learned that she has the right to choose her life; more importantly, she has also learned to choose in reality and in difference. Analogously, Cazeau, whilst experiencing an overwhelming sense of loss after she has fled their home, considered that 'the loss of self-respect seemed to him too dear a price to pay for a wife' (438). This is not patriarchy speaking; it is an individual recognising that love can exist only in difference and that difference can exist as true dialogue only when selfness and self-respect exist on both sides.

Motherhood is an important theme in many of Chopin's stories, notably in *The Awakening*, where Edna scandalises Madame Ratignolle by telling her that 'she would never sacrifice herself for her children or for anyone', elaborating, 'I would give up the unessential; I would give my money, I would give my life for my children, but I wouldn't give myself. I can't make it more clear; it's only something which I am beginning to comprehend, which is revealing itself to me' (929). In this respect, Edna is regarded as strange, even unnatural. Earlier, we learn that it would have been a difficult matter for Mr Pontellier to 'define to his own satisfaction or anyone else's wherein his wife failed in her duty toward their children' (887). A few lines later, the text proclaims 'In short, Mrs Pontellier was not a mother-woman' (888). Mother-women are somewhat ironically characterised as 'women who idolised their children, worshipped their husbands, and esteemed it a holy privilege to efface themselves as individuals and grow wings as ministering angels' (888), the most perfect embodiment of such women being Adèle Ratignolle. What is interesting in the novel is that motherhood is always perceived and described from an adult point of view. Even when we learn that her sons tend simply to pick themselves up, brush themselves down and go on playing after a fall, rather than rushing in tears to their mother's arms, this is related from an adult point of view. In other words, motherhood in the novel is always conceived and presented as an institution rather than a relationship. This is brought home forcefully when Edna has to leave Robert just after she has confessed her love for him, in order to attend Adèle's labour. She attends 'with an inward agony, with a flaming, outspoken revolt against the ways of Nature, she witnessed the scene of torture' (995), and, when bending to kiss her friend goodbye, 'Adele, pressing her cheek, whispered in an exhausted voice, '"Think of the children Edna, oh think of the children! Remember them!"' (995). It is, of course, not the children whom she must remember, but the institution of motherhood.

Later, she tries to explain her position to Dr Mandelet: 'But I don't want anything but my own way. That is wanting a good deal, of course, when you have to trample upon the lives, the hearts, the prejudices of others – but no matter – still, I shouldn't want to trample on the little lives' (996). This is no monster speaking, simply someone who is trying to understand what she wants and why she wants it so badly. When she asks the doctor not to blame her for anything, it is not because she fears his moral judgement or that of society; rather, she is recognising evermore that she has different attitudes from those of her entourage. In western societies, women who abandon their children are invariably stigmatised as monstrous or emotionally stunted or inadequate. Society judges such mothers harshly, without allowing them the right to an individuality and identity that emerges from within themselves rather than from their roles as mother/wife-woman. In 1977, Julia Kristeva pointed out in 'Stabat Mater' that the Virgin Mary, who for centuries had been the central icon of self-sacrificing motherhood, was becoming less and less appropriate a model for women in the late twentieth century,[9] and, in 1979, in 'Woman's Time',[10] she stressed that motherhood is creation in its highest form, an activity that entails being deeply attentive to a child, bonded to it in enveloping gentleness and in a love that is forgetful of the self. However, she stresses that this selfless love should neither necessitate nor imply the sacrifice of the mother's own self, be this emotional, intellectual or professional. Kristeva proposes a notion of motherhood which is certainly selfless in the love for the child but which also strengthens the selfness of the mother. This maintenance of selfness is, for Kristeva, to be seen not as a source of guilt but as a source of creation and creativity in all senses of the term.[11] More recently, Élisabeth Badinter argued that modern women can exercise more choice than Beauvoir ever imagined and that they can now conceive of motherhood as a fundamental part of their lives, which is none-theless only a part, a parenthesis between their lives before and after mother-hood.[12] Badinter's use of the term 'parenthesis' is to be read not only in temporal but also in emotional and conceptual terms. A mother does not begin and end her motherhood at particular times; rather, the amount of attention she can focus on herself and her own becoming is greater when her children are less dependent on her, and she needs to recognise that she has responsibility for defining herself.

When Edna and Adèle argue about self-sacrificing motherhood, the narra-tor alerts us to the fact that Edna is beginning to understand the reality of difference: 'the two women did not appear to understand each other or to be talking the same language' (929). And as well as learning about difference, Edna is beginning to learn about selfness.

On the evening when she finally swims out into the sea, she is presented herself like a child: 'That night she was like the little tottering, stumbling, clutching child, who of a sudden realises its powers, and walks for the first time alone, boldly and with over-confidence' (908). This is a strangely inappropriate metaphor to use for someone who is learning to swim, yet this very strangeness draws attention to the issue of motherhood, for in her decisions Edna is like a motherless child with no one to help or guide her, and with no one to share proudly in her journey towards selfness.

In *Powers of Horror*, Julia Kristeva considers the role of the mother in the child's development: 'Toward the mother there is convergence, not only of survival needs but of the first mimetic yearnings. She is the other subject, an object that guarantees my being as subject.'[13] So, from the child's point of view as from the husband/father's, the mother is to be an object, and her subjectivity is restricted by the fact that the child wants her to be the guarantor of its subjectivity rather than recognising her as the centre of (an)other subjectivity.

As Edna swims out ever further, again like a child wading through a blue-grass meadow, 'She thought of Léonce and the children. They were a part of her life. But they need not have thought they could possess her, body and soul'; her last thoughts are 'Goodby – because, I love you' (1000). In sense and in syntax this is odd, the comma acting as both bridge and hiatus between justification and statement to herself, leaving the reader to speculate rather than arbitrate on her choice of suicide.

As Adrienne Rich argues in *Of Woman Born*, we need to differentiate between motherhood as an institution and motherhood as a series of individual experiences and practices. It is with the institutional dimension that Chopin mainly engages in her fiction. However, it is interesting to note that she also gives examples of motherhood as creative and reparative, especially when motherhood is an adopted rather than natural role. As already seen, for Mamzelle Aurélie, the elderly spinster of 'Regret', to tend and care for her neighbour's four young children, despite all the disorder they bring, is to learn the joy that comes from mothering as well as the ache of her own loneliness. In 'A Matter of Prejudice', Mme Carambeau lives irritatedly with her widowed daughter Cécile Lalonde and her grandson, tolerating only grudgingly that Gustav be allowed a birthday party every year. Her own lack of interest as a mother is demonstrated by the fact that she has not spoken for a decade to her son Henri, because he had married an American girl and decided to live in the English-speaking suburbs of New Orleans. During the party, a little girl runs into Mme Carambeau's room and leaps into her lap, throwing her arms around the old lady's neck, and stays there, 'panting and fluttering like a frightened bird' (283). Irritated, Mme Carambeau tries to remove the child, but the little girl does not understand French and stays resting her cheek against the old lady's dress. Realising that the flushed child has a fever coming, she decides to look after the child in her own house until she is well enough to be sent home. Although the child is 'sweet [...] gentle and affectionate' (285), she inevitably cries a lot throughout the night. To this is added the fact that 'Madame in all her varied experience with the sick, had never before nursed so objectionable a character as an American child' (285). However, she gradually realises that the only 'objectionable' dimension of the child is the fact that she is not Creole and does not speak French, and her prejudices are dispelled by the 'touch of the caressing baby's arms [...] and the feeling of the hot lips when the child kissed her believing herself to be with her mother' (285). The sick child is, in fact, her son Henri's daughter, and eventually the family rift born out of prejudice is healed due to the therapeutic powers of surrogate motherhood.

If surrogate motherhood can liberate from prejudice, in 'Beyond the Bayou' it liberates from personal trauma and emotional scarring. Jacqueline, 'La Folle', a thirty-five-year-old black woman, had been 'frightened literally "out of her senses" in childhood' when the young master on the plantation had staggered into her mother's cabin, 'black with powder and crimson with blood' after being shot in the Civil War (175). Manic in that she refuses to leave the area around her cabin or to cross the bayou, La Folle is nonetheless often visited by the children of the young master who now owns the Bellissime estate, and especially by his ten-year-old son, Chéri, who one day shoots himself in the leg, close to her cabin. Desperate to save the boy whom she calls 'Mon bébé, mon bébé, mon Chéri', La Folle realises that, despite 'her fear of the world beyond the bayou, the morbid and insane dread she had been under since childhood' (177), she has only one choice and must wade across the bayou with Chéri in her arms. Her surrogate motherhood drives her on until she can finally lay the boy in his father's arms. Then, abruptly, 'the world that had looked red to La Folle, suddenly turned black – like that day she had seen powder and blood' (178). She collapses and awakes only to find herself at home. She recovers quickly and then returns to cross the bayou again to visit the boy she saved. Having made a choice as to who she is and what she loves, she has learned the power of autonomy and selfness and can now, like many of Chopin's heroines, discover and exult in the beauty of the world around her: 'All the world was fair about her, and green and white and blue and silvery shinings had come again instead of that frightful fancy of interminable red!'[14]

In 'Charlie', Charlotte, the seventeen-year-old second daughter of an often silent father is a tomboy, who 'filled the place of that ideal son he had always hoped for, and that had never come' (644). However, after accidentally shooting a young man in the forest, she is sent to a private boarding school in New Orleans to learn to be a lady and gradually acquires the appropriate social skills. She also develops an infatuation for her accidental victim, and when she discovers that he is in love with her elder sister Julia, she flies into a rage, fulminates against her sister's treachery and tears off on her horse across the country. The mad ride paradoxically soothes her, and she experiences shame, regret and 'humiliation such as she had never felt before' (667). This leads her suddenly to grow up: 'The girlish infatuation which had blinded her was swept away in the torrents of a deeper emotion, and left her a woman' (667). After her father is severely maimed in an accident at the sugar mill, Charlie takes the reins of their home, and 'with all the dignity and grace which the term implies, she was mistress of Les Palmiers' (669). She has made a choice and becomes surrogate mother to her younger sisters, the main support of her father and the partner in running the estate of Mr Gus, who has long been in love with her and finally dares to propose to her. Her response is that they should wait, 'since she couldn't dream of leaving Dad without a right arm' (669) and also could not abandon the twins because 'I have come to be a sort of mother to them instead of a sister, and you see I'd have to wait till they grew up' (669). However, this is no refusal masquerading as a deferral. She has learned about herself and about what she can, must and chooses to do. She thus has grown into selfness, as well as into a certain (chosen) selflessness, telling him that 'It seems to me I have always liked you better than anyone, and that I'll keep on liking you more and more!' (669). She has found and chosen her place in the world and knows that she will go on growing.

Chopin's fictional world can appear to be a very hierarchical one. Men are masters of society, the Creoles are superior to the Anglophone Americans, 'old money' families look down on 'new money' families, the landowners (usually) look after their servants well but live in a world above and apart from them. However, in this world, Chopin's women are often learning that relations are more complex and varied than society's traditional vertical power relations and can be horizontal, fluid and changing. If awakening is a key theme in much of her work, the nature of the awakening is more subtle and complex than is often recognised, being about coming into a sense of relationality rather than into strengthened oppositionality: her women are learning about how to engage with the world rather than simply impose themselves as autonomous, self-driven individuals within that world.

Early in *The Awakening*, we find a statement about Edna that applies to many of Chopin's characters: 'In short, Mrs. Pontellier was beginning to realize her position in the universe as a human being, and to recognize her relations as an individual to the world within and about her. [...] But the beginning of things, of a world especially, is necessarily vague, tangled, chaotic and exceedingly disturbing' (893). Edna's emotional journey is one of learning to make connections, as when she suddenly sees the connection between the ocean and a meadow, between swimming and walking (897).

This is equally a journey of the discovery of differences, a journey shared by many of Chopin's heroines, albeit in different ways.

Edna's quest is not one 'primarily for sensual experience',[15] nor is she drawn into 'anti-feminism', wherein she has 'accepted a masculinist definition of selfhood', betraying all women as 'she is gradually revealed as a woman who cannot really like or value other women.'[16] Much has been made of the difference between Edna and Adèle. However, the two are united in a sororal friendship that is precisely built on difference: Edna's 'sensuous susceptibility to beauty' (894) draws her to Adèle, who is drawn to Edna because of 'the graceful severity of poise and movement, which made Edna Pontellier different from the crowd' (894). Their friendship grows mysteriously out of difference – which makes possible a genuine dialogue and sympathy: 'who can tell what metals the gods use in forging the subtle bond which we call sympathy, which we might as well call love' (894).

In Chopin's world, women have no male other to whom they can relate: the men are usually distant or absent and offer no dialogic otherness, nor even the potential for such dialogue. Irigaray argues that 'women almost always privilege the relationship between subjects, [...] the relationship between two', whereas 'man prefers a relationship between the one and the many, between the I-masculine subject and others: people, society, understood as *them* and not as *you*.'[17] Her insistence on relational identity illuminates the reading of Chopin's world, where women struggle with their solitude and where they essentially seek not so much sex or sensuality or even independence but someone with whom to *dialogue in difference*. This is why Mlle Reisz becomes a privileged interlocutor for her: not only because of her artistry as a pianist but especially because she makes Edna think – and think differently. A counterexample can be found in the ironic 'At Chênière Caminada', where, when Claire Duvigné finally realises that the fisherman Tonie is infatuated with her, 'a feeling of complacency took possession of her with this conviction. There was some softness and sympathy mingled with it' (314). Her sympathy can rise only because he now has some presence for her in his radical difference from all that she is and stands for. Of course, she has no real interest in him, and he is left with 'a terrible, and overmastering regret, that he had not clasped her in his arms when they were out there alone, and spring with her into the sea' (315). Plunged into depression, Tonie becomes his bright self once more only when he discovers that Claire has died and can therefore never have suitors or a husband but is in heaven where 'there is no difference between men. It is with the soul that we approach each other there. Then she will know who has loved her best' (318). In their individual ways, both Tonie and Claire live in the realm of fantasy; they recognise difference in each other but have no sense of the similarity within difference that is essential to true intersubjectivity. What is lacking in both their emotional make-up is the sense of what Irigaray calls a 'relationship-to', which is built on the desire for the other *as* other and on the recognition that s/he will always remain irrevocably different.[18]

Irigaray's notion of 'in-direction' between two individuals, of transcendence and mutual respect aids us to understand the frequent failure of Chopin's women to achieve full selfness – because for them there is often no real other. They want to be individual subjects who both desire and are desired in their difference. In Irigaray's terms, they want to be able to say 'I love *to* you' rather than simply 'I love you'; they want to experience caresses that are awakenings to intersubjectivity and to 'a life different to the arduous everyday' rather than modes of 'ensnarement, possession and submission of the freedom of the other'.[19] Yet, frequently, they adapt meekly to the role of mother-woman and the pleasures of conjugal life. Yet, even here, there are occasional moments of escape, as in 'The Storm', where Calixta finally gives in to her desire for Laballière, then enthusiastically welcomes back her husband and son, while Clarisse Laballière happily agrees to her husband's suggestion that she stay away a month longer, as she can rediscover for a while 'the pleasant freedom of her maiden life': 'devoted as she was to her husband, their intimate conjugal life was something which she was more than willing to forego for a while' (596).

Edna and Charlie are important heroines precisely because they come to a sense of selfness through recognising difference in others. In Charlie's case, full union in difference is deferred but promised, as she and Mr Gus, as well as she and her father (and even her sisters), have learned to respect difference and bring it into their lives. As for Edna, she comes to understand the nature of the 'soul's slavery' in which she could be imprisoned by her family and discovers the way to 'elude' her children (999); more importantly even, she has learned to dialogue in difference with both Adèle and Mlle Reisz. Yet, this is not enough, for she needs more than difference in sorority. She needs difference-in-equality with a man. However, she realises that 'there was no one thing in the world that she desired. There was no human being whom she wanted near her except Robert' (999), and she knows equally that even he will eventually vanish from her thoughts. She is alone, in solitude that she perceives as absolute, hence her swimming out into oblivion, into fusion with the sea, which, for all its seductive sensuality, is ultimately the abolition of the possibility of individuation through, and selfness in, differentiation.

Chopin's tales are very much of their time and place; therein lies their charm. However, as we read her today through various lenses, and especially through that of contemporary French feminist theory, we discover a world that speaks powerfully to us not only of the difficulties of ever finding selfness but also of the abiding need to establish it and to discover ourselves in our relations with others.

NOTES

1. Alice Hall Petry (ed.), *Critical Essays on Kate Chopin* (New York: G. K. Hall and Co, 1996), 58.
2. Petry, *Critical Essays*, 14.
3. Eliane Jasenas, 'The French Influence in Kate Chopin's *The Awakening*', *Nineteenth-Century French Studies*, 4, 3 (spring 1976), 312–22.
4. Simone de Beauvoir, trans. H.M. Parshley, *The Second Sex* (New York: Alfred Knopf, 1993).
5. Luce Irigaray, trans. Carolyn Burke and Gillian C. Gill, *An Ethics of Sexual Difference* (London: Athlone Press, 1993), 52.
6. Biddy Martin and Chandra Talpade Mohanty, 'Feminist Politics: What's Home Got to Do with It?', in Teresa de Lauretis (ed.) *Feminist Studies/Cultural Studies* (Bloomington, Ind.: Indiana University Press, 1986), 191–212.
7. Irigaray, *Ethics*, 52 and 101. For insights into Irigaray's more recent thinking on dwelling spaces, see, for instance, 'How Can We Live Together in a Lasting Way?', *Key Writings* (London: Continuum, 2004), 123–33.
8. Gaston Bachelard, *La Terre et les rêveries du repos* (Paris: Librairie José Corti, 1948), 102.
9. Julia Kristeva, 'Stabat Mater', in Toril Moi (ed.) *The Kristeva Reader* (Oxford: Basil Blackwell, 1986), 160–86.
10. Julia Kristeva, 'Women's Time', in Toril Moi (ed.) *The Kristeva Reader* (Oxford: Basil Blackwell, 1986), 188–213. I am grateful to Gill Rye for her insights on motherhood and mothering in contemporary French literature and thought: see her forthcoming book, *Narratives of Mothering: Women's Writing in Contemporary France*.
11. Kristeva, 'Women's Time', *The Kristeva Reader*, 206.
12. Élisabeth Badinter, 'La Revanche des mères', *Le Monde*, supplement 'L'Avenir des femmes: du *Deuxième Sexe* de Simone de Beauvoir à la parité', 22 April 1999, 4.
13. Julia Kristeva, trans. Leon S. Roudiez, *Powers of Horror: An Essay on Abjection* (New York: Columbia University Press, 1982), 32.
14. This sentence does not appear in the *Complete Works* (1969), but is to be found in Kate Chopin, in Pamela Knights (ed.) *The Awakening and Other Stories* (Oxford: Oxford University Press, 2000), 171.
15. Paul Christian Jones, 'A Re-Awakening: Anne Tyler's Postfeminist Edna Pontellier in *Ladder of Years*', *Critique: Studies in Contemporary Fiction*, 44 (March 2003), 276.
16. Katherine Kearns, 'The Nullification of Edna Pontellier', *American Literature*, 63, 1 (March 1991), 76.
17. Irigaray, 'The Wedding Between the Body and Language', *Key Writings* (London: Continuum, 2004), 13.
18. Irigaray, 'The Wedding', 17.
19. Irigaray, 'The Wedding', 20.

8

ELIZABETH NOLAN

The Awakening as literary innovation
Chopin, Maupassant and the evolution of genre

the artist must possess the courageous soul ... The soul that dares and defies.
(946)

Any literary succession is first of all a struggle, a destruction of old values and a
reconstruction of old elements

Jurrii Tynyanov (1921)[1]

Kate Chopin's well-documented descent into literary obscurity after the publication of *The Awakening* (1899) is most often attributed to her engagement
with the taboo issues of female sexual desire and infidelity. Her marginalisa-
tion, however, may have been as much a result of her overt rejection of
traditional literary form and blatant transgression of conventional genre
boundaries. While reviews of Chopin's earlier collections of short stories, in
particular *Bayou Folk* (1894), had focused on the 'quaintness', 'charm' and
distinctly regional flavour of the writing and had positioned her firmly within
the framework of local-colour fiction, *The Awakening* resisted such generic
categorisation. The highly original style and voice that Chopin established in
this impressionistic narrative, with its lyrical, sensuous prose, symbolism,
unusual circular structure and its focus on the inner consciousness of its
heroine, evidently unsettled the expectations of critics. Although C.L. Deyo,
writing in the *St Louis Post-Dispatch* in May 1899, recognised Chopin's
originality and innovation, observing that 'The work is more than unusual.
It is unique',[2] many interpreted the text as an 'aberration', a radical departure
for a writer who had previously adhered to convention. Few critics actually
attempted definitions of genre, their commentaries relying primarily on moral
condemnation of the novel's controversial themes.

In fact, if close attention is paid to Chopin's writings, both fiction and non-
fiction, what is revealed is a long-standing opposition to the constraints of
literary tradition and, from her earliest compositions, a willingness to experiment with form and genre. Her dissatisfaction with existing literary models
is everywhere apparent. Emily Toth, Chopin's biographer, identifies her as

having studied and understood literary tradition – and always with a critical eye – noting that as a fledgling writer she copied passages from famous authors into her commonplace book, only to rewrite and simplify their lines.[3] Later, as a literary critic, Chopin would lament the 'provincialism' of the Western Association of Writers who, she suggested, would not produce an artist of vision until they learned to transcend the local, the immediate and move beyond 'past and conventional standards' to engage with 'human existence in its subtle, complex, true meaning, stripped of the veil with which ethical and conventional standards have draped it' (691). And, throughout her career, she fictionalised her own frustrations and desires in the portrayal of women artists, who, circumscribed by the modes available to them, struggled to achieve creative expression. In *The Awakening*, disappointed with her early, mimetic sketches, Edna Pontellier embarks on a journey of artistic experimentation. Seeking to free herself from the limits of realistic representation, she begins to paint intuitively. Surrendering herself to the vagaries of feeling and mood, she attains moments of transcendence during which she can work spontaneously with 'sureness and ease' (956). But 'Elizabeth Stock's One Story' (1898) is a bleaker meditation on women's relationship to art, in this case the written word. The heroine who 'always felt as if [she] would like to write stories', agonises over an 'original' composition in the face of sustained discouragement from a male relative who believes she should stick to dressmaking. The story she does manage to tell is her own, and it explores the consequences for women who participate in the culture of literacy: when a good turn reveals she has read the content of an open postcard, Elizabeth Stock encounters censure and dismissal from her position as postmistress. In this story, women's artistic aspirations are further circumscribed by an unsympathetic narrative voice that defines female authorship as 'scribbling' and announces the protagonist's relapse into 'a silence that remained unbroken to the end' (586).

Since the critical reappraisal of Kate Chopin, which began in earnest in the 1960s, we have become very familiar with the idea of her as a groundbreaking artist. Now, her writing is quite properly considered in terms of its sophisticated engagements with romanticism, transcendentalism, literary realism, naturalism and New Woman fiction and as anticipating the concerns of feminism and literary modernism. Any reductive categorisation of her work as local colour has been disputed as scholars have brought fresh insight to her relationship with nineteenth-century literary currents, particularly highlighting her manipulation of form and genre. Elaine Showalter, for example, places *The Awakening* into the context of its literary precursors, offering a comprehensive overview of the genres in which American women writers had, up to this point, articulated their artistic vision and examining the manner in which Chopin both engaged with these and distinguished herself from them. Figuring Adelle Ratignolle and Mademoiselle Reisz as 'the proto-heroines of sentimental and local color fiction' who suggest 'different plots and conclusions' for Edna Pontellier's story, Showalter interprets Edna's failure to follow either model as Chopin's 'rejection of the conventions of women's writing'.[4] Janet Beer has explored the Louisiana stories in terms of the considerable range of interpretative possibilities they allow. She notes that although rich in the language and culture of their specific locale, these tales have a significance that transcends the mediation of a nostalgic, sentimental version of the American South to a northern audience. She suggests Chopin's development as a writer of short fiction was, in fact, informed by the search for the new and alternative means of expression which would be realised in *The Awakening*. Beer discusses the way in which Chopin makes use of the 'screen' of local colour – a tradition 'whose conventions apparently support the status quo' – to address contentious issues and examines her accomplished manip-ulation of the medium which, for example, sees her provide traditional end-ings that distract attention from more significant and controversial themes embedded at other points in the narrative.

Showalter's and Beer's assessments make bold interventions in the study of Chopin's literary innovation: Showalter labels *The Awakening* 'a revolution-ary book'[5] and Beer makes 'extravagant'[6] assertions about Chopin's techni-cal expertise in the construction of the short story. But such examinations of the author's work in the development of new and original forms of expression can be usefully extended in two ways: by considering her writings through the lens of contemporary theories of genre and through the reconfiguration of her oft-cited relationship with the French writer Guy de Maupassant. Tzvetan Todorov has drawn attention to the ideological nature of genre systems, noting, 'a society chooses and codifies the acts that correspond most closely to its ideology; that is why the existence of certain genres in one society, their absence in another, are revelatory of that ideology'.[7] Thus, his insistence on the conflict involved as genres change and artists invoke previous models to subvert, revise and transform them, implies a corresponding ideological struggle in which the attitudes informing those models are also interrogated. Thomas O. Beebee identifies these transitional stages in the evolution of new genres – the 'cusps' of genre – as 'a most advantageous place from which to observe the workings of ideology in literature'.[8] As Showalter and Beer demonstrate, we can locate Chopin on such a 'cusp': poised between the Victorian and modernity, she challenges the conditions of existence for women in nineteenth-century American society through a reorientation of its literary forms. But this is not the only 'cusp' or intersection that is relevant here. For Kate Chopin's French ancestry and immersion in the French Creole culture of Louisiana also connects her to European traditions and places her writing into dialogue with a more diverse body of work. Chopin's cross-cultural literary engagements are actually most often interpreted in terms of their potential to liberate her from the limitations of those models accepted as specifically female forms rather than as conflicts of genre and ideology in themselves.

This is, perhaps, not surprising, given that in 1896, reflecting on the development of her artistic consciousness, Chopin revealed a deep appreciation for the work of Guy de Maupassant, identifying him as a trigger for her creative awakening:

> I had been in the woods, in the fields, groping around; looking for something big, satisfying, convincing [...] It was at this period of my emerging from the vast solitude in which I had been making my own acquaintance, that I stumbled upon Maupassant. I read his stories and marvelled at them [...] Here was a man who had escaped from tradition and authority, who had entered into himself and looked out upon life through his own being and with his own eyes; and who, in a direct and simple way, told us what he saw. (700–1)

So attuned to his particular artistic vision was she that she expressed a desire for an exclusive, profound connection with him, admitting to having cherished 'the delusion that he has spoken to no one else so directly, so intimately as he does to me' (701). Her words are often cited by critics, many of whom interpret her admiration for the French writer, who had died three years previously, in terms of posthumous mentorship. Chopin's literary innovation is rarely discussed without her indebtedness to Maupassant being invoked. That she followed his lead in breaking from convention and dispensing with the 'old fashioned mechanism and stage trapping' (700) of traditional literary form is not in doubt. Elements of his style, his narrative construction and his exploration of the individual psyche, are evident in many of her compositions, not least *The Awakening*. In a detailed analysis of their respective short stories, Richard Fusco traces Maupassant's influence on the development of Chopin's technique, identifying striking structural similarities across the writing and discussing her judicious 'borrowing' of his trademark surprise ending, a feature she employs in stories such as 'Désirée's Baby' (1892) and 'The Story of an Hour' (1894).[9] In addition, Maupassant's frank treatment of such themes as illicit love, divorce, madness and suicide held particular appeal for Chopin, informing her rebellion against the predictable subject. But to focus too closely on what Chopin may have learned from Maupassant, and to imply that she adopted his style unreservedly is to suggest, wrongly, a master–disciple relationship. As Heather Dubrow reminds us, 'the choice of a literary form functions less as the willing admission of indebtedness [...] than as a proud assertion of originality',[10] and, despite Chopin's obvious admiration for him, it is fair to say she revised Maupassant's literary model much as she revised those of her American predecessors. In addition, her hybrid identity gave her a unique insight into the ideological genre systems of two cultures. Far from rejecting what Beebee terms the 'writing lessons' of one to embrace and reproduce those of the other, Chopin collapses the boundaries of conventional American modes *and* those of French psychological realism, reworking genre in order to accommodate and express a vision all her own.

The selections Chopin made as a translator of Maupassant's stories are revelatory of the particular inspiration his work afforded her. His 'Solitude', for example, a version of which Chopin published in the *St Louis Life* in December 1895, expresses the isolation of the individual and the existence of an essential self which can never be known by others: 'we are always alone. I have dragged you out into the night in the vain hope of a moment's escape from the horrible solitude which overpowers me. But what is the use! I speak and you answer me, and still each of us is alone; side by side but alone.'[11] The parallels between this piece and *The Awakening*, originally titled 'A Solitary Soul', are clear. Towards the end of the novel, Edna Pontellier recognises the fragility and impermanence of human relationships: 'There was no human being she wanted near her except Robert; and she even realized that the day would come when he, too, and the thought of him would melt out of her existence, leaving her alone' (999). In aligning Edna's journey towards the assertion of an immutable 'self' so closely with Maupassant's meditations on individual solitude, and in punctuating her narrative with explorations of the inner world of her heroine, Chopin demonstrates the way in which he had spoken to her 'so directly, so intimately'. But there are important points of difference between the visions of the two writers, and it is in elucidating these that we can gain insight into the revisionary nature of Chopin's engagement with her French counterpart.

The chief difference to note is the gendered perspective each writer brings to their art. The adoption of Maupassant's focus on the inner consciousness is central to Chopin's subversion of genre. By placing emphasis on the psyche of her protagonist, she enacts a variation on realism, posing a challenge to its depiction of external reality. But she also brings a gender-specific approach to her innovative practices. Amy Kaplan has argued that realism, in its traditional form, functions as a tool of patriarchy, 'complicit[y] with structures of power [...] a fictional deceit, packaging and naturalizing an official version of the ordinary'.[12] That *The Awakening*'s unconventional psychological explorations lead to the depiction of a distinctly female selfhood and gesture towards the limitations imposed on the woman in a male-orientated society, suggests a critique of ideology as well as a revision of form. In *Feminist Fiction*

(1990), Anne Cranny Francis explores the ways in which feminist writers of the late twentieth century appropriate and subvert literary genres, 'consciously encoding an ideology which is in direct opposition to the dominant gender ideology of western society, patriarchal ideology'.[13] Examining the work of Angela Carter, Marge Piercy and Ursula Le Guin, among others, Cranny Francis focuses on the 'structural' and 'semantic' consequences that result when science fiction, fantasy and utopian narrative, detective fiction and romance are subjected to a robust interrogation by feminist discourse. She suggests that in their attempts 'to show the ideological processes (of patriarchy) in (textual) operation',[14] these writers rework and disrupt genre to the point of breakdown, so that 'the texts function differently' and sometimes 'do not seem to function at all'.[15] Writing a century earlier, Kate Chopin did not espouse a self-consciously feminist perspective, but she was interested in the conditions of existence for women whose society defined them in terms of domesticity and maternal responsibility. Whilst her subtle probing of the limits of genre contrasts with the outright assaults on form mounted by her feminist successors, it effects a similar exposure of the conservative ideology encoded in traditional literary forms.

Chopin, then, subverts genre, formally and thematically, by placing the woman's experience at the heart of her text and constituting her as the *subject* of the narrative. Maupassant, however, had little interest in the female experience. Mary Donaldson-Evans argues that in his writings, women become merely the site on which male fears and desires are played out: 'Women are objects of erotic delight, intended for the pleasure and adornment of the male, and their physical beauty is paramount [...] The pleasure that the possession of a beautiful woman affords is entirely physical and is coupled with an absolute disdain for her *being*.'[16] The articulation of such an androcentric position is clearly at odds with the woman-centred nature of Chopin's literary innovation. Edna Pontellier's soul-searching is driven by the necessity of expressing her 'being'. So, whilst elements of Maupassant's technique and style undoubtedly facilitate Chopin's transcendence of unsatisfactory modes, imitation will not suffice. Ultimately, his model, too, is inadequate to accommodate and express her ambitions for her writing, and, in *The Awakening*, Chopin revises what might be termed the masculinist discourse of Maupassant to suit her purposes.

One of the ways in which Maupassant presents his women is, according to Mary Donaldson-Evans, by aligning them symbolically with nature. She suggests, for example, that in equating aquatic imagery with the feminine, Maupassant figures the woman/nature as simultaneously attractive and dangerous, an elemental force capable of seducing, corrupting and engulfing his hero: 'nature becomes an accomplice of woman herself [...] the eternal temptress in Maupassant's work who lies in wait for men.'[17] Since Chopin also draws heavily on Maupassant's technique in the use of symbolism, a comparison of their troping illustrates the point at which their artistic visions diverge. The depiction of their protagonists' encounters with bodies of water marks a key point of difference, centred on gender, which indicates Chopin's development and extension of the Maupassantian technique. Donaldson-Evans reads the tale of 'Little Louise Roque'[18] as Maupassant's evocation of the mythological siren. In this narrative, she suggests, the 'sexual symbolism' of the woman/water combination leads to corruption, violence and death.[19] Observing the adolescent Louise splashing naked in a stream awakens a powerful carnal desire in the town's mayor, who rapes and brutally murders the girl. Tormented by the baseness of his actions, he later leaps from the high walls of his home, strikes his head on a boulder and dies in the stream that was the site of his initial corruption. Here, the deadly feminine element is seductive and also, ultimately, the agent of the hero's destruction.

There are clear echoes of Maupassant's riverside scene in Chopin's 'A Vocation and a Voice' (1896), where an encounter with Suzima, his female travelling companion, bathing naked in a pool, arouses the passions of the young protagonist: 'His face, all his skin, to the very soles of his feet, was burning and pricking, and every pulse in his body was beating, clamouring, sounding in his ears like confused, distant drum-taps' (539). Although exploring the experience of a male figure, in Chopin's tale the desires kindled at the water's edge lead not to a frenzied sating of lust but to a consensual act that marks the boy's sexual initiation. In *The Awakening*, the revision of Maupassant's theme is bolder. Here, the eroticising effects of the water are transferred from a male to a female protagonist. In the novel, it is the heroine who is seduced by the 'whispering, clamouring, murmuring' voice of the sea as she surrenders to its sensuous touch, a touch that enfolds 'the body in its soft, close embrace' (893). Again, the sexual connotations are unmistakable – it is after swimming in the ocean that Edna Pontellier experiences 'the first-felt throbbing of desire' (911). She too recognises the awesome power of the waves and their capacity to engulf and overwhelm her. Alone in the 'vast expanse' of the ocean, a 'quick vision of death smote her soul' (908). And, in common with Maupassant's male protagonist, it is in the water that she will meet her end. But, in *The Awakening*, the sea functions more as a site of empowerment for the woman than as a corruptor of the male. As in Maupassant, it is an important agent in engendering passionate, natural impulses, but for Chopin these are not violent, brutal urges but a sensual awakening that plays a key role in the assertion of an autonomous female self. Here, water is figured in terms of renewal and rebirth as well as death. When Edna swims for the first time, her achievement is expressed in terms of 'joy' and 'exultation'. Buoyed by the waves, she is opened up to new sensations that will bring about momentous changes in her life; she feels as if 'some power of significant import had been given to her to control the working of her body' (908). Her return to the shore is immediately identified with limitation as her euphoria is diminished by her husband's reductive comments on her success, but the sea remains as a site of freedom and possibility for the heroine – an alternative space, beyond the reaches of those who seek to define her. Even as the medium of death, the water is representative of defiance and a refusal to compromise rather than a defeat. Alone on the beach, Edna knows there is a way to 'elude' those who would 'drag her into the soul's slavery for the rest of her days' (999), and her final immersion allows her to resist being engulfed by the demands of familial responsibility.

The sexual impulses that are awakened in Edna by the sensuous touch of the waters of the Gulf signal Chopin's engagement with literary naturalism. Again, the standard conventions of genre are modulated for purpose. Broadly defined, naturalism is the literary representation of human beings incapable of exercising free will, governed by their instincts and passions and conditioned and controlled by environment, heredity, economics or chance. But *The Awakening* is not the narrative of a grim fight for survival in the brutal urban environment depicted in Frank Norris's *McTeague* (1899), nor is it hampered by the accumulation of minute realistic detail, as in Émile Zola's *Lourdes*, which, Chopin complained, was, 'swamped beneath a mass of prosaic data, offensive and nauseous description' (697), and, as Per Seyested notes, neither is it characterised by an emphasis on the significance of heredity.[20] The narrative is clearly informed by the work of the social and natural scientists, but Chopin is subtle in her effects, making selective use of naturalistic devices. She takes from the generic template only those elements which will enable her to free her protagonist from an identity and existence determined by social convention. Edna's story does, however, answer to Donald Pizer's definition of the form as the dramatisation of 'the limitations placed on the human will by the biological and social realities within which the will attempts to find its way'.[21] So, the primary attraction of naturalistic fiction for Kate Chopin lies in its emphasis on the importance of natural instincts in determining behaviour. In an essay, written in 1894, she expressed her belief in the enduring, universal truth of the human condition, remarking: 'human impulses do not change' (693). A means of expressing this condition, in its natural state, unencumbered by the structures and discourses that seek to define and regulate individuals and the relationships between them, is empowering for a writer concerned with the female protagonist at odds with the legal and societal apparatus that circumscribe her existence. Through the lens of social and natural science, it is possible to bypass Edna

Pontellier's conventional role as wife and mother, figuring her instead as a human animal, subject to primal instincts, impulses and passions. This kind of exploration is clearly at work in the depiction of Edna as a 'beautiful, sleek animal waking up in the sun' (952) and in the description of the way in which she satisfies her basic appetite for food. Awakening from sleep on a visit to Madame Antoine with Robert Lebrun, Edna is hungry and bites into a 'brown loaf, tearing it with her strong, white teeth' (918). On another occasion, she rummages in the larder for a late-night snack to satisfy her ravenous hunger. The language used in these scenes does not describe the etiquette of the polite dining room and is also suggestive of appetites of a different kind. Edna's trip to the cupboard for beer and cheese follows a trip to the races with a group which includes Alcée Arobin, and which marks the beginning of a relationship that will result in an extramarital sexual encounter. Chopin extends the range of natural, animal instincts that drive Edna's behaviour, claiming powerful physical desires for her female protagonist.

In so doing, she challenges the theory underpinning the genre. As Bert Bender has argued, whilst Chopin found the alignment of human impulses with those found in the animal kingdom liberating, she also found the positioning of women within the hypothesis limiting. Engaging intellectually with Darwin's *The Descent of Man and Selection in Relation to Sex* (1871), Chopin took issue with its 'analysis of the female's [passive] role in sexual selection'[22] – that is, the woman's role as regulator of the male's powerful urges through modesty and maternal, asexual instinct. In her creation of Edna Pontellier, Bender notes, Chopin offers a bold rejection of elements of Darwin's thesis, depicting not only a woman who seeks the freedom actively to select a mate but also a mother who expresses sexual desire: 'It was the first kiss of her life to which her nature had really responded. It was a flaming torch that kindled desire' (967). Edna's passions are clearly expressed; Chopin's depiction of the sexualised mother in *The Awakening* is consistent with the entire body of her work in its refusal of moral intent. Her treatment of this figure represents another point of comparison with Guy de Maupassant who, Donaldson-Evans notes, always punishes 'the mother who has an illicit love affair [...] or who places sexual attractiveness above what should be instinctive maternal sentiments.'[23] In 'A Parricide', for example, a carpenter, conceived as a result of an adulterous affair and consequently abandoned, encounters his mother in later life and bludgeons her to death with a 'long iron spike'[24] before throwing her body into the river. In common with her experiments with Maupassant's psychological realism, Chopin's engagement with naturalism in *The Awakening* constitutes a bold, woman-centred vision. As her sexualised mother-figure becomes attuned to her basic natural impulses, she becomes increasingly alienated from her socially defined role. For the awakened Edna, authentic experience is to be found in moments of solitude during which her impulses can be indulged. Her disconnection from her conventional existence is symbolised by a series of removals; of clothing – the markers of the middle-class wife and mother – and to various abodes in the search for a life free from someone else's expectations and routines.

While the novel represents Chopin's most sustained and experimental engagement with naturalism, it is not her first, and, again, 'A Vocation and a Voice' serves as a useful illustration of her staged development and adaptation of genre. Tracing its male protagonist's movement between an ordered social world, represented by conventional religion, and the elemental, natural world, the short story explores the potential of environment to awaken inherent impulses and drives but also of contemplative solitude to facilitate the recognition of an essential 'self'. Travelling through a drowsy, rural landscape in the company of fortune-teller Suzima and her partner Gutro, the young man is confronted with his capacity for sexual desire for the former and violent, jealous rage against the latter. The language employed in the tale is decidedly naturalistic. Instinctively reaching for a knife to protect Suzima from the physically abusive Gutro, the boy recognises 'a devil lurking unknown to him, in his blood, that would some day blind him, disable his will and direct his hands to deeds of violence' (542). Despite seeking refuge in the church, ultimately his natural urges will not be denied. The stone wall he builds around his 'holy refuge' cannot contain his essential inner being, and he is lured back to the landscape and uninhibited expression of the self by the entrancing singing voice of Suzima. Peggy Skaggs reads the tale's focus on the male experience as evidence of Chopin's interest in the human, rather than specifically feminine condition. But, in common with her development of the water trope across the short story and the longer narrative, transference of the naturalistic treatment from the male to the female subject marks a growth in Chopin's confidence and a stage in her evolution of genre.

Another staple of the naturalist genre that Chopin exploits in *The Awakening*, as indeed she had previously in 'A Vocation and a Voice', is the significance of environment. As noted, her character's existence is not determined by interaction with the threatening, brutal urban environment depicted in the work of some of her contemporaries, but the various geographical, social and cultural locations Edna inhabits are of great importance to her recognition of 'her relations as an individual to the world within and about her' (893). Her awakening to the truth of the human condition and to her own appetites, passions and desires is facilitated to a great extent by the faintly exotic, sultry and seductive atmosphere of Grand Isle which brings her close to the natural world, and, in particular, to the ocean. Edna is responsive to the physical surroundings but also to the alien cultural milieu in which she finds herself. Her encounters with Creole society – flirtatious and characterised by a lack of inhibition, even whilst strictly adherent to conventional morality – engender some of her most powerful awakenings. For example, the morning she spends on the beach with the charming and tactile Adelle Ratignolle arouses her to a heightened awareness of herself as a potentially sexual being. The mood created by their exchanges of confidence and the clasping and stroking of hands unsettles Edna's sense of self, inducing a languid, dreamlike state and generating feelings, homoerotic in tone, which 'muddled her like wine, or like a first breath of freedom' (899).

A consideration of Chopin's use of environment and location again places her work into relationship with that of Maupassant. In his analysis of the composition of the French writer's stories and their influence on Chopin, Richard Fusco describes his deployment of the complex 'sinusoidal structure' to which geographic setting is central. Typically, these tales are 'tripartite' and involve movement between locations. In most cases, an interlude in a 'Romantic' landscape during which a character escapes from the reality of their existence to achieve 'a transcendent grasp of his plight', is framed by a beginning and end located in the realms of grim reality. The narrative progression, according to Fusco, is from pessimism to possibility with a return to pessimism more keenly felt, which 'reconfirms Maupassant's notion of the ephemeral nature of happiness'.[25] *The Awakening* represents a version of the sinusoidal narrative, but Chopin's adaptation of the form is apparent. As in Maupassant, place and movement between locations is significant. Here, too, the 'Romantic' setting is the site of awakenings, facilitating the heroine's 'transcendental grasp' of her place in the universe. But, in Chopin's narrative, this 'other', ideal space frames the text, with Edna's everyday life in the city providing the backdrop for the interlude. Edna's darkest, most challenging moments take place in the New Orleans section placed at the centre of the text. During this time, her presence at the birth of Adele Ratignolle's child confronts her with the greatest impediment to her personal freedom, and Robert Lebrun's inability to recognise her as an autonomous individual leads her to the realisation that life with him will ultimately replicate that which she shared with her husband. The arrangement of episodes in this way signals a reversal of Maupassant's narrative patterning. Failing in her attempts to express her newly awakened desires and passions within the framework of her everyday environment, Edna returns to the 'Romantic' setting of Grand Isle. Her journey towards a realisation of self takes her from possibility to pessimism and back to possibility. Having glimpsed an alternative existence, she refuses to compromise and, in suicide, achieves a form of transcendence.

In considering the ways in which *The Awakening* functions as a naturalistic fiction, it is useful to examine a tension that complicates the typical determinist narrative. Edna is depicted variously as being directed by external forces and as active agent in her own destiny. An example of the former can be found in the short, lyrical Chapter VI, one of several episodes during which there is a shift in narrative perspective as Chopin adopts the passive voice: 'A certain light was beginning to dawn dimly within her [...] At that early period it served but to bewilder her. It moved her to dreams, to thoughtfulness, to the shadowy anguish which had overcome her the midnight when she had abandoned herself to tears' (893). The effect of this narrative mode is to create Edna as passive recipient of the action. Here, it seems that she is acted upon rather than exercising free will, and she appears to have little control over the feelings arising within her. This rousing of unbidden emotion is echoed in the effect of Mademoiselle Reisz's music on Edna: 'the passions themselves were aroused within her soul, swaying it, lashing it, as the waves daily beat upon her splendid body' (906). Conversely, there are instances in which her behaviour appears to be self-directed: when Robert Lebrun posits the idea of her being 'set free' by Leonce so that they can marry, she issues a bold rebuke, insisting on her own agency: 'I give myself where I choose' (992).

A similar ambiguity is evident in the ending of *The Awakening*. As noted, Edna makes a conscious decision – a choice – to 'evade' the responsibilities that compromise her individual freedom. The primary responsibility implied here is that associated with her role as a mother. Indeed, as she stands at the water's edge, 'The children appeared before her like antagonists who had overcome her; who had overpowered and sought to drag her into the soul's slavery for the rest of her days' (999). Her entry into the water represents a rejection of their and her husband's right to 'possess her, body and soul' (1000). But Edna's fate is often interpreted as the defeat of the woman by nature. Awakened to the realisation that there is no possibility of an existence without contingencies, her death by drowning can be read as the inevitable consequence of her inability to reconcile a desire for freedom and individuality with the biological and societal functions of motherhood. In common with her dissatisfaction with other literary modes, it appears that Chopin finds naturalism an insufficient vehicle for the complexities of her gynocentric vision. Once more, a woman's attempts to transcend limitations cannot be accommodated, and, again, she draws attention to the limitations of form.

In 1924, Edith Wharton wrote: 'General rules in art are useful chiefly as a lamp in a mine, or a hand-rail down a black stairway; they are necessary for the sake of the guidance they give, but it is a mistake, once they are formulated, to be too much in awe of them.'[26] To be in 'awe' of artistic principles and models is not a 'mistake' Kate Chopin made. As mentioned at the outset, her writing is now recognised for its sophisticated engagements with the major literary movements of the nineteenth century, and, in *The Awakening*, many of these are invoked in order for their limitations to be exposed and challenged. *The Awakening*'s rejection of local-colour and sentimental traditions has already been discussed, but in this narrative Chopin also poses a challenge to other forms which are specifically masculine in authorship and audience. For example, Chopin's insistence on her heroine's individuality, her affinity with the natural environment and her open sexuality owes much to Walt Whitman, whose verse she quotes at a moment of sexual tension in the story, 'A Respectable Woman' (1894), but Edna's falling asleep whilst reading Emerson – whose 'American Scholar' address in many ways articulates with Chopin's own desire to break away from models of the past – has been interpreted as a comment on the inadequacy of transcendentalism to articulate a woman's experience.

Thomas O. Beebee has said: 'the meaning of a literary text can depend on the play between its generic categories [...] the truly vital meanings of a text are often contained not in any specific generic category into which the text may be placed, but rather in the play of differences between its genres.'[27] As has been argued here, Kate Chopin engaged in a restless movement between genres. She sustained a relationship with the work of Guy de Maupassant, reacting to his technique throughout her career. But, whilst his psychological realism/naturalism provided her with an inspirational spark, it failed to accommodate fully her artistic vision. The same is true for literary naturalism, described by Donald Pizer as 'the principal innovative movement in American fiction of the 1890s'.[28] Ultimately, Chopin's literary debts take their place in the play of genres that *The Awakening* enacts, as traditions to be transcended in the quest for a distinctive voice through which to articulate the 'vital meaning' of the woman's life.

NOTES

1. Quoted in Boris Eichenbaum, 'The Theory of the Formal Method', in *Russian Formalist Criticism*, ed. Lee T. Lemon and Marion J. Reis (Lincoln, Nebr.: University of Nebraska Press, 1965), 134.
2. C.L. Deyo, *St Louis Post-Dispatch*, 20 May 1899, reprinted in Margo Culley (ed.), *The Awakening* (New York: W.W. Norton & Company, 1994), 164.
3. Emily Toth and Per Seyersted (eds.), *Kate Chopin's Private Papers* (Bloomington, Ind.: Indiana University Press, 1998), 9.
4. Elaine Showalter, 'Tradition and the Female Talent: *The Awakening* as a Solitary Book', in Wendy Martin, (ed.), *New Essays on The Awakening* (Cambridge: Cambridge University Press, 1988), 33–57, 42–3.
5. Showalter, 'Tradition and the Female Talent', 34.

6. Janet Beer, *Kate Chopin, Edith Wharton and Charlotte Perkins Gilman: Studies in Short Fiction* (Basingstoke: Palgrave, 2005), 18.
7. Tzvetan Todorov, *Genres in Discourse* (Cambridge: Cambridge University Press, 1990), 19.
8. Thomas O. Beebee, *The Ideology of Genre: A Comparative Study of Generic Instability* (Pennsylvania, Pa.: Pennsylvania State University Press, 1994), 17.
9. Richard Fusco, *Maupassant and the American Short Story: The Influence of Form at the Turn of the Century* (Pennsylvania, Pa.: Pennsylvania State University Press, 1994).
10. Heather Dubrow, *Genre, The Critical Idiom* (London: Methuen, 1982), 13.
11. Guy de Maupassant, 'Solitude', trans. Kate Chopin, in Thomas Bonner, Jr., *The Kate Chopin Companion* (New York: Greenwood Press, 1988), 195.
12. Amy Kaplan, *The Social Construction of American Realism* (Chicago, Ill.: University of Chicago Press, 1988), 1.
13. Anne Cranny Francis, *Feminist Fiction: Feminist Uses of Generic Fiction* (Cambridge: Polity Press, 1990), 1.
14. Francis, *Feminist Fiction*, 6.
15. Francis, *Feminist Fiction*, 1.
16. Mary Donaldson-Evans, *A Woman's Revenge: The Chronology of Dispossession in Maupassant's Fiction* (Lexington, Ky.: French Forum Publishers, 1986), 14.
17. Donaldson-Evans, *A Woman's Revenge*, 19.
18. Guy de Maupassant, 'Little Louise Roque', available at <http://www.gutenberg.org/files/3090/3090-h/3090-h.htm#2H_4_0031>. (Accessed 17 August 2007.)
19. Donaldson-Evans, *A Woman's Revenge*, 21.
20. Per Seyersted, *Kate Chopin: A Critical Biography* (Baton Rouge, La.: Louisiana State University Press, 1980), 108.
21. Donald Pizer, 'A Note on Kate Chopin's *The Awakening* as Naturalistic Fiction', *Southern Literary Journal*, 33, 2 (2001), 5.
22. Bert Bender, 'The Teeth of Desire: *The Awakening* and *The Descent of Man*', *American Literature*, 63, 3 (1991), 461.
23. Donaldson-Evans, *A Woman's Revenge*, 34.
24. Guy de Maupassant, 'A Parricide', available at <http://www.gutenberg.org/files/3090/3090-h/3090-h.htm#2H_4_0035>. (Accessed 17 August 2007.)
25. Fusco, *Maupassant*, 84–5.
26. Edith Wharton, *The Writing of Fiction* (1924, New York: Touchstone, 1997), 33.
27. Beebee, *The Ideology of Genre*, 249–50.
28. Pizer, 'A Note on Kate Chopin's *The Awakening*', 5.

9

AVRIL HORNER

Kate Chopin, choice and modernism

Much of the best work on Kate Chopin's fiction over the past two decades has sought to contextualise her writing firmly within the discourses and contexts of the nineteenth century. Valuable and influential essays have been written, for example, on Chopin's debts to French nineteenth-century authors such as Maupassant and Flaubert; on Chopin and the New Woman; on New Orleans and the figure of the female flâneur; on Chopin and other women authors of the *fin-de-siècle* period such as Willa Cather and Edith Wharton; on Kate Chopin as part of the nineteenth-century American literary tradition; on Chopin and Darwinism. Indeed, the essays in this volume continue and richly develop work in these areas. By contrast, publications on the connections between Kate Chopin's work and modernism have been halting and piecemeal. Moreover, they have invariably focused on *The Awakening*, either dwelling on its formal and experimental aspects or emphasising its relation to the New Woman, sexuality and feminist thought. Michael T. Gilmore's essay, 'Revolt Against Nature: The Problematic Modernism of *The Awakening*' is a good example of the former approach, stressing as it does similarities between Chopin's work and impressionist painting and music.[1] Marianne DeKoven's essay 'Gendered Doubleness and the "Origins" of Modernist Form' extends consideration of the formal experimental qualities of *The Awakening* into an argument that elements of ambivalence and contradiction in the story are not only typical of early modernist writing but also that they result in a 'self-cancelling narrative stance' that indicates an ambivalence about feminism itself: 'given the depth and intractability of the fear of punishment for female anger and desire [...] inherent doubleness of modernist form is precisely what allows the expression of feminist content at all.'[2]

Later claims for Chopin as modernist have been less tentative. In her article on *The Awakening*, gender and modernism, published in 1998, Sarah Klein draws on numerous definitions of modernism, including those offered by Norman Cantor and Peter Faulkner, in order to argue that 'The Awakening [...] tentatively explores, and from a gendered point of view to be sure, the uncharted waters of Modernism.'³ During the same year, Emily Smith-Riser, in one of the few articles on modernism and Chopin that draws on texts other than *The Awakening* to make its case, claimed that 'Chopin expresses a modernist's disillusionment with Victorian society's conventions through her treatment of religion; in short, we will see that Kate Chopin was a modernist before her time.'⁴ Like several other critics, Smith-Riser sees Chopin's use of irony, ambiguous juxtaposition and ambivalence as anticipating modernism. Joseph Allen Boone, in his book *Libidinal Currents*, links Chopin's narrative strategies evoking 'states of interiority' both with Freud's attempt in the 1890s to explore the unconscious and with recent theories of women's writing. The ambivalences and contradictions noted by DeKoven in Chopin's work, Boone sees as a very modern attempt to represent a divided consciousness, and he therefore confidently defines Chopin as both protomodernist and protofeminist.⁵ In 1999, in an American radio programme, Elizabeth Fox-Genovese described Chopin as 'very important as one of the earliest examples of modernism in the United States [...] I think one reason that some of her stories were very short was because she was self-consciously experimenting with stylistic concerns every bit as thematic ones.'⁶

I agree that Chopin's work anticipates modernism in both form and content – and that *The Awakening* can justly be described as a modernist text. However, I want to offer a rather different way of looking at her work in this respect – one that also considers the reader's response to the complexities and ambiguities of her writing. In this essay, I shall argue that Chopin's stylistic concerns, the thematic content of her work, the reader–narrator relationship she sets up and her modernism all cohere through her emphasis on, and use of, choice. Chopin's implicit engagement with various influential discourses of the nineteenth century, including Catholicism and Darwinism, resulted in sophisticated fictions that presage the techniques and concerns of many modernists, including their focus on the choices facing the modern subject. She also shows, however, that such choice does not necessarily result in a deeper sense of authenticity. Indeed, her characters often make choices that seem against their best interests or that puzzle the modern reader – and which sometimes result in endings that seem curiously at variance with the main drift of the narrative.⁷ Like many modernist writers – including Lawrence, who rejected 'the old stable ego of the character'⁸ – she sought new modes of expression to express the dilemmas that face her characters. Focusing on choice as an aspect of modernism enables us to move beyond *The Awakening* to look at other texts by Chopin which can then be seen as protomodernist. To test this theory, I have chosen to focus on three works quite different from each other in terms of content: a story in which the main character is male and

Catholic – 'A Vocation and a Voice'; a tale which seems to undermine New Woman credos – 'Athénaïse'; and, briefly, *The Awakening*. I shall argue that the emphasis on choice in these three stories, for both character and reader, typifies them as modernist works.

The final choices made by many of Chopin's characters – as in 'A Vocation and a Voice' and 'Athénaïse' – might first appear as apparently emphatic and unambiguous. They seem initially to confirm the influence of Darwin's ideas upon Chopin's depiction of love and sexual desire, suggesting characters whose choices are influenced by a biological agenda beyond their conscious control. However, notwithstanding her deep interest in Darwin, choice in Chopin's fiction is not driven wholly by the selfish gene. Although rarely do we see in Chopin's work what Martin Halliwell describes in his book on modernism as the modern 'individual's inability to decide between possible choices' (what we might call the Prufrockian syndrome), we do see her characters expressing, through their choices, 'an intense dissatisfaction with social values and (the implication) that new codes of living should be devised to challenge and supersede them'.[9] However, Chopin's refusal to provide narrative explanations for her characters' decisions leaves them open to different interpretations. This is typified most clearly by the end of *The Awakening*. Whereas many of Chopin's contemporaries read this tale as illustrating Edna's choice of suicide as the proper wages of sin,[10] its closure has since provoked a number of interpretations that present Edna's death variously as a despairing act of suicide, a metaphorical rebirth, a defeat for the modern woman and as a triumphant assertion of the female artistic or sexual self. In emphasising the importance of choice in the modern world and in playing out various ethical dilemmas on the page, Chopin leaves her reader with puzzles to resolve. What we see in Chopin's work, in fact, is a move into 'the realm of experiential morality' which Halliwell and others have recently begun to identify strongly with the modernist movement.[11] Leaving us to make sense of her protagonists' choices, Chopin helps to create the active reader of modernist texts. In focusing on the moral dilemmas which face her characters, she foregrounds an ethics of choice that is, according to Halliwell, a preoccupation of modernist authors.

Above all, the reader is invited to see her fiction as a lens through which to view life itself as a choice of narratives. Such narratives include: a scientific approach that privileges rationality and scepticism (in particular, Darwinism); religion and art (including Romanticism) which offer mysticism and transcendentalism as a way of understanding life; 'the garb of romance' (537) or the love between a man and a woman as the great driver of human experience; Victorian notions of woman as the angel of the house and man as provider – social constructions of gender that present themselves (falsely) as 'natural'; or, the self as an economic unit in a material world. The message of Chopin's writing seems to be that each of these narratives makes sense of life in a particular way but they can all be imprisoning if used as the sole explanation and driver of human behaviour. In this respect, Chopin anticipated the later critical insight that plurality offers a healthy antidote to dominant ideologies. In her work, elements of Darwinism jostle with New Woman credos, and lyricism sits next to satire in what is a complex representation of the possibilities for 'self' in the modern world. Chopin's writing, I shall suggest, is resonant with conflict, choice, ambiguity and irresolution in a way that anticipates both the content and the techniques of much modernist writing. Her work should thus be seen in the context of what Martin Halliwell calls 'Transatlantic Modernism', which he defines as 'both a zone of moral experimentalism and a zone of moral danger'.[12]

Chopin's 'A Vocation and a Voice', which appears on the surface to be one of her least experimental stories, provides an interesting starting point.[13] Its main character, 'the boy', suffers as a child from 'a vague sense of being unessential' (521). Finding some sort of identity in joining forces with a couple of travellers, the fifteen-year-old adolescent is increasingly attracted to the woman, Suzima, who is five years older than himself and companion to a frequently drunken and sometimes violent man named Gutro. In 'the Patch', he was drawn to Catholicism – the rituals of the Catholic Church having provided the only beauty and order in his life – and thus to the idea of living a ritualised and disciplined life. But his response to nature, as he walks the open roads, melds these two dominant instincts: he reacts sensually – the 'soft wind caressed him with a thousand wanton touches' (521) – and also with a quasi-religious intensity – 'he felt as if he were [...] holding communion with something mysterious, greater than himself [...] something he called God' (530). These represent conflicting narratives between which the boy must eventually choose.

The dark-eyed Suzima earns money occasionally as 'The Egyptian Fortune Teller'; she also has a beautiful voice which takes on a siren-like quality as the story develops. She comes to represent all that is exotic, adult and sexual for Chopin's adolescent, who finds himself besieged by conflicting feelings and passions: part of him wants to settle down and 'lead an upright, clean existence before God and man', but, at the same time, 'a savage instinct stirred within him' and pulls him towards the freedom of the countryside and to the 'shadowy form of Suzima lurking nearby' (536). When the sexual lure suggested by Suzima's 'Egyptian wisdom' combines with the surge of spring, then – Chopin implies – nature and culture combine to form an irresistible attraction. In a scene that anticipates Stephen Dedalus's epiphany when he sees the girl on the beach in Joyce's *The Portrait of the Artist as a*

Young Man,[14] Chopin describes the boy's 'awakening' on seeing Suzana naked for the first time: 'He saw her as one sees an object in a flash from a dark sky – sharply, vividly. Her image, against the background of tender green, ate into his brain and into his flesh with the fixedness and intensity of white-hot iron' (538–9). The transition is from 'boy' to man, from innocence to experience, and Suzima's gesture of clutching her clothes to her breast when she sees him acknowledges this. The boy's initiation into adult sexuality makes him feel part 'of the universe of men and all things that live' (541): in Darwinian terms, he has begun to fulfil his biological destiny. However, the same Darwinian agenda – to secure and keep a mate – also results in his threatening Gutro with a knife. Such passion, such loss of control, horrifies him; it is not surprising, then, that the next section, set a few years later, sees the boy transformed into Brother Ludovic. The reader is left to deduce the reason for his decision to take orders: presumably he was so appalled by the violence of his impulses that he has given up Suzima and his freedom in order to overcome his 'natural' propensity to evil. In the penultimate section of the story, we see him obsessively building a stone wall round the monastery (known as 'The Refuge'), indicative of his desire to keep the world and passion at bay. One day, he is distracted from his task by 'the scent of approaching danger', which reawakens his physical being: he feels his 'pulses [...] clamoring' and his flesh 'tingled and burned as if pricked with nettles'. Suzima appears, alone, singing 'the catchy refrain from an opera' (546). Without reflection he goes to her: 'He was conscious of nothing in the world but the voice that was calling him and the cry of his own being that responded. Brother Ludovic bounded down from the wall and followed the voice of the woman' (546).

James Joyce's short story 'Araby', written in 1905, three years after the publication of 'A Vocation and A Voice' and later included in *Dubliners* (1914), deals with analogous subject matter. The narrator is an unnamed boy, whose entry into puberty similarly results in a passion of conflicting desires. Brought up by his aunt and uncle in a Catholic household, he yearns for escape. The possibility of freedom manifests itself in two ways that become fused in an exotic 'other' which constantly 'calls' to him, just as Suzima's voice calls the boy. He has a friend called Mangan, whose sister, with her white curving neck and soft hair, arouses his sexual desire: 'her name was like a summons to all my foolish blood'.[15] Araby, the 'Grand Oriental Fête' (which was actually held in Dublin in 1894) stands for all that is different from the dark, damp routine of his daily life in the Irish city: 'The syllables of the word *Araby* were called to me through the silence in which my soul luxuriated and cast an eastern enchantment over me.'[16] The girl and the fête become linked in the story, the exotic nature of the oriental bazaar suggesting the erotic strangeness of the girl's body and vice versa. Both hint at a world of temptation and exciting possibilities that might result in a new self. The narrator, like Chopin's 'boy', becomes besieged by conflicting emotions and passions but decides to embrace them instead of renouncing them. He promises Mangan's sister that he will bring her something back from the bazaar, but his plan is ruined by the fact that his uncle – who has promised to fund the outing – is late home from work. Arriving at the bazaar well into the evening, he finds it almost over, and his quest – for a gift, for the exotic, for escape, for another 'self' – is defeated: 'Gazing up into the darkness I saw myself as a creature driven and derided by vanity; and my eyes burned with anguish and anger.'[17]

Although both tales feature sensitive young boys who try to escape the 'nets' of an ordinary life, the endings of the two stories are quite distinct. Chopin's story closes in a way that seems more in tune with the life-affirming choices of Molly Bloom or Stephen Dedalus than with the stasis of 'Araby' which – like most of the stories in *Dubliners* – emphasises entrapment and stagnation. Both stories, however, leave many questions unanswered. Joyce's tale leaves us to work out the nature of his narrator's insight into himself and its consequence for his future life. What is the cause of his 'anger'? Does the word 'vanity' suggest that he has suddenly seen through what Chopin calls in her story 'the garb of romance' (537), just as he has seen through the bazaar as a rather cheap money-making exercise? Does it suggest that he will return to the fold of Catholicism and the Christian vision of life on this earth as mere 'vanity'? Or will his disappointment confirm his need for escape from the nets of Catholicism and dreary Dublin, presaging the choices made by Stephen Dedalus? Chopin's story is also more ambiguous than it might at first seem. Read from a Catholic perspective, 'A Vocation and A Voice' is the story of a fall into temptation, of a man unable to transcend his own physical instincts despite his desire to dedicate himself to God. Read from a Darwinian perspective, the ending is predictable and endorses the notion that the instincts we all share are, for most of us, irresistible. Seen through the lens of romantic love, the tale seems to follow – almost to the point of parody – the plot convention of the happy ending in which true love triumphs over all. It can also be interpreted as a portrait of the artist as a young man who finally chooses sensuality, sexuality and art rather than religion, asceticism and the Church. Chopin's closure suggests all of these possibilities but privileges none of them. 'For nothing', as James thinks to himself in Woolf's *To the Lighthouse*, 'was simply one thing'.[18]

The insight that life itself is given meaning through a choice of competing narratives is something we associate more commonly with the twentieth century than with the nineteenth, but writers such as Chopin were edging towards it during the *fin de siècle*. The nameless 'boy' is indicative of all mankind (driven by needs and rites of passage we recognise as universal), whereas the tale of Brother Ludovic is the tale of an individual who makes choices. His choices pose further questions for the reader. How far do the boy's various rebellions – rejecting family life for a life on the road, then rejecting the road in order to follow God, finally rejecting the monastic life in order to follow the call, or the 'voice', of the body – presage 'intense dissatisfaction' with tradition and convention? Can transcendence be found in the flesh as well as the spirit? Which is the 'vocation' and which is the 'voice'? Why have they become so diametrically opposed in the western world? In what ways do Freud's theories of the unconscious (he was working on *The Interpretation of Dreams* during the 1890s) force us to reconsider the suppression of sexual desire demanded by Christianity, especially in its Catholic form? How will Catholicism survive in a world that adopts a Darwinian or a Freudian narrative in order to explain human behaviour?[19] How far does the conflict between such 'grand narratives'[20] or metanarratives replicate and coincide with the divided consciousness of the modern subject? These are questions endemic to much modernist writing. They also more starkly inform Chopin's 'Two Portraits' (earlier entitled 'The Nun and the Wanton'), a story that gives us alternative narratives for the life of the same woman and that daringly explores the idea that spirituality and sexuality are two sides of the same coin. The woman's different choices – in one version, man and sexual pleasure, in the other, God and 'holy' ecstasy – result, in Janet Beer's words, in 'lives curtailed almost at the moment of birth by dedication to a single purpose'.[21] The implication is that the reader should not mimic the woman's choice – should not privilege one narrative above another – but should rather embrace plurality and multiplicity. Not surprisingly, 'Two Portraits' was rejected for publication during Chopin's lifetime. In contrast, 'A Vocation and a Voice', written a year later, suffered neither censorship nor rejection, Chopin presenting her ideas in a more palatable form for the genteel reader, but it does not quite offer the easy resolution it might at first seem to promise. Instead, the story prompts reflection on the workings of various grand narratives – and leaves the discerning reader to evaluate the collision between them as an aspect of late modernity.

Perhaps it was the curious ending of 'Athénaïse' that led the editor of the *Atlantic Monthly* to add the subtitle, 'A Story of Temperament', presumably in order to help clarify the meaning of the tale for magazine readers used to more straightforward narratives.[22] Superficially, this story addresses the plight of a young woman who married 'because she supposed it was customary for girls to marry when the right opportunity came' (430). Her escape to the city, aided by her brother, her residence in the house of Madame Sylvie, the friendship with Gouvernail – and his infatuation with her – all lead her back from whence she came, as biology proves to be destiny, and she returns willingly to her husband, seemingly reconciled both to him and to her future as a mother. One can imagine how conservative magazine readers of the 1890s might have seen this tale as that of a young woman brought to her senses by a combination of physiology and duty, her 'temperament' tamed by the fate in store for most young women of the time. More recently, of course, feminist readers have been puzzled by the story since it seems – unlike *The Awakening* – to capitulate to the idea that happiness lies not in rebellion but in conforming to the expectations of one's family and of society. Indeed, it can be read as a conservative text that expresses nervousness about the vulnerability of the modern woman in the city: Helen Taylor notes that as 'New Orleans was a perilous site for women [...] Athénaïse was much safer back with her dull husband on Cane River.'[23]

But Cazeau is not dull. He might be uneducated and unsophisticated compared to M. Gouvernail, but he is not dull. He is dark, 'distinguished-looking', serious and somewhat overbearing, evincing both respect and fear from those who know him. Financially astute, he is also charismatic and, it is hinted, a very sensuous man with a strong libido. At the beginning of the story, however, he regards his young wife as merely another of his possessions, worrying less about her than about the pony she used to visit her family – and is so preoccupied with his list of tasks that 'there was not a moment in which to think of Athénaïse'. He is well aware of her 'growing aversion' to him (427) – fuelled, he suspects, by her visits to her family ten miles away. His solution to this unhappy situation is to seek control: 'He would find means to keep her at home hereafter' (418). Chopin makes it clear within the first two sections of the story that Cazeau sees his wife as both object of desire and as a child to be disciplined: she is a possession and in no way to be regarded as his equal. In this respect, he typifies the traditional nineteenth-century male attitude to women, so it is not surprising to find that the young woman's parents regard him highly and feel that their daughter has made a good marriage. They are therefore shocked at her decision not to return to her husband. Athénaïse's brother Montéclin, whose love for his sister seems unusually intense, thinks otherwise. Indeed, he encourages her to consider separation and to pursue a settlement.

Athénaïse realises, however, that she has none of the normal grounds for such a separation. Her husband does not abuse her in any obvious way; like the later Edna Pontellier, she merely hates the state of marriage: 'I hate being Mrs. Cazeau, an' would want to be Athénaïse Miché again' (431). Although, as readers, we are drawn to sympathise with Athénaïse's feelings and situation, at the same time, Chopin's narrator provides counterbalances which prevent us from sentimentalising her and demonising her husband. It is made clear, for example, that Athénaïse is emotionally immature, 'perhaps too childlike' (432). In particular, a key incident forces the reader to reassess Cazeau and see him from a perspective other than his wife's. It occurs during the journey home from Athénaïse's parents' house, when the sight of an oak tree vividly reminds Cazeau of an incident from his childhood:

> He was a very small boy that day, seated before his father on horse-back. They were proceeding slowly, and Black Gabe was moving on before them at a little dog-trot. Black Gabe had run away, and had been discovered back in the Gotrain swamp. They had halted beneath this big oak to enable the negro to take breath; for Cazeau's father was a kind and considerate master, and every one had agreed at the time that Black Gabe was a fool, a great idiot indeed, for wanting to run away from him. The whole impression was for some reason hideous [...] (433)

The reader has to deduce why – apart from a revulsion at the spectacle of slavery itself – Cazeau suddenly finds the memory of this scene 'hideous'. It is, presumably, because he sees for the first time the parallel between himself as husband and his father as slave owner – and he realises, with sudden shock, how complacent he has been. Because he can provide for his wife and has not abused her, he thinks of himself as a good husband. In one moment, he realises that, in forcing his wife to return to him, he has allowed her no freedom, no choice. He has regarded her as one of his possessions, just as his father had regarded Black Gabe. This experience changes him profoundly. From this moment on, Cazeau renounces his traditional and legal authority as husband, and, when Athénaïse disappears for a second time, he writes to her, stating that he does not want her to come back unless she comes 'of her free will' (439). In so doing, he accords her freedom of choice. But Athénaïse is more concerned at this time with her choice of new gowns – and decides that one of them should be 'pure white' (442), indicating a nostalgia for her premarital virginal state. Indeed, what she enjoys at first when living at Madame Sylvie's is 'the comforting, comfortable sense of not being married' (444). This soon, however, turns into a feeling of loneliness which makes her glad of M. Gouvernail's company and conversation. This intelligent and wise man quickly comes to understand Athénaïse better than she understands herself: he realises she adores her volatile brother, Montéclin, 'and he suspected that she adored Cazeau without being herself aware of it' (446). For Athénaïse, her relationship with Gouvernail contrasts starkly with her marriage: 'She could not fancy him loving any one passionately, rudely, offensively, as Cazeau loved her' (449). In this one short sentence, Chopin subtly suggests that the young and ignorant Athénaïse has been sexually traumatised by a husband whose physical lust for his wife combined with nineteenth-century narratives of a husband's 'rights' so as to blind him to her feelings. The memory of the Black Gabe incident, however, has – it is implied – forced him to recognise her as a separate individual whose emotions, wishes and choices must be respected in order for him to have any self-respect. In this episode, Cazeau discards the value system of the old, pre-war South that has been shored up by insidious metanarratives of race and gender, and that has socialised him to treat both slaves and women as inferior. He rejects an order which has privileged him and given him a secure definition. Instead, he becomes a modern subject: a man whose identity is no longer secured by tradition but who is dependent on his own integrity from one moment to the next for his sense of self.

Athénaïse also unwittingly functions as an agent of change for Gouvernail. A man of integrity and a journalist who specialises in questions of the law and individual rights, it nevertheless takes a relationship with a naïve and beautiful young woman to bring home to him the ethical aspects and emotional pain associated with the matter of choice in love. Although he prides himself on his sophisticated liberalism – 'That she was married made no particle of difference to Gouvernail' (450) – he comes to recognise that his own happiness lies in her right to choose. This urbane and autonomous man is suddenly made aware that accepting the emotional freedom of the other person – less tangible but as important as any legal right – is a very painful business:

> When the time came that she wanted him, – as he hoped and believed it would come, – he felt he would have a right to her. So long as she did not want him, he had no right to her, – no more than her husband had. It was very hard to feel her warm breath and tears upon his cheek, and her struggling bosom pressed against him and her soft arms clinging to him and his whole body and soul aching for her, and yet to make no signs. (450)

However, Athénaïse's realisation that she is pregnant transforms everything, bearing her on 'a wave of ecstasy' towards a new sense of self. Looking in the mirror she sees a face 'transfigured [...] with wonder and rapture [...] Her whole passionate nature was aroused as if by a miracle' (451). No longer feeling emotionally isolated (even identifying with an oyster-woman who holds a 'dirty little' baby in her arms), Athénaïse feels suddenly happy: 'No one could have said now that she did not know her own mind' (452). On the surface, all seems resolved. However, Chopin's use of quasi-religious language suggesting transcendence ('ecstasy', 'transfigured', 'wonder', 'rapture', 'miracle'), together with the subsequent description of her as 'Eve after losing her ignorance' (453), sharply modulates a sentimental reading of the tale and suggests that we should not take Athénaïse's apparent transformation into a

Madonna figure at face value. Does she really know her own mind? Will the problems of the marriage really be resolved by a child? Will the physical maturation of becoming a mother be matched by a corresponding emotional maturity? And, of course, there is further irony in Chopin's statement that 'All day long she had not once thought of Gouvernail' (453), when we remember how Cazeau was implicitly damned in almost the same words for emotionally neglecting his wife. Indeed, Gouvernail's final acts of kindness are offered without any indication of his own pain, and he, perhaps, is offered as a touchstone for emotional maturity in this tale.

In the story's final section, Athénaïse returns to her husband thinking 'of nothing but him'. Athénaïse, suddenly sexually adult, returns her husband's ardent desire for the first time: 'He felt her lips for the first time respond to the passion of his own' (454). But the story contains clues that we should consider it as a self-reflexive work that invites the reader to think beyond the ending. One of these is Gouvernail's choice of reading matter for Athénaïse. Dismissing poetry and philosophy as 'out of the question' and not knowing her literary tastes, he gives her a magazine. This entertains her, and she particularly enjoys the pictures, although a 'New England story had puzzled her, it was true, and a Creole tale had offended her' (446). Chopin no doubt realised that this story, first published as a magazine story in the *Atlantic Monthly*, would similarly puzzle or offend some readers. Furthermore, Chopin's tale ironically frames three patriarchal narratives for woman. Montéclin, superficially the most rebellious and unconventional male character, almost entraps his sister in an early nineteenth-century Byronic tale of romance and transgression, perhaps as much to enhance his own glamour as to solve her problems. While recognising that she returns of her own choice, he therefore 'could not help feeling that the affair had taken a very disappointing, an ordinary, a most commonplace turn, after all' (454). He thinks he has given her choice but he has not really done so; instead, he tried to orchestrate her conflicting emotions to suit his own romantic agenda. On the other hand, Gouvernail represents a free-thinking, educated and very modern approach to life and is an attractive character who anticipates more liberal twentieth-century attitudes to relationships between men and women. But Athénaïse does not choose to become his city mistress. She chooses her husband, the rather surly dark man who has made her pregnant but who seems at least to have reassessed his own nineteenth-century views on women and marriage. The three men in her life have thus provided Athénaïse with three possible narratives: the tragedy of the romantic rebel whose destiny, like that of Madame Bovary, would inevitably be despair and then death; the story of the transgressive modern woman who chooses freedom above security; and the tale of the repentant wife. Whether her choice is driven by a

Darwinian biological agenda or whether it is a choice made out of a new awareness of self – or whether it is a compromise – is something Chopin leaves us to decide. She refuses to resolve the puzzle for the reader; the ending is intellectually inconclusive although the plot closes definitively with reconciliation.

In such instances, the ambiguous endings of Chopin's stories resonate interestingly with those of Katherine Mansfield. The closure of 'The Daughters of the Late Colonel' (1922), for example, leaves us unclear whether the death of their father will enable middle-aged Connie and Jug to exercise their new freedom of choice or whether they will remain forever trapped in emotional adolescence and uncertainty about their lives. Similarly, Beryl's sense of herself as desperately inauthentic ('I'm never my real self for a moment') lends the closure of 'Prelude' (1917) a rather melancholy air.[24] Mary Anne Gillies and Aurelea Mahood have noted that 'The pivotal moment in a Mansfield story is the instant in which competing or contradictory impulses converge and conflict.' This observation lends itself equally well to Chopin's fiction, as does their comment that:

> the continuing power of Mansfield's work can in part be attributed to its powerful and compelling analysis of sexual relations in the early twentieth century. Her characters struggle with the personal implications of the era's prevailing attitudes with regard to courtship, marriage and parenting [...] Individuals consistently emerge as socially constituted, and it is on these terms that her stories [...] evince an ongoing concern with the difficulties particular to emotional, physical, and sexual relations.[25]

The Awakening is, of course, resonant with such struggles and conflicts, and much ink has been spilt in the cause of their interpretation. Rather than retread such ground, which has been so well and skilfully covered by a number of critics, I wish to draw attention to the *way* in which Chopin focuses on conflicting impulses and competing narratives in order to emphasise choice. Elaine Showalter has noted that in the novel 'Scenes of lyricism and fantasy [...] alternate with realistic, even satirical, scenes of Edna's marriage.'[26] Section VI presents such tensions in miniature. It opens:

> Edna Pontellier could not have told why, wishing to go to the beach with Robert, she should in the first place have declined, and in the second place have followed in obedience to one of the two contradictory impulses which impelled her. A certain light was beginning to dawn dimly within her, – the light which, showing the way, forbids it. (893)

The Awakening is, above all, an exploration of 'contradictory impulses'. In the few hundred words that constitute Section VI, the stimulation of society (culture) pulls against the sublimity of the sea (nature); the warm company of others (sociability) competes with the lure of solitude. Edna is presented as a bundle of conflicting desires and choices, and this is illustrated elsewhere in the novella by the tension she experiences between the sensual fulfilment offered by motherhood and its obliteration of her as an individual. These tensions and themes are also, of course, the subject matter of Virginia Woolf's *The Voyage Out* (1915), in which the marriage of a gifted young pianist seems to threaten a similar obliteration of self and results in her drift into death – and of *To the Lighthouse* (1927), in which the conflict between Mrs Ramsay, the Victorian Angel of the House, and Lily Briscoe, the modernist female artist, must result in the death of one of them. However, it is not just in terms of content that Chopin anticipates twentieth-century writing. Her prose simultaneously draws attention to different ways of perceiving such conflict and its relation to Edna's situation as mother, wife, lover and putative artist. The language of Section VI moves between a lyricism that privileges Romantic values – 'The voice of the sea is seductive; never ceasing, whispering, clamouring, murmuring, inviting the soul to wander for a spell in abysses of solitude' (893) – and a briskly humorous and ironic representation of Edna's situation that encourages the reader to take a far more objective and perhaps rather sceptical view of her turmoil:

> In short, Mrs. Pontellier was beginning to realize her position in the universe as a human being, and to recognize her relations as an individual to the world within and about her. This may seem like a ponderous weight of wisdom to descend upon the soul of a young woman of twenty-eight – perhaps more wisdom than the Holy Ghost is usually pleased to vouchsafe to any woman. (893)

The difference in tone between these two passages signals to the reader that Chopin is self-consciously playing out different narrative positions, just as she did in 'Athénaïse'. She is also, of course, drawing attention to the possibility of a range of interpretations and narratives, both for character and for reader. In this sense, and many others, *The Awakening* anticipates what we now recognise as metafictional devices, presaging the way in which twentieth-century fiction will be drawn – both by modernism and postmodernism – to declare its interest in plurality. Certainly, the way in which her central characters struggle to find coherent identities while experiencing conflicting desires and fears anticipates the struggles experienced by characters created later by Joyce, Mansfield, Lawrence and Woolf. The fact that Chopin's characters often fail in their quests to realise an essence of self anticipates a major preoccupation of twentieth-century fiction: that the awakening of the sexual self is often accompanied by a sense of internal division and by feelings of turmoil and alienation. Even in her stories which carry 'happy' endings, authenticity is elusive for Chopin's characters: they remain isolated consciousnesses in a changing world. Choice is endemic to freedom, but Chopin's works seem to imply, to enter the 'zone of moral experimentalism' is also to enter a 'zone of danger'. Her writing provides no simple answers but plays out the consequences of choice in the face of sexual, social and emotional dilemmas. Both in style and content, then, Chopin anticipates modernism. This is not to deny the importance of authors such as Maupassant and Flaubert in her development as a writer. Indeed, as Morag Shiach – referring to the work of Peter Nicholls – has recently suggested, 'modernism begins when poetic writing develops a specific capacity for ironic distance, and it begins in nineteenth-century France.'[27] Kate Chopin's subtle use of irony and her emphasis on choice combine to mark the dawn of modernism in a particularly interesting way.

NOTES

1. Michael T. Gilmore, 'Revolt Against Nature: The Problematic Modernism of *The Awakening*', in Wendy Martin (ed.), *New Essays on 'The Awakening'* (Cambridge: Cambridge University Press, 1988), 59–87.
2. Marianne DeKoven, 'Gendered Doubleness and the "Origins" of Modernist Form', *Tulsa Studies in Women's Literature*, 8, 1, Special Issue 'Towards a Gendered Modernity' (spring 1989), 19–42, 36. Not all readers found this portrait of Chopin as a rather ambivalent feminist convincing: Anne Ardis, for example, did not accept that Chopin's use of the modernist form resulted in 'the muting of feminist content' in her work: Ann Ardis, *New Women, New Novels: Feminism and Early Modernism* (New Brunswick, NJ: Rutgers University Press, 1990), 201. DeKoven's article later became part of Chapter 5 in her book *Rich and Strange: Gender, History, Modernism* (Princeton, NJ: Princeton University Press, 1991), and she reiterates her reading of Chopin's modernism in her essay 'Modernism and Gender' in Michael Levinson (ed.), *The Cambridge Companion to Modernism* (Cambridge: Cambridge University Press, 1999), 183–4.
3. Sarah Klein, 'Writing the "Solitary Soul": Anticipations of Modernism and Negotiations of Gender in Kate Chopin's *The Awakening*', at <http://www.womenwriters.net/domesticgoddess/klein.html> (accessed 7 August 2007).
4. Emily Smith-Riser, 'Kate Chopin as Modernist: A Reading of "Lilacs" and "Two Portraits"', at <http://www.womenwriters.net/domesticgoddess/smith.html> (accessed 7 August 2007).
5. Joseph Allen Boone, *Libidinal Currents: Sexuality and the Shaping of Modernism* (Chicago, Ill.: University of Chicago Press, 1998), 80 and 76.
6. *Kate Chopin: A Re-Awakening*, a Louisiana Public Broadcasting production, first broadcast 23 June 1999 on PBS. See <http://www.pbs.org/katechopin/program.html>.
7. See Janet Beer, *Kate Chopin, Edith Wharton and Charlotte Perkins Gilman: Studies in Short Fiction* (Basingstoke: Palgrave Macmillan, 1997; 2nd edn 2005), 45–63 for an interesting discussion of the endings of Chopin's short fictions.
8. D.H. Lawrence wrote in a letter to Edward Garnett on 5 June 1914, 'You mustn't look in my novel for the old stable ego of the character', quoted in Vassiliki

Kolocotroni, Jane Goldman and Olga Taxidou (eds.), *Modernism: An Anthology of Sources and Documents* (Edinburgh: Edinburgh University Press, 1998), 407.

9. Martin Halliwell, *Transatlantic Modernism: Moral Dilemmas in Modernist Fiction* (Edinburgh: Edinburgh University Press, 2001; 2nd edn, 2006), 3.

10. Elaine Showalter, *Sister's Choice: Tradition and Change in American Women's Writing* (Oxford: Clarendon Press, 1991), 81.

11. Halliwell, *Transatlantic Modernism*, 3.

12. Halliwell, *Transatlantic Modernism*, 6.

13. 'A Vocation and A Voice' was written in November 1896 and published in the *Mirror* (St Louis) on 27 March 1902 (1027).

14. Stephen's sight of the beautiful girl in Chapter 4 of *A Portrait of the Artist as a Young Man* (published 1916) inspires both sexual desire and an aesthetic reverence for beauty and works against the pull of Catholicism in the novel.

15. James Joyce, *Dubliners* (Ware: Wordsworth Classics, 1993), 18.

16. Joyce, *Dubliners*, 19.

17. Joyce, *Dubliners*, 21.

18. Virginia Woolf, *To the Lighthouse* (1927, Oxford: Oxford University Press, World's Classic series, 1992), 251.

19. This particular question continues to provoke debate, of course. See, for example, Richard Dawkins' *The God Delusion* (London: Bantam Press, 2006).

20. See Jean-François Lyotard, *The Postmodern Condition: A Report on Knowledge*, trans. Geoff Bennington and Brain Massumi 1979, (Manchester: Manchester University Press, 1984), in particular, Chapter 10, 'Delegitimation'.

21. Janet Beer, 'Sexuality, Spirituality and Ecstatic Communion in the Short Fiction of Kate Chopin', in Michael A. Hayes, Wendy Porter and David Tombs (eds.), *Religion and Sexuality* (Sheffield: Sheffield Academic Press, 1998), 148 and 154.

22. See Per Seyersted's note to the story (1025).

23. Helen Taylor, 'Walking through New Orleans: Kate Chopin and the Female Flâneur', *Symbiosis*, 1, 1 (April 1997), 69–85, as extracted in Janet Beer and Elizabeth Nolan (eds.), *Kate Chopin's The Awakening: A Sourcebook* (London and New York: Routledge, 2004), 82.

24. *The Collected Stories of Katherine Mansfield* (Harmondsworth: Penguin Books, 1981), 59.

25. Mary Anne Gillies and Aurelea Mahood, *Modernist Literature: An Introduction* (Edinburgh: Edinburgh University Press, 2007), 50.

26. Elaine Showalter, *Sister's Choice*, 72.

27. Morag Shiach, (ed.), *The Cambridge Companion to the Modernist Novel* (Cambridge: Cambridge University Press, 2007), 7. She refers here to Peter Nicholls, *Modernisms: A Literary Guide* (London: Palgrave Macmillan, 1995).

10

HELEN TAYLOR

'The perfume of the past'
Kate Chopin and post-colonial New Orleans

Like many other 'regional' – that is, not Boston or New York – writers of the late nineteenth century, Kate Chopin participated in an ambitious post-Civil War publication project designed to open up the diverse richness of the USA to a growing reading public. The 'Local Color' movement involved making strange or exotic the particular and parochial – in terms of landscape, character, dialect and so on – and expanding the range and scope of the 'national' literature. One of many who took Louisiana as her subject, Chopin is recognised as having captured brilliantly the state's atmosphere, fine detail, ethnic and racial mixtures, fleshing out as she does the nature of this post-colonial society in a bruised post-bellum world.[1] Chopin takes pains to emphasise the specific linguistic and social differences between French-speaking regions of Louisiana and the rest of the USA. Quotation marks are frequently appended to phrases, sayings and aspects of Louisiana life and artefacts, and her use of dialects – mainly Negro and French Acadian, though also French Creole – is authoritative. Writing at a distance in St Louis, Missouri, following the deaths of her husband and mother, she was involved in interpretation and explication, not only to portray for readers the essence of a state that fascinated her but also to record a world that was disappearing fast into the maw of 'Americanness'. Much of her fiction records what a newly post-colonial state felt like within a larger homogenising nation, particularly in terms of the impact on its French Creole and French Acadian peoples.

Kate Chopin had a complex relationship with Louisiana's French culture, offering multiple perspectives on *fin-de-siècle* issues of gender, ethnicity and language. Her work has rightly been celebrated for its subtle treatment of the changing face of southern life, and especially of southern women. In all her work, female characters embody the tensions and transformations within post-bellum life. Louisiana, the state she adopted after marriage, became an increasingly exotic site, evolving imaginatively as she gained confidence in publishing fiction based on its mixed Catholic/Protestant, Native American/ French/Spanish/African American/English cultures. She had a good eye for the literary market, and her fiction played into readers' fantasies and desires, especially about the Francophone Acadians of Louisiana's Red River community and the French Creoles who moved between Paris and that notorious southern city, New Orleans.[2]

The latter was well known from earlier writers' work: Francophone, such as Alfred Mercier, Sidonie de la Houssaye and Armand Lanusse, as well as Anglophone George W. Cable, Grace King, Alice Ruth Moore (later Dunbar-Nelson) and others, who had already provided conflicting versions of a city known for its long history of colonial (French and Spanish) and postcolonial (American) interaction and exchange. New Orleans already lived in popular imagination as a city of unique racial mixtures, including the largest community of free people of colour, sexual pleasure and immorality, and it was often compared with the erstwhile colonial city of Paris – specifically in relation to a metaphoric femininity, with both seen as sites of romance, glamour and sexualised street life, particularly prostitution. By the end of the nineteenth century, both were defined as the sex capitals of their nations. This went against an American discursive tendency to masculinise cities as sites of power, capital and labour, contrasted with the reputedly simple small towns of America's regions, where women's domestic and parochial roles ruled the day. For Kate Chopin, New Orleans was a natural setting for much of her fiction (she lived there for the first nine years of her marriage and motherhood), while her Creole French heritage and marital links led her to interrogate what that 'American Paris' might be.

At the same time as this young married woman was enjoying her adopted New Orleans, an artist was on a visit to the city that would help to transform his career. In 1872–3, Edgar Degas, the only French Impressionist painter to visit America, stayed a mere five months in New Orleans, his mother's native city; having arrived in New Orleans in a state of crisis about the future direction of his work, he left with some sketches, paintings and a clearer sense of purpose about artistic production. Emily Toth and others have noted the interesting coincidence of residence in that city by Degas and Kate Chopin, living in similar areas, sharing business and social connections, and possibly meeting to gossip and share artistic concerns.[3]

The city they inhabited in the early 1870s was undergoing rapid change. The elite French Creole families, to whom Kate Chopin's husband, Oscar, and Degas's mother had belonged, retained a tight social stranglehold on the city at the same time as their economic wealth and cultural standing were in sharp decline. Degas was installed in grand style on Esplanade Street (the street in which Edna Pontellier lives in *The Awakening*) and produced the now-famous painting *A Cotton Office in New Orleans*, which appears to celebrate a thriving Creole city business. It features members of his own family but was actually completed after the collapse of the firm Musson, Prestidge, & Co, as the small cotton brokerage was swept away by larger national firms. Degas's sketches and painting, as well as his comments in letters and elsewhere about the city, reflect this loss of French hegemony, as well as economic crisis from the decline of the cotton trade and breakdown of urban infrastructure. The city was still badly damaged following the Civil War; its slave population had fled while freedmen and women were entering the city, needing work and shelter; there was widespread crime and disease. Meanwhile, the Creoles – cosmopolitan and urbane – continued to speak French and talk as if they were Parisians; they read French newspapers, visited French relatives and discussed French politics. Degas picked up the strongly nostalgic and backward-looking tone of the Creole community, suggesting that 'the perfume of the past has not quite evaporated'.[4]

Degas's perspective, coming as it did from a French artist of complex mixed-race heritage visiting his mother's native city, demonstrates both the familiarity of such a culture to European sensibility but also its utter strangeness. For New Orleans has always been (despite its claims to be utterly unique) a *southern* city, and Degas witnessed its struggle – cosmopolitan as it was but still in thrall to its rural hinterland – to position itself economically and culturally within a challenging post-colonial and post-bellum period. Although Degas was apparently dazzled by the city's colours, racial mixtures and visual delights, he reflected little of this in his subdued portraits of domestic interiors, such as *Children on a Doorstep* (1872), in which four children are guarded by a shadowy quadroon nurse, or his three portraits of his brother René's pregnant, blind wife. Rather than a hub of cotton, banking and land management run by interrelated wealthy planters and agents, his New Orleans remains a private, feminised Catholic city of racial and sexual secrets, shadows and patriarchal surveillance.

Like Degas, Chopin – from mixed Irish and French background and married into a conservative French Creole family – was fascinated by this city in which she was always somewhat an outsider and treated her experience there in tourist fashion, walking the streets for hours at a time.[5] She too portrayed it as a city of agricultural commerce, linked to the rest of the state by its cotton, banking and land-management firms. In *The Awakening* (1899), she also gestures at the fragile state of the cotton market: when Edna provocatively moves out of the marital home, her broker husband is concerned not about *sexual* scandal but about loss of 'financial integrity', since it might look as if there were 'reverses' which would 'do incalculable mischief to his business prospects' (977). But, for Chopin, this private city's secrets and surveillance are focused on a woman who is not a native New Orleanian and whose gloomy Presbyterian Kentucky perspective is transformed by its seductive ambience. Like Degas, she was mesmerised by the city, but because she then lived on Red River among small rural communities that felt very far away, her work complicates easy assumptions about the contrast between simple pastoral life and characters and urban sophistication and knowingness. She demonstrates the dialectical relationship between the two, showing transformations of mood and feeling as characters inhabit unfamiliar realms. She also challenges literary expectations about a hierarchy of Louisiana character types, perhaps deliberately confusing the reader with dialects, languages and colloquialisms of the French Acadians, black plantation workers, black and mixed-race New Orleanians, French Creoles and white Protestant 'Americans'.

From the beginning of her short-fiction publication, Chopin subverts readers' lazy 'local-color' expectations. 'A No-Account Creole' (1894) is a good example. Wallace Offdean, a young, wealthy New Orleans man, visits as land inspector what his family firm describes as '"a troublesome piece of land on Red River"' (81) in Natchitoches parish. His fantasy about such a visit is to retire into this land as 'a sort of closet' where he can 'take counsel with his inner and better self'. Placide, the jealous Creole whose family originally owned the land, dismisses him as 'that d— Yankee' (88), and, despite Euphrasie telling him 'he's a Southerner, like you, – a New Orleans man', the Creole refuses to recognise any communality: 'he looks like a Yankee.' The 'darkies' (who read the white community better than most) all conclude quickly that Offdean is courting Euphrasie, foreseeing trouble between Placide and the New Orleans visitor. Offdean's business interest in the plantation ceases abruptly when he hears that Euphrasie (whose letters about its refurbishment had interested him greatly) is visiting New Orleans for Mardi Gras. The city offers sexual opportunities to out-of-town planters/landowners; Placide's brother Hector would have been willing to make his knowledge of the city 'a more intimate one', but Placide 'did not choose to learn the lessons' his brother was ready to teach – given his own agenda with Euphrasie. However, Euphrasie's attitude to her country-boy fiancé Placide is disturbed by her interest in Offdean, whom she seeks by 'scann[ing] the faces of passers-by' (93). Describing a 'business' meeting between her and Offdean, Chopin captures the sensual atmosphere of a warm New Orleans afternoon: moist air, rattling shutters and perfume from the courtyard parterres. The fact the couple are 'scintillant with feeling' (94) is then expressed through a passionate kiss conferred on Placide – a recurrent trope in Chopin's work, whereby passion aroused by one man is expressed to another by a confused and inexperienced woman.

The story to date appears to confirm an educated reader's expectations of the difference between a sophisticated urban lover and his rural hot-headed counterpart. The 'no-account Creole' – popular but also hot-headed – is the only one of the Santien brothers to work the plantation neglected by their father after the war, and, unlike his peers who become professional/city men, stays on at Red River, engaged to his childhood sweetheart, the overseer's daughter. Realising his love has been supplanted, he plans to kill his rival, and we anticipate a bloody end. The story unsettles expectations, however, when he absorbs that man's advice about thinking of his fiancée's happiness and quits the plantation with dignity, scattering the word that he has been jilted.

In a couple of early stories, Chopin appears to present the city/country contrast in conventional terms, albeit with uneasy closure. 'The Going Away of Liza' (1892) presents an Emma Bovary-style female victim who is foolishly swayed by her reading of novels into a life of sin. However, there is little doubt as to where Chopin's sympathies lie. Liza's novel-reading is the subject of colloquial speculation which demonstrates a limited patriarchal understanding of female desires and dissatisfactions: the local 'traditional prophet' predicts disaster because 'constant readin' in them paper-covered books thet come to her through the mail, an' readin's boun' to fill the mind up with one thing another in time' (112). To be different, or to be suspected of class aspirations directed toward urban life, is interpreted by the (male) community as false consciousness rather than legitimate restlessness with a dreary marital lot. When Liza returns 'bedraggled' to the marital farm, this 'hunted and hungry thing' embodies unspecified disgrace and failure. As with many a disgraced Victorian fallen woman, 'Whatever sin or suffering had swept over her had left its impress upon her plastic being', (114), and this 'impress' is one that recurs in Chopin's stories and novels about women's resistance to the constraints of their communities.

In 'Doctor Chevalier's Lie' (1893), another story about female victimhood, Chopin explores the relationship between claustrophobic rural community and anonymous city by focusing on a familiar tragedy in New Orleans's daily life. Doctor Chevalier is called to yet another murder scene, clearly a whorehouse where this was an 'oft-recurring event[s]' involving '[t]he same scurrying; the same groups of tawdry, frightened women bending over banisters' (147). The figure of surveillance, as often in Chopin, is the professional man – in this case the doctor who lives in an 'unsavory quarter' and mediates between the murdered prostitute and her family at home in an Arkansas cabin, causing gossip for a while. The sketch repeats the old story of a girl 'going away to seek her fortune in the big city', and, despite the twist of gossip that the doctor had 'cared for a woman of doubtful repute' (148), the focus is the repetitive nature of such a tragedy, together with the shrugging of society's shoulders. Throughout her writings, Chopin returns to the fate of 'fallen women' who were all too prevalent and constituted a subject of great civic concern in the American city of the 1890s.[6]

Chopin often offers playful variations on the familiar tropes of wicked city life and innocent, sexless Arcadia. In the sketch, 'A Harbinger' (1891), painter Bruno decides to revisit his rural model, Diantha, after a winter in the big city that 'seemed too desolate for endurance' following his summer idyll. Chopin prepares us for rural cliché, choosing a classical-sounding name, giving her hair 'the color of ripe wheat' and beauty 'crisp with morning dew' (145). He is clearly drawn to her as the epitome of a rural childlike innocence. However, there is a very un-Arcadian sexual explosiveness between urban artist and rural subject: when first leaving, Bruno kisses her, and 'the baby look went out of her eyes and another flashed into them' (145). As previously mentioned, the sexual awakening works to the advantage of another man since, when Bruno returns for a second summer, he sees Diantha's wedding; he had been 'only love's harbinger' (146) and – having been catalytic to desire – must get back on the train.

In 'A Sentimental Soul' (1895), Mademoiselle Fleurette's occupation of the New Orleans streets directly reflects her shifting emotional state. This respectable Catholic single shopkeeper, gradually realising she is in love with a married man, observes Monsieur Lacodie walk down the street from her shop doorway; she then self-consciously walks down Chartres Street past Lacodie's store not 'with her usual composed tread' but seeming 'preoccupied and agitated' – a clear allusion to sexual excitement (389). Having visited the dying man despite her Catholic priest-instilled guilt, she returns home in the darkness 'like a slim shadow […] glid[ing] rapidly and noiselessly along the banquette' (394), shaken that he did not request a priest at his bedside. Finally, after his death and the indecent haste of his widow's remarriage, Mlle Fleurette goes to confession a car-ride away from her usual priest and – volunteering this time nothing of her adulterous desires – walks home. 'The sensation of walking on air was altogether delicious; she had never experienced it before' (396). This is a decisive transformation in her emotional, and, clearly, religious life, allowing her to acknowledge her love and – in defiance of his widow – to tend her beloved's grave and appropriate his memory. Occupying the street with freedom and joy both empowers the sinful Catholic woman and – another familiar Chopin trope – liberates her to indulge her romantic desires alone.[7]

This epiphany anticipates the first solitary journey onto city streets by the eponymous Athénaïse (1896), who, staying in New Orleans during a trial separation from her husband, ventures forth having discovered her pregnancy and finds a new self-assurance alone in public space: 'She walked along the street as if she had fallen heir to some magnificent inheritance' (452). As with

Mlle Fleurette, she has gained a new proprietorial sense of her physical and social status which takes the form of embracing an oyster-woman's baby and demanding money from her husband's merchants. Both of them relish their surrender to a state of narcissistic indulgences, which is also vividly described in the brief story, 'A Pair of Silk Stockings' (1897), in which Mrs Sommers, a normally judicious and dutiful mother, unexpectedly acquires fifteen dollars which – despite herself – she spends on herself. Having bought luxury goods – stockings, shoes, gloves, magazines and a restaurant meal – Mrs Sommers enters a theatre to attend a play, sitting 'between brilliantly dressed women who had gone there to kill time and eat candy and display their gaudy attire'. The reference to the display of gaudy dress signals the woman of ill repute, next to whom she sits, and with whom she weeps over the tragedy, discusses the play and shares candy. Such mutual acknowledgement of female desires and appetites, in a theatre where the woman would automatically be associated with prostitution (regarded as one of the greatest threats to social order in the city of the 1890s), is gently reinforced by the reference to a man 'with keen eyes' (503–4) studying her face in the cable car returning home. Ever alert to gendered social regulation and control, Chopin alludes to the dangerous pleasures for independent women on the street and in public spaces usually barred to them.

For this writer, Frenchness – so central to New Orleans life and culture – signifies style and grace, as well as a certain emotional and social liberalism, lacking the hypocrisy and self-righteous morality of white Anglo-Saxon culture. An old gentleman in 'At the 'Cadian Ball' reads Parisian newspapers and praises the conduct of Creole planter Alcée Laballière as '*chic, mais chic*' and showing '*panache*' (223). 'Miss McEnders' is a study of Anglo-French non-communication, located in the St Louis of the New Woman, women's clubs and middle-class women's movements to clean up cities. As with 1890s New Orleans, the Anglo-American Miss McEnders prides herself on her surveillance of female morality and propriety, visiting Mademoiselle Salambre, the French seamstress of her wedding trousseau, in order to see for herself whether the 'whisper here and there' about character has any foundation. Miss McEnders is exposed as both a voyeur of a class and ethnic group defined as inferior to her own and also as a ruthless judge of her fellow women. Observing a child playing with 'mademoiselle', and being told the white lie that the child belongs downstairs, Miss McEnders explodes with high-handed rage at the seamstress, whose response is significantly nonchalant. Conceding that she has to lie about her single parenthood in order to obtain employment, Salambre claims McEnders would not understand, taunting the privileged woman with a French phrase she utters with crocodile tears: '"Life is not all *couleur de rose*, Mees McEndairs; you do not know what life is, you!"' (206). Similar French terms are then used to mock the limited moral perspective of this member of the Women's Reform Club. Miss McEnders's fiancé is described by the narrator as a '*viveur*' and by Mlle Salambre as '"*c'est un propre, celui la!*"' as she sarcastically praises McEnders for preaching sermons in '"*merveille*"' (207, 209). The seamstress – 'living in her sin' (207) – teaches the New Woman about the tainted fortune which funds her own 'white-souled' nature (205). This is classic Chopin: describing the ways women feel they must maintain barriers of difference and distance while ignoring the very real – and often compromised – ways their lives complement and mirror one another. In 'Miss McEnders', the New Woman and working single mother share a fragile class and social position. The protagonist's father and fiancé are well known for their moral turpitude not only to the seamstress but to every man on the street. In *The Awakening*, Edna Pontellier knocks on many doors in order to find out how others live and how to evaluate other lives. Unlike the sermonising Miss McEnders, the mildly Presbyterian Edna offers no judgement on others but, like the St Louis suffragist, she comes to understand the tensions and slippages within urban and racial identities and how fundamental to urbane bourgeois life is the art of hypocritical concealment or denial of uncomfortable truths.

The pressure of the city on confident female identity also features in 'Lilacs' (1896), in which Adrienne, Parisian singer-dancer (a profession suggesting dubious morality) makes an annual visit at lilac-time to the convent she abandoned in order to live in the city. Her visit saves her from her own thoughts and 'despondency', let alone the city's 'boulevard, its noises, its passing throng' (358). On her return, Paris 'engulfed her' (360). Her erratic behaviour towards her suitor/employer and employees is complemented by her dismissal of Zola's realist urban novels as so weighty that they 'cannot fail to prostrate you' (362). Her abrupt decision to visit the convent for the fourth time is described by her old *bonne* as insanity, something needing to be watched. Indeed, Chopin hints that the level of surveillance in Paris by manager, lovers, maids, is one of the main causes of Adrienne's annual flight. Naïvely so, however, for this is echoed within the convent, when her dangerous seductive powers (working their magic on at least one of the nuns) do not go unnoticed. She is barred entry, and her lilacs are swept from the portico.

'Caline' (1893) is a characteristic Chopin story of an unawakened young countrywoman stirred into awareness of life's possibilities, in this case by a train, en route from the North to New Orleans, broken down in her Cajun community. In a classic 1890s trope, the railroad offers journeys to new worlds and away from small, insular communities. Caline becomes the focus of displaced passengers, who cannot communicate with her because she speaks only Acadian French, while a young man sketches her as local colour and captures her heart. Caline moves to New Orleans but soon realises that finding her portrait sketcher is her sole purpose. The city lures with false promise and can offer only the pleasures of urban modernity to a girl who – through representation as a colourful and unique pastoral subject – has been sensually aroused. Like other such fictional figures, Caline cries alone and will doubtless return home to the log cabin and cotton field, because the young man who sketched her has inevitably disappeared into the crowd. Because its size and anonymity invite fantasies about fresh identities, the city offers erotic potential to several Chopin characters – not only Caline but also Esmée ('The Return of Alcibiade', 1892), Suzanne ('In and Out of Old Natchitoches', 1893) and Athénaïse. Return to the country follows early disillusionment – usually in reaction to absent or detached flâneuring men. Caline is lonely and homesick, her portraitist invisible; Suzanne is warned away by Hector, self-proclaimed '*bon à rien*' (265); Athénaïse's pregnancy saves her from a casual and destructive affair.

All these women walk the streets with dubious characters who act as part-chaperon, part-tempter, and Chopin uses this to suggest the gendered nature of urban spaces. In 'In and Out of Old Natchitoches', the boundaries of female presence in the public realm are spelled out. To the theatre and opera go two women, Suzanne and Madame Chavan, 'unaccompanied by any male escort', a journey described in terms of 'trotting along, arm in arm, and brimming with enjoyment'; however, to vespers, accompanied by Hector as far as the church door, they must walk abreast, almost occupying 'the narrow width of the banquette' (263). Chopin contrasts here the excessive, formal occupation of mixed-sex pavement space with the euphoric, playful female engagement with a patriarchal civic arena. This is followed by a description of a more orthodox meeting in a private house between suitor Laballière and Suzanne. Doors – front, parlour and side – open and close; these invite the entrance of Suzanne who bows 'a little stiffly' (263). That carnivalesque scampering about the streets is dampened to demure passivity indoors – where Suzanne learns the price of public surveillance as Laballière explains the dangers of being seen on the streets in the company of a dis-reputable man, convincing her to return home to Natchitoches. The story ends with Hector Santien, by public repute 'the most notorious gambler in New Orleans' (267), making light of his flirtation with Suzanne, walking alone down Canal Street blatantly inviting public gaze: 'He might have posed, as he was, for a fashion-plate' (266). Strutting one's stuff is appropriate for gamblers or discredited women, but female innocence is in peril in urban contexts. There is an echo of this, too, in 'At Chênière Caminada', when the young Claire Duvigné, who imitates a romance heroine in giving the boy Tonie a provocative gift, is soon to die '"from a cold caught by standing in thin slippers, waiting for her carriage after the [New Orleans] opera"' (316). Tonie's shock at hearing the news is rendered ironic by a singing mockingbird and also the coarseness of some women passing by, who 'laughed and tossed their heads' (317); these are the far-from-innocent women who can survive in the city.

In 'Charlie' (1900), Chopin creates a country-girl protagonist who aspires in vain to urban sophistication. For Charlie, New Orleans offers ideal versions of femininity: 'entertainment such as Charlie had not yet encountered outside of novels of high life', involving lots of shopping, perambulating, 'perpetual flutter, and indescribable excitement'. Chopin describes her poignant and risible attempts to shine in city fashionable life in order to appeal to young Mr Walton: from feeling sentimental attachment to her mother's engagement ring, she now 'look[s] upon it as an adornment'; and she uses curling irons on her short cropped hair until her head resembles 'a prize chrysanthemum'. Her enthusiastic response to the extravagances of city shops ('ribbons and *passementeries*') is regarded as slightly insane and vulgar but, undeterred even when in the Seminary, Charlie determines to 'transform herself from a hoyden to a fascinating young lady, if persistence and hard work could do it' (656–8). The story satirises this process of producing white ladyhood, as when Charlie asks her bewildered father if her moisturised hands are now as soft and white as her sister's and suggests she may one day become queen of the Carnival. This hubris is rendered ludicrous when Charlie returns to the plantation after her father's serious accident at the sugar mill; while watching near his bedside, she continues to fix her hair, mix ointments to whiten skin and polish her nails 'till they rivalled the pearly rose of the conch-shells which Mme. Philomel kept upon either side of her hearth' (665). When Walton's engagement to sister Julia is announced, the fruitless nature of such hard labour is revealed, and Charlie (her father's 'ideal son') reverts with relief to the 'hoyden' of masculine garb and horse-riding, throwing away her sentimental love poem and deciding to give Julia her mother's ring (the black servant, Aunt Maryllis, appropriates the sweet-smelling handgrease). The unusually moral conclusion of the story for Chopin, with uncanny echoes of Jane Austen's *Emma*, returns Charlie to the bosom of her home, close to her father and family friend, Gus, whose tentative proposal she now accepts. The artificial worlds of New Orleans and Paris – where her more 'naturally' feminine sisters are taken – contrast with the genuine affections and qualities of rural plantation life.

In Chopin's first published novel *At Fault* (1890), the life of leisured women in cities is similarly stifling and absurd. Fanny, divorced wife of the novel's female protagonist's suitor, David Hosmer, lives in St Louis a life that is 'very blank in the intervals of street perambulations and matinées and reading of morbid literature' (779),[8] while one of Fanny's friends, Mrs Worthington, uses her husband's books to support a bureau's legs or to hold down dry goods. She and Fanny have no sympathy for the southern plantation life that draws together Hosmer and Thérèse Lafirme. By a classic reversal of expectation, Chopin makes the St Louis women drably philistine and even uses the word about Mrs Worthington (781), while the rural Louisiana women are sophisticated and urbane. The most notable example of this is the least expected – Thérèse's black '*grosse tante*', her nurse from childhood, who is a Creole from New Orleans brought with the white woman to the plantation. In semi-retirement, Marie Louise is – in cuisine-obsessed New Orleans terms – truly classy: the most famous cook in the state, she was trained by the great Lucien Santien, 'a *gourmet* famed for his ultra Parisian tastes' (807), her only task now to act as '*chef de cuisine*' for her mistress's important dinners. Status- and class-conscious like all Chopin's black and white characters, she has no time for her fellow blacks, the plantation hands, whom she dismisses as '"*ces néges Américains*"' (807). The scene between the two women, when Thérèse visits her old nurse for coffee, is the most tender in the novel, spiced with French expressions and vocabulary that remind the reader of the women's alienation from Protestant culture and modes of expression.

The relationship between French Creole Thérèse Lafirme and Fanny, once she remarries Hosmer, anticipates that between *The Awakening*'s Edna Pontellier and Adèle Ratignolle, with the French woman's sensuality and tenderness, described as 'pretty Creole tact' (843), meeting an emotional response from the repressed northern woman (801). Fanny's lack of knowledge of French, however, underlines her lack of sophistication and, by inference, emotional intelligence: for instance, she refers to the famous New Orleans carnival as '"Muddy Graw"' (836). Her husband demonstrates his greater sensitivity by beginning to learn a few French words. Frenchness is always, however, under threat: Thérèse's nephew, Grégoire, is shot dead after rising to a taunt of being 'Frenchy' (851), a poignant death made more so by his mother's 'living now her lazy life in Paris' and one of Grégoire's brothers 'idling on the New Orleans streets' (853). In a soberly joyful conclusion, Thérèse Lafirme sails to Paris for six months following the accidental death of David's wife, returning sensualised and with a new awareness of her body in terms of clothes, other possessions and reading matter. She travels through New Orleans, where she is identified with the city itself, the air being 'soft and strong, like the touch of a brave woman's hand' (869). Urban pleasures and commodities, in both Paris and New Orleans, offer reparation and renewal to a woman who is coming to terms with her own moral culpability.

Throughout her urban fiction, Chopin alludes to social and racial difference which is also linguistic, suggesting the ways in which languages confirm identity and relationship, as well as foment tension and social or familial conflict. In 'A Matter of Prejudice' (1895), Chopin's critique of monolinguism and French Creole insularity is articulated through Madame Carambeau, whose heart is melted by her own granddaughter, whom she inadvertently protects and befriends. The lack of understanding between American English-speaking child and French-speaking grandmother is resolved when Carambeau crosses the physical and metaphoric line between the French and American communities, visiting the Garden District where her son lives with his American wife – who, in a neat ironic twist, speaks faltering French which her French husband, having been rejected by his prejudiced mother, refuses to teach his daughter. Lack of intelligibility, and thus understanding, is focused on language: Madame refuses to let the child be cared for by an Irish maid because of her 'original theory that the Irish voice is distressing to the sick' (285), while the black maid mumbles to herself in language 'unintelligible to any one unacquainted with the negro patois' (284). Like 'Charlie', unusually for a Chopin story, this appears to offer a moral resolution, with the family reunited happily and the matriarch resolving to teach French to her young granddaughter from whom she will learn English. There is surely also a political rebuke to Creole isolationism, anticipating the stronger critique four years later, in *The Awakening*. In 'La Belle Zoraïde', a more typically pessimistic story, the tale of the wronged '*café au lait*' quadroon maid is related by Negro maid Manna-Loulou to her white mistress, in standard English to its conclusion – until the narrator informs the reader that the two women 'really talked to each other' (308) in French Creole patois. Language can include and exclude, and its various traces in post-colonial Louisiana are mapped attentively in Chopin's fiction.

Significantly, in *The Awakening*, a novel which uses much French dialogue and expression, Chopin makes no effort to translate or footnote. The novel begins by offering a linguistic challenge (via a French-speaking parrot) and continues in that vein – frequently reminding the reader that its female protagonist cannot understand all the language around her and is thus uneasy about her ability to read and understand others. I would suggest that this late novel comes from a less reserved writer than the composer of short fiction who wished to explicate and translate French Louisiana culture, since Kate Chopin most completely found her own vocation and voice in this, her best work. *The Awakening* constitutes a sustained attack on the insularity of the Creole community and its inability to communicate with a wider Anglophone world, to which – by the end of the century – it had become increasingly irrelevant (something Edna Pontellier's own physical and emotional movement away from the community underlines). Edna is drawn to the quintessentially Creole Ratignolles: 'There was something which Edna thought very French, very foreign, about their whole manner of living' (936). Yet, paradoxically, Madame Ratignolle – despite all that 'lofty chastity' – is described as a woman with an 'entire absence of prudery' (889) who, along with other Creoles, makes Edna blush with tales of adultery, prostitution and *accouchements*. The Creoles are inveterate storytellers, mingling a Catholic French emphasis on propriety and a rather salacious delight in sinful or wayward behaviour; the fact that Edna understands only intermittently their language and discourse allows her to slip recklessly into their culture without understanding the possible consequences. As if referring surreptitiously or longingly to her fellow outsider in New Orleans, Edgar Degas, Chopin describes Edna's proposed trip to Paris, partly for her picture dealer who requests 'some Parisian studies to reach him in time for the holiday trade in December' (988). Edna's attraction to the Creoles' inclination for sexual obsession and fantasy (disguised as community tittle-tattle) proves fatal because of her cultural and emotional isolation and desperation. In post-colonial, post-bellum New Orleans, her social group has run out of time, energy and purpose, but there is nowhere else to go. Edna's fate is to challenge the hypocritical rigidity of the city's Francophone elite rump, since – like Kate Chopin herself – she aspires to social and sexual mores that are ahead of her time and space. Degas's 'perfume of the past' smelled rancid from the distance of St Louis, and the cool critical reception of *The Awakening* confirmed the explosive nature of this tale of female urban anomie.

NOTES

1. Janet Beer, *Kate Chopin, Edith Wharton and Charlotte Perkins Gilman: Studies in Short Fiction* (1997, Basingstoke: Palgrave Macmillan, 2005), Chapter 2.
2. For further information about New Orleans history (and complex terms such as 'Creole'), see Arnold R. Hirsch and Joseph Logsdon (eds.), *Creole New Orleans: Race and Americanization* (Baton Rouge, La.: Louisiana State University Press, 1992), and for information about its literary history, Helen Taylor, 'Paris and New Orleans: The Transatlantic Cultural Legacy of Prostitution', in Richard Gray and Waldemar Zacharasiewicz (eds.), *Transatlantic Exchanges: The American South in Europe – Europe in the American South* (Vienna: Verlag der Osterreichischen Akademie der Wissenscaften, 2007), 309–34.
3. See Christopher Benfy, *Degas in New Orleans: Encounters in the Creole World of Kate Chopin and George Washington Cable* (Berkeley, Calif.: University of California Press, 1997) and Emily Toth, *Unveiling Kate Chopin* (Jackson, Miss.: University Press of Mississippi, 1999).
4. Quoted by Christina Vella in Jean Sutherland Boggs, *Degas and New Orleans: A French Impressionist in America* (New Orleans, La.: New Orleans Museum of Art in conjunction with Ordrupgaard, 1999), 36.
5. Emily Toth, *Kate Chopin* (New York: William Morrow, 1990), Chapter 5.

6. See Alecia P. Long, *The Great Southern Babylon: Sex, Race, and Respectability in New Orleans, 1865–1920* (Baton Rouge, La.: Louisiana State University Press, 2004).

7. For a discussion of the female flâneur in Chopin's fiction, see Helen Taylor, 'Walking through New Orleans: Kate Chopin and the Female Flâneur', *Symbiosis: A Journal of Anglo-American Literary Relations*, 1, 1 (April 1997), 69–85 and Janet Beer, 'Walking the Streets: Women Out Alone in Kate Chopin's New Orleans', in Janet Beer and Elizabeth Nolan (eds.), *Kate Chopin's* The Awakening: *A Sourcebook* (London and New York: Routledge, 2004), 92–7.

8. Kate Chopin often alludes to literature (especially European fiction) as having a powerful influence on women's fantasy lives and personal dilemmas.

11

BERNARD KOLOSKI

The Awakening
The first 100 years

Because it was so far ahead of the times, *The Awakening* has had a turbulent history. It was rejected when it appeared in 1899, forgotten for thirty years, rejected again in the 1930s and forgotten for another generation, rediscovered in the 1950s and 1960s by scholars in Europe and the USA, embraced in the 1970s by feminists in the USA and the UK – and then accepted ecstatically by teachers, students and readers of all kinds. Today, it is reprinted in dozens of editions and textbooks, as well as in several translations, and is one of America's most widely read, most widely loved classic books.

It took 100 years for all this to play out, and there were contradictions along the way. Not all readers rejected the novel or forgot it, not all feminists liked it, and not everyone today is pleased with its omnipresence in bookstores and classrooms – but scholars are virtually unanimous about the ups and downs of its reception. We should, however, distinguish between the history of *The Awakening* and that of Kate Chopin's short stories. The 100 or so stories Chopin wrote throughout the 1890s were, by almost any writer's standards, more than merely accepted in her own time. Many of them appeared in America's most prestigious magazines, including *Vogue*, the *Century*, *Youth's Companion*, the *Atlantic Monthly* and *Harper's Young People*. Several were syndicated by the American Press Association. Twenty-three were published by Houghton Mifflin in *Bayou Folk* (1894) and twenty-one others by Way and Williams in *A Night in Acadie* (1897), and both anthologies were well received by critics across the country who praised the regional charm of the stories, their local colour, their realistic treatment of Louisiana Creole and Acadian life. When *The Awakening* appeared in 1899, Kate Chopin had every reason to think that her national reputation would ensure the success of her novel.[1]

But she misjudged the mood of the country. She had, it is true, been publishing short stories with unconventional subjects and themes – 'A Respectable Woman', 'The Story of an Hour', 'A Pair of Silk Stockings' and 'Désirée's Baby', among them – but those and fifteen other stories had appeared in *Vogue*, edited by Josephine Redding, which had a readership accepting of controversial ideas. The better part of Chopin's stories had appeared in more conservative magazines, some in family magazines, such as *Youth's Companion*, whose editors made clear to their contributors that the publications would be read by adolescents and children, as well as by adults, and that submissions needed to be prepared with that in mind. Kate Chopin was quite willing to compose stories suitable for children – she was, after all, raising six children herself – and she was comfortable writing for both traditional and progressive audiences.

The Awakening, however, went out to everyone. And this was America, not France, whose books and magazines Chopin knew intimately, because she had from childhood lived among French-speaking as well as English-speaking people and had read French as well as English and American literature. It was one thing for Guy de Maupassant, George Sand or Émile Zola to write in French about women exploring sex and adultery. It was quite a different thing for Kate Chopin to do that in English in the USA. Perhaps Chopin thought book reviewers would resemble her character Gouvernail, a newspaperman who attends Edna Pontellier's dinner party in Chapter 30 of *The Awakening* and whom Chopin presents in her short story 'Athénaïse' as a man of '"advanced"' opinions, 'a liberal-minded fellow' (444).

The critics were not at all like Gouvernail. They lashed out at the novel. We cannot know if they wrote out of conviction or out of an understanding of what editors and readers expected of them. They needed to be prudent in reviewing books, because the newspapers and magazines they worked for spoke mostly to mainstream tastes, to conventional values, to the religious and ethical beliefs of Americans well off enough to purchase them. A few reviewers praised the artistry of Chopin's book, its local colour and its realistic presentation of life, but most focused on condemning Edna Pontellier's behaviour – her sexual behaviour, especially – and her suicide, calling the novel vulgar, disturbing, morbid, disagreeable. 'It is nauseating to remember that those who object to the bluntness of our older writers will excuse and justify the gilded dirt of these latter days', one critic wrote. And Willa Cather, who went on to become one of America's major twentieth-century novelists, added that the theme of the book was 'trite and sordid. [...] Next time', she added, 'I hope that Miss Chopin will devote that flexible iridescent style of hers to a better cause.'[2]

The novel had hit a nerve. Even a decade later, Percival Pollard continued to rage against the book, although he believed it had been 'utterly forgotten'. He is bitter, vicious. He sees Edna Pontellier as representing a dangerous type of modern woman:

Edna became utterly unmanageable. She neglected her house; she tried to paint – always a bad sign, that, when women want to paint, or act, or sing, or write! – and the while she painted there was a 'subtle current of desire passing through her body, weakening her hold upon the brushes and making her eyes burn.' [...]

Ah, these sudden awakenings of women, of women who prefer the dead husband to the quick, of women who accept the croupier's caresses while waiting for hubby to come up for the week-end, and of women who have been in a trance, though married! Especially the awakenings of women like *Edna*! [...]

Ah, these married women, who have never, by some strange chance, had the flaming torch applied, how they do flash out when the right moment comes![3]

Pollard's presenting Edna's behaviour as a threat to society captures a dominant mood in Kate Chopin's America.

From all we can tell, the early reviews took their toll, and *The Awakening* was not much read for the next half century, although Emily Toth, Chopin's newest biographer, and other scholars have not been able to verify often-repeated claims that the book had been banned or removed from library shelves or that Kate Chopin had been denied membership in something critics called the St Louis Fine Arts Club. Recently discovered evidence, however, does show that in 1902 at least one public library, Evanston, Illinois – as discussed by Pamela Knights – did, in fact, take the novel out of circulation.[4] Chopin's short stories also dropped out of the public's mind for a few years, but, by the 1920s, anthologists were again reprinting her work, and at least eight of her stories were available in the USA before the Chopin revival of the 1960s and 1970s brought them all into print.[5] In 1930, Dorothy Anne Dondore spoke well of the novel, noting that 'it is one of the tragedies of recent American literature that Mrs. Chopin should have written this book two decades in advance of its time.'[6] But, in 1932, Daniel Rankin published the first Chopin biography, and *The Awakening* was once again dealt a blow.

Rankin stands at the midpoint between the 1899 publication of *The Awakening* and the 1969 appearance of Per Seyersted's critical biography and his *Complete Works of Kate Chopin*. As the only person to write a book about Chopin in the sixty-five years between her death and the publication of the *Complete Works*, he demands our attention. He had, in fact, what no other Chopin scholar would ever have again: access to Kate Chopin's children, relatives, friends and at least one of her publishers. Half a century later, Emily Toth needed to build her argument that Chopin had an affair by working with stories passed down to their families by people who knew Kate Chopin. Rankin was able to talk with those people himself. It is through his work that we learned much of what is to be known about Kate Chopin's life. Both Per Seyersted and Emily Toth depend upon Rankin for information.

Rankin admired Kate Chopin. An 'original genius', he calls her. She writes, he says, 'poetic realism' with 'exquisite care', she has a 'remarkable skill with dialect', and there is 'truth in all her writings'. But, he is convinced, it is with the short stories that Chopin shines – as *Kate Chopin and Her Creole Stories*, the title of his 1932 book, suggests. 'In Sabine', he writes, is a 'glittering weave of humor'; 'A Very Fine Fiddle' is 'one of the most quietly moving fragments in modern writing'; and 'Désirée's Baby', he says, is perhaps 'one of the world's best short stories' – an assessment echoed by critics and scholars ever since.[7]

But Rankin's critical judgement was impaired by his calling. His Chopin biography is unambiguously presented from the point of view of a Roman Catholic priest seeing life through what he understood to be Catholic dogma in the 1930s. Beginning with an introductory note, in which he lists his residence as 'St Mary's Manor', 'Father Rankin', as Per Seyersted would later call him, judges Kate Chopin's life and work by the standards of his church.

He cannot see Edna Pontellier except as a 'selfish', 'restless' and 'capricious' woman without 'courage' whose life is 'vacant', who has an 'unholy' love for Robert Lebrun and who awakens to the 'shifting, treacherous, fickle depths of her own passionate nature'. *The Awakening*, as he sees it, is 'exotic in setting, morbid in theme, erotic in motivation. [...] The reader, following Edna as she walks for the last time down to the beach at Grand Isle – well, what does he feel? Merely that human nature can be a sickening reality.'[8] Rankin forms no emotional bond with Edna Pontellier, feels no sympathy for her, finds nothing to respect about her. He is, as Daniel Aaron so eloquently phrased it, 'disqualified by taste and temperament from doing justice to the original qualities of Kate Chopin's mind'.[9] But his influence was great. Scholars accepted what he said and repeated his judgements, which were similar to those of the critics in 1899. Kate Chopin was a first-rate local colourist, a fine realist, a brilliant writer of short stories. *The Awakening* was an unfortunate mistake.

The Great Depression and the Second World War demanded that people pay attention to other matters, but by the 1950s a new generation of scholars began to recognise that Chopin's novel spoke powerfully to their times. The first hints of revival were in the air.

Cyrille Arnavon translated the novel into French and added an introduction praising it. Robert Cantwell wrote that *The Awakening* 'seems to me to be the finest novel of its sort written by an American, and to rank among the world's masterpieces of short fiction'. Kenneth Eble edited a paperback version of the book, saying it is 'a novel uncommon in its kind as in its excellence' and its theme 'offers little offense today'. Edmund Wilson, one of America's best-known critics, described the book as 'quite uninhibited and beautifully written'. And Warner Berthoff argued that the novel has the easy candor and freedom appropriate to its theme. It admits that human beings are physical bodies as well as moral and social integers and that the spirit acts not only by sublimation but directly through the body's life. Not many English or American novels of the period had come so far.[10]

These critics of the 1950s and 1960s confronted what had been written about *The Awakening* at the turn into the twentieth century and later. They rejected Daniel Rankin's insights and enticed people to read the novel for themselves. They threw the considerable weight of their critical reputations behind Kate Chopin and her novel. In fifteen years, they dismantled half a century of hostility to the book.

Larzer Ziff built on their work, devoting a chapter in his important 1966 study, *The American 1890s: Life and Times of a Lost Generation*, to Sarah Orne Jewett, Mary Wilkins Freeman and Kate Chopin. *The Awakening*, he writes,

> was the most important piece of fiction about the sexual life of a woman written to date in America [...] It did not attack the institution of the family, but it rejected the family as the automatic equivalent of feminine self-fulfilment, and on the very eve of the twentieth century it raised the question of what woman was to do with the freedom she struggled toward.[11]

Then, in 1969, Per Seyersted published the volumes that were to give Kate Chopin an international reputation.

Seyersted's work is about changing context. His critical biography and his introduction to *The Complete Works of Kate Chopin* position *The Awakening* in relation to Chopin's other work, examine it alongside two millennia of western writers and wrest Kate Chopin free from her six-decade-long niche as an American local-colour writer or realist by anchoring her firmly in the canon of women's literature. Almost certainly, *The Awakening* would not have acquired the reputation it enjoys today without the insights and influence of Per Seyersted. His work has been expanded upon and corrected, but the fundamental directions he established for appreciating the novel have not been challenged. The way he saw the book in 1969 is, in many respects, the way most readers see it today.

By gathering together Chopin's writings, Seyersted shows us how *The Awakening* fits with her other work. We can read the novel in the light of Chopin's 100 short stories, her other novel, her poetry and her literary criticism. We can see how 'A Pair of Silk Stockings', 'The Story of an Hour', 'Athénaïse' and 'The Storm' set out themes and motifs that the novel integrates into its narrative.

In his discussion of *The Awakening*, Seyersted sets up comparisons with a host of western writers, invaluable for future critics of her work and its

context: Guy de Maupassant, Gustave Flaubert, Margaret Fuller, Victoria
Woodhull, Euripides, Edwin Arlington Robinson, George Sand, Émile Zola,
Thomas Hardy, Madame de Staël, Henrik Ibsen, Jean-Paul Sartre, Simone de
Beauvoir, Erich Fromm, Joel Chandler Harris, Walt Whitman, Sigmund
Freud, W.H. Auden, Gaston Bachelard, Lord Byron and Charles Darwin –
along with the Bible. It is important to Seyersted, as it was important to Kate
Chopin, that people be aware of what he calls her 'southern setting' as well as
her 'global view'.[12]

Most important for Seyersted, however, was Chopin's place in the tradition
of women's fiction. His *Critical Biography* sets the tone in its preface, describing Chopin's 'ever-increasing openness and the growing artistry with which
she described woman's sexual and spiritual self-assertion'. His view of *The
Awakening* is complex and nuanced, and he goes out of his way to present the
book and the author of the book in the context of the 1890s. At one point in
the novel, he notes, Chopin introduces 'a discreet feminist touch', but, he
argues, she 'was never a feminist in the dictionary sense of the term, that is, she
never joined or supported any of the organizations through which women
fought to get [what one dictionary calls] "political, economic, and social
rights equal to those of men."'

> The great achievement of Kate Chopin was that she broke new ground in
> American literature. She was the first woman writer in her country to accept
> passion as a legitimate subject for serious, outspoken fiction. Revolting against
> tradition and authority; with a daring which we can hardy fathom today; with an
> uncompromising honesty and no trace of sensationalism, she undertook to give
> the unsparing truth about woman's submerged life. She was something of a
> pioneer in the amoral treatment of sexuality, of divorce, and of woman's urge
> for an existential authenticity. She is in many respects a modern writer, particularly
> in her awareness of the complexities of truth and the complications of freedom.
> With no desire to reform, but only to understand; with the clear conscience of the
> rebel, yet unembittered by society's massive lack of understanding, she arrived at
> her culminating achievements, *The Awakening* and 'The Storm.'[13]

Per Seyersted's work sparked an explosion of energy. The remaining years
of the twentieth century were heady ones for *The Awakening*. Almost, it
seemed, overnight, the English-speaking world discovered Kate Chopin.
Redbook, a mass-market women's magazine, reprinted *The Awakening* in
one 1972 issue. In the same year, the *New York Times* ran a headline: 'There's
Someone You Should Know: Kate Chopin'. Paperback editions of the novel
and of Chopin short stories, scholarly books and articles, Ph.D. dissertations,
newspaper pieces, teaching aids, study guides, films, videos and other materials appeared everywhere. A graduate student at Columbia University in New
York complained publicly that he had been assigned the novel in several

courses but *Moby Dick* in none. And Robert Stone published *Children of Light*, a novel about a production company making a movie of *The Awakening*.

Readers from all walks of life responded powerfully to Chopin. Here was her classic novel speaking to contemporary women's issues. And here was 'The Story of an Hour' and 'A Pair of Silk Stockings' and 'A Respectable Woman' and – almost too good to be true – 'The Storm', a remarkable story, a lovely story, a story decades ahead of its time, and one, no less, that had never been published. Teachers and book clubs took up Chopin with a hunger that had not often been seen in their environment, almost as if readers needed to make up for lost time, as if lavish attention today would correct half a century of neglect. And scholars published impressive books that have had lasting influence.

Barbara Ewell writes that the central question of *The Awakening* is 'How does one (especially one female) achieve personal integrity in a world of conventional restraints?' The novel, she adds, 'quietly implicates us in its probing of such moral questions as the nature of sexuality, selfhood, and freedom, the meaning of adultery and suicide, and the relationship between biological destiny and personal choice.' Peggy Skaggs argues that 'Edna's sense of herself as a complete person makes impossible her role of wife and mother as defined by her society; yet she discovers that her role of mother also makes impossible her continuing development as an autonomous individual.' Anna Shannon Elfenbein points out that

> while white male authors [...] broached the subject of women's sexuality, they permitted sexual passion only to lower-class women [...] Edna gains an independent sense of herself as a sexual being; and she defies race, class, and gender conventions regarding woman's sexual nature as she moves by fits and starts to a partial understanding of the obstacles to her personal freedom and fulfillment.[14]

Helen Taylor, although complaining that Chopin does not engage herself 'in the problems of race and southern blacks', writes that *The Awakening* 'challenges sexual taboos most radically'. Conflicts in the novel, she notes,

> center round Catholic sexual codes: the indissolubility of marriage is used by the creole community as both a constraint on sexual freedom (especially for women) and also as license for ritual sexual games. These must be played according to unspoken rules, the breaking of which inevitably signals ostracism and (in the case of Edna) ultimately death.[15]

Mary Papke echoes Seyersted in arguing that Chopin and Edith Wharton

> are not, to be precise, feminist writers. Neither woman aligned herself with the feminist movements of her day, nor did either label herself a feminist. Each did, however, produce what one might call, for want of a better term, female moral

art in works that focus relentlessly on the dialectics of social relations and the position of women therein.[16]

In *The Awakening*, she adds, 'Edna's death is unspeakable tragedy, yet one does hear in her story the constant murmur, whisper, clamor of another vision of life. Through her work, Chopin invites the reader to imagine a world in which woman's experience and desire are no longer marginalized or effaced but have become critically central.'[17]

Joyce Dyer devotes an entire chapter to Edna's suicide, concluding that the novel's 'universality and twentieth-century appeal come precisely from Chopin's decision *not* to complete Edna's journey toward selfhood [...] Because [Edna's] story ends prematurely, ends exactly as it does, we are forced to think hard about her life, and about our own.' And Christopher Benfey reads *The Awakening* in the context of the American Civil War, comparing it to Stephen Crane's *The Red Badge of Courage*. His 1997 study is important here not so much because of what it offers us about the novel but because of what it tells us about just how deeply rooted Kate Chopin has become in American culture. The book, titled *Degas in New Orleans: Encounters in the Creole World of Kate Chopin and George Washington Cable*, is only indirectly about literature.[18]

The most influential Chopin scholar active today is Emily Toth – in part because of her decades-long, tireless efforts to promote Chopin studies and in part because of her two Chopin biographies. Toth worked from the ground up. In 1975, she launched the *Kate Chopin Newsletter*, which, during its two-year run, published anything and everything that scholars and others knew or were discovering about Chopin's life and work. The *Newsletter* printed biographical data, original articles, abstracts of published books and articles, bibliographies of dissertations, schedules of scholarly meetings, calls for papers for upcoming conferences, notes about works in progress – whatever Toth could unearth that might shed light on Kate Chopin. The journal played an important part in Chopin's rising popularity among university teachers and students. It helped build a network of Chopin specialists and gave legitimacy to the field of Kate Chopin scholarship. Over the next three decades, Toth produced a host of articles and conference presentations about Chopin and her work.

She focused on how Chopin's life shaped her fiction. In her 1990 biography, she gives us not a new reading of *The Awakening* but a better understanding of how Chopin came to write the novel, how her childhood and family, her marriage and years in Louisiana, her friendships and, perhaps, her loves, shaped the book. 'How', she asks in the introduction to the book, '*had* Kate Chopin known all that in 1899?'[19] With this question as her starting point,

Toth set out to uncover whatever Rankin and Seyersted may have missed, to review the records, to talk with whoever was still available.

She concentrated much of her energy in Cloutierville, the Louisiana village where Chopin had lived with her husband. There she interviewed descendants of people who had known Kate Chopin, and she describes how 'the wisdom of a community of women' in Cloutierville convinced her that Chopin had an affair with a local planter. 'Embedded in her Louisiana short stories', she writes, 'and in *The Awakening*, was the romance of her life – the man she loved, then left behind, in pursuit of something that mattered much more. At a critical moment in her life, Kate Chopin had made the same choice that Edna Pontellier makes: She chose herself.'[20]

Working with what she frankly calls 'the gossip in Cloutierville', along with other evidence, including legal records, newspaper announcements and textual elements in the short stories and *The Awakening*, Toth builds the argument that after her husband died, Chopin had an affair with a man named Albert Sampite before moving herself and her children back to St Louis where she began her career as a writer. And, in a shorter, pithier, more confident, more personally grounded biography published in 1999, the centennial of the publication of *The Awakening*, Toth enhances her picture of Kate Chopin. She makes *Unveiling Kate Chopin* more woman-centric than her earlier biography, more inspirational, more therapeutic. The book, Toth writes, is not only about the content of Chopin's life but about the 'content of her character', about why she did what she did. And Toth speaks now in a new voice, speaks to women in the new century, the twenty-first century. 'We need to know', she says, 'about that kind of woman', the kind Kate Chopin was, 'a courageous woman [...] a solitary soul, a tough and resilient character who had opinions and who dared and defied. In a new millennium, we need to create – as she did – new and distinctive ways of awakening, living, thinking, and growing.' 'When we read her', Toth says at the close of her book, 'we know that she opened windows, and she gave us wings.'[21]

Other scholars worked at other projects. Thomas Bonner's *Kate Chopin Companion*, a dictionary of the 900 characters and 200 locations in Chopin's stories, including maps and other materials, has been an invaluable tool for scholars. Emily Toth, Per Seyersted and Cheyenne Bonnell's *Kate Chopin's Private Papers* updates Seyersted and Toth's earlier *Kate Chopin Miscellany*. It includes primary materials not printed in *The Complete Works of Kate Chopin*, as well as other documents important for Chopin studies. Paperback editions of *The Awakening*, with or without some short stories, were published by Avon, Rinehart, Bantam, Penguin, Signet, the Modern Library and other houses, as well as by bookstore chains Barnes and Noble and, recently, Borders, and some of those editions are introduced and edited by distinguished scholars – Lewis Leary, Sandra Gilbert, Nina Baym and Barbara H. Solomon. Margo Culley's Norton Critical Edition adds extensive background materials – including 1890s reviews – and is (in a second edition) widely used today.[22]

The Norton has been especially influential because it includes scholarly comments about *The Awakening*. Essays about Kate Chopin in published volumes are more likely to be cited by other scholars than those which appear in scholarly journals. The Norton includes edited versions of twenty-seven previously published essays or book chapters on the novel, ranging from Percival Pollard's 1909 commentary to a 1991 essay by Elaine Showalter. Bernard Koloski's *Approaches to Teaching Chopin's 'The Awakening'* is also widely cited. The volume contains twenty-one original essays about the background of the novel, the book's treatment of women's experience and the ways teachers use the book in their classrooms. And other anthologies of essays are often referred to by scholars. Harold Bloom's volume in the Modern Critical Views series gathers together versions of ten previously published essays or book chapters. Wendy Martin's anthology contains four original works. Lynda Boren and Sara deSaussure Davis's collection includes fourteen new essays, several focused on *The Awakening*. Alice Hall Petry's book of essays combines previously published works with seven new pieces. Other collections of Chopin essays have also appeared and can be found listed in bibliographies, and the website for the Kate Chopin International Society contains links to lists of books and articles.[23]

At the time of writing, in excess of eighty-five Ph.D. dissertations focused in whole or in part on Kate Chopin's work have been completed since Per Seyersted published the *Complete Works* in 1969: Robert Arner's being the first in 1972.[24] The Modern Language Association's online international bibliography of books and articles about literature and language – available at larger public libraries and at colleges and universities – lists over 350 entries related to *The Awakening*, in English, but also in French, Spanish, German and Japanese, among other languages, with additions appearing throughout the year.[25]

About half such entries are articles in scholarly journals – and many of those articles are in one way or another feminist in nature or focused on matters of gender. But many others are not, and the variety of subjects all of them treat is impressive:

- contexts for Edna's revolt: conformity, confinement, resistance, the search for selfhood, for self-discovery, for identity
- feminine sexuality, resistance to gender conformity, gender and power, gender and ethnicity, feminist cartographies

- maternity, pregnancy and birth imagery
- Robert, Adèle, Mademoiselle Reisz, Léonce, other characters
- Edna's suicide, the novel's ending, the relationship between Thanatos and Eros, sexuality and death
- the novel as a political romance, as a southern work, as naturalistic writing, as part of the American literary tradition
- homosexuality and phallic power in the novel, homoeroticism, gay and transgendered sensibility, Edna as a metaphorical lesbian
- narrative control, narrative stance, modes of disclosure, conversational analysis, maternal discourse, tensions between disparate discursive registers
- influences and intertexualities: Arishima Takeo, Simone de Beauvoir, Willa Cather, Theodore Dreiser, George Egerton, Ralph Waldo Emerson, Gustave Flaubert, William Dean Howells, Henrik Ibsen, Paule Marshall, Carson McCullers, Toni Morrison, Arthur Schopenhauer, Carol Shields, Algernon Charles Swinburne, Virginia Woolf, Zhang Jie
- Edna as Icarus, as Psyche, as Aphrodite
- psychosexuality and prospective shifts, depression
- the semiotics of food, the structure of dinners
- feminist criticism, the new historicism, psychoanalytic criticism, deconstruction, reader-response analysis, Foucauldian analysis
- the economics of the body, the economics of tension, Edna's expenditures, exchange value and the female self, women as commodity
- the significance of music, the role of romantic music, of Wagner's *Tristan und Isolde*
- strategies of art, of painting
- the Mexicanist presence, Hebrew metaphors, dress and undress, the novel as Utopia
- dissenting opinions on the novel's importance.

Kate Chopin would surely be pleased that a century after her death *The Awakening* has become a classic and that it is read as widely as almost any other American novel of her time. She would be astonished with how people today understand her book. And she would be happy, though not surprised, that much of its fame is tied to feminist insights. But she would object to being thought of as seeking to advance an ideology. 'Social problems', she writes, 'social environments, local color and the rest of it are not *of themselves* motives to insure the survival of a writer who employs them' (693). Inspired by the fiction of her French contemporary Guy de Maupassant, she wanted above all to tell the truth about what she had seen in her life. And 'truth', she argues, 'rests upon a shifting basis and is apt to be kaleidoscopic' (697). She seeks, she tells us, to record 'human existence in its subtle, complex, true meaning, stripped of the veil with which ethical and conventional standards have draped it' (691).

Chopin would be impressed with the subtle, complex nature of recent commentaries on *The Awakening*, with our attempts to recover the truth of what she is saying, with our need to discover our own truths in her work. 'Kaleidoscopic', she would call our efforts – exactly what she would want them to be.

We might ask, then: Is the novel no longer ahead of the times? Have we now caught up with it? Perhaps. But even a cursory look at recent published articles should give us pause. Like so much of the world's great literature, the book grows with us, reveals to us only what we are ready to see. Many of us find something fresh each time we read. *The Awakening*'s first 100 years may be just the beginning of its history.

NOTES

1. Information about Kate Chopin's life and work is drawn from Per Seyersted, *Kate Chopin: A Critical Biography* (Baton Rouge, La.: Louisiana State University Press, 1969) and the appendix to Per Seyersted (ed.), *The Complete Works of Kate Chopin*, 2 vols. (Baton Rouge, La.: Louisiana State University Press, 1969); from Emily Toth, *Kate Chopin* (New York: William Morrow, 1990) and *Unveiling Kate Chopin* (Jackson, Miss.: University Press of Mississippi, 1999); and from Emily Toth, Per Seyersted and Cheyenne Bonnell, *Kate Chopin's Private Papers* (Bloomington, Ind.: Indiana University Press, 1998).

2. Janet Beer and Elizabeth Nolan (eds.), *Kate Chopin's The Awakening: A Sourcebook* (London: Routledge, 2004), 58–60. These and other contemporary reviews of *The Awakening* are included in Margo Culley (ed.), *Kate Chopin, The Awakening*, 2nd edn (New York: Norton, 1994).

3. Percival Pollard, *Their Day in Court* (New York: Neale, 1909), 40–3.

4. Bernard Koloski, 'Kate Chopin: The Critics, the Librarians, and the Scholars', in Earl Yarington and Mary De Jong (eds.), *Popular Nineteenth-Century American Women Writers and the Literary Marketplace* (Newcastle: Cambridge Scholars Publishing, 2007), 471–85, 477–9.

5. Bernard Koloski, 'The Anthologized Chopin: Kate Chopin's Short Stories in Yesterday's and Today's Anthologies', *Louisiana Literature*, 11 (1994), 18–30.

6. Dorothy Anne Dondore, 'Kate O'Flaherty Chopin', in Allen Johnson (ed.), *Dictionary of American Biography*, Vol. IV (New York: Scribner's, 1930), 91.

7. Daniel Rankin, *Kate Chopin and Her Creole Stories* (Philadelphia, Pa.: University of Pennsylvania Press, 1932), 133, 138, 139, 168, 174, 177.

8. Rankin, *Kate Chopin*, 171–2, 175–6.

9. Daniel Aaron, 'Per Seyersted: Kate Chopin. A Critical Biography', *Edda: Scandinavian Journal of Literary Research*, 71 (1971), 342.

10. Cyrille Arnavon (trans.), *Edna* (Paris: Club Bibliophile de France, 1953). Robert Cantwell, '*The Awakening* by Kate Chopin', *Georgia Review*, 10 (1956), 489. Kenneth Eble, Introduction, *The Awakening* (New York: Capricorn, 1964), vii, xiv. Edmund Wilson, *Patriotic Gore: Studies in the Literature of the American*

Civil War (New York: Oxford University Press, 1962), 590. Warner Berthoff, *The Ferment of Realism: American Literature, 1884–1919* (New York: Free Press, 1965), 89.

11. Larzer Ziff, *The American 1890s: Life and Times of Lost Generation* (New York: Viking, 1966), 304.

12. Seyersted, *Biography*, 75.

13. Seyersted, *Biography*, 10, 102, 141, 198.

14. Barbara C. Ewell, *Kate Chopin* (New York: Ungar, 1986), 142–3, 158. Peggy Skaggs, *Kate Chopin* (New York: Twayne, 1985), 111. Anna Shannon Elfenbein, *Women on the Color Line: Evolving Stereotypes and the Writings of George Washington Cable, Grace King, Kate Chopin* (Charlottesville, Va.: University Press of Virginia, 1989), 142–3.

15. Helen Taylor, *Gender, Race, and Region in the Writings of Grace King, Ruth McEnery Stuart, and Kate Chopin* (Baton Rouge, La.: Louisiana State University Press, 1989), 155.

16. Mary E. Papke, *Verging on the Abyss: The Social Fiction of Kate Chopin and Edith Wharton* (New York: Greenwood, 1990), 2, 87–8.

17. Papke, *Verging on the Abyss*, 88.

18. Joyce Dyer, *The Awakening: A Novel of Beginnings* (New York: Twayne, 1993), 117. Christopher Benfey, *Degas in New Orleans: Encounters in the Creole World of Kate Chopin and George Washington Cable* (New York: Knopf, 1997). See also Nancy Walker, *Kate Chopin: A Literary Life* (Basingstoke: Palgrave, 2001).

19. Toth, *Kate Chopin*, 9.

20. Toth, *Kate Chopin*, 10.

21. Toth, *Kate Chopin*, 140. Toth, *Unveiling Kate Chopin*, xxii, 244.

22. Thomas Bonner, Jr., *The Kate Chopin Companion: With Chopin's Translations from French Fiction* (New York: Greenwood, 1988). Toth, Seyersted, and Bonnell, *Private Papers*. Culley, *The Awakening*.

23. Bernard Koloski (ed.), *Approaches to Teaching Chopin's The Awakening* (New York: Modern Language Association, 1988). Harold Bloom (ed.), *Kate Chopin* (New York: Chelsea, 1987). Wendy Martin (ed.), *New Essays on The Awakening* (New York: Cambridge University Press, 1988). Lynda S. Boren and Sara deSaussure Davis (eds.), *Kate Chopin Reconsidered: Beyond the Bayou* (Baton Rouge, La.: Louisiana State University Press, 1992). Alice Hall Petry (ed.), *Critical Essays on Kate Chopin* (New York: G.K. Hall, 1996). See also *Perspectives on Kate Chopin*: Proceedings from the Kate Chopin International Conference, 6, 7, 8 April 1989 (Natchitoches, La.: Northwestern State University Press, 1992); Nancy Walker, *Kate Chopin: The Awakening* (New York: St Martin's, 1993); the special Kate Chopin section of *Louisiana Literature*, 11 (1994), 8–171; and Donald Keesey, *The Awakening: Contexts for Criticism* (Mountain View, Calif.: Mayfield, 1994). For the website, see <http://www.katechopin.org>.

24. Robert Arner (ed.), Special issue of *Louisiana Studies*, 14 (1975), 11–139.

25. A recent thorough bibliography in printed form is Suzanne Disheroon Green and David J. Caudle, *Kate Chopin: An Annotated Bibliography of Critical Works* (Westport, Conn.: Greenwood, 1999).

FURTHER READING

Kate Chopin's novels and stories are available in various reprints and editions; those referred to by essayists are included in the **Primary texts** below. Throughout the volume the textual references are all to *The Complete Works of Kate Chopin*, edited by Per Seyersted. Full bibliographical references to articles, books and other texts are included in the endnotes to each essay. The **Selected Critical and Biographical Studies** below are to be considered as the starting point to any study of Chopin's life and works.

Primary texts

Bonner, Thomas, Jr. *The Kate Chopin Companion* (New York: Greenwood Press, 1988).

Chopin, Kate, *The Complete Works of Kate Chopin*, ed. Per Seyersted 2 vols (Baton Rouge, La.: Louisiana State University Press, 1969).

Kate Chopin, The Awakening, ed. Margo Culley (New York: Norton, 1976).

The Awakening and Selected Stories, ed. Sandra Gilbert (Harmondsworth: Penguin, 1986).

The Awakening and Other Stories, ed. Pamela Knights, (Oxford: Oxford University Press, 2000).

At Fault, ed. Bernard Koloski (New York: Penguin, 2002).

Kate Chopin: The Awakening, ed. Nancy A. Walker (Boston, Mass.: Bedford Books, 1993).

Seyersted, Per with Emily Toth (eds.), *A Kate Chopin Miscellany* (Natchitoches, La.: Northwestern State University Press, 1979).

Toth, Emily, Per Seyersted, and Cheyenne Bonnell, (eds.), *Kate Chopin's Private Papers* (Bloomington, Ind.: Indiana University, 1998).

Select critical and biographical studies

Beer, Janet, *Kate Chopin, Edith Wharton and Charlotte Perkins Gilman: Studies in Short Fiction* (Basingstoke: Palgrave, 1997).

Beer, Janet and Elizabeth Nolan (eds.), *Kate Chopin's The Awakening: A Sourcebook* (London: Routledge, 2004).

Benfy, Christopher, *Degas in New Orleans: Encounters in the Creole World of Kate Chopin and George Washington Cable* (Berkeley, Calif.: University of California Press, 1997).

Bloom, Harold (ed.) *Kate Chopin* (New York: Chelsea, 1987).

Boren, Lynda and Sara deSaussure Davis (eds.), *Kate Chopin Reconsidered: Beyond the Bayou* (Baton Rouge, La.: Louisiana State University Press, 1992).

Ewell, Barbara C., *Kate Chopin* (New York: Ungar, 1986).

Hirsch, A.R. and Joseph Logsdon (eds.), *Creole New Orleans: Race and Americanization* (Baton Rouge, La.: Louisiana State University Press, 1992).

Koloski, Bernard (ed.), *Approaches to Teaching Chopin's The Awakening* (New York: Modern Language Association, 1988).

    Kate Chopin: a Study of the Short Fiction (New York: Twayne/Simon & Schuster, 1996).

Martin, Wendy (ed.), *New Essays on The Awakening* (New York: Cambridge University Press, 1988).

Papke, Mary E., *Verging on the Abyss: The Social Fiction of Kate Chopin and Edith Wharton* (New York: Greenwood, 1990).

Petry, Alice Hall (ed.), *Critical Essays on Kate Chopin* (New York: G. K. Hall, 1996).

Rankin, Daniel, *Kate Chopin and Her Creole Stories* (Philadelphia, Pa.: University of Pennsylvania, 1932).

Schuyler, William, 'Kate Chopin.' *Writer*, 7, (August 1894).

Seyersted, Per, *Kate Chopin: A Critical Biography* (Baton Rouge, La.: Louisiana State University Press, 1979).

Showalter, Elaine, *Sister's Choice: Tradition and Change in American Women's Writing* (Oxford: Clarendon, 1991).

Taylor, Helen, *Gender, Race and Religion in the Writings of Grace King, Ruth McEnery Stuart, and Kate Chopin* (Baton Rouge, La.: Louisiana State University Press, 1989).

Toth, Emily, *Kate Chopin: A Life of the Author of 'The Awakening'* (London: Century, 1990).

    Unveiling Kate Chopin (Jackson, Miss.: University of Mississippi Press, 1999).

Walker, Nancy A., *Kate Chopin: A Literary Life* (Basingstoke: Palgrave, 2001).

INDEX

Kate Chopin is denoted by KC

Cambridge Companions To ...

AUTHORS

Edward Albee edited by Stephen J. Bottoms

Margaret Atwood edited by Coral Ann Howells

W.H. Auden edited by Stan Smith

Jane Austen edited by Edward Copeland and Juliet McMaster

Beckett edited by John Pilling

Aphra Behn edited by Derek Hughes and Janet Todd

Walter Benjamin edited by David S. Ferris

William Blake edited by Morris Eaves

Brecht edited by Peter Thomson and Glendyr Sacks (second edition)

The Brontës edited by Heather Glen

Frances Burney edited by Peter Sabor

Byron edited by Drummond Bone

Albert Camus edited by Edward J. Hughes

Willa Cather edited by Marilee Lindemann

Cervantes edited by Anthony J. Cascardi

Chaucer, second edition edited by Piero Boitani and Jill Mann

Chekhov edited by Vera Gottlieb and Paul Allain

Kate Chopin edited by Janet Beer

Coleridge edited by Lucy Newlyn

Wilkie Collins edited by Jenny Bourne Taylor

Joseph Conrad edited by J.H. Stape

Dante edited by Rachel Jacoff (second edition)

Don DeLillo edited by John N. Duvall

Charles Dickens edited by John O. Jordan

Emily Dickinson edited by Wendy Martin

John Donne edited by Achsah Guibbory

Dostoevskii edited by W.J. Leatherbarrow

Theodore Dreiser edited by Leonard Cassuto and Claire Virginia Eby

John Dryden edited by Steven N. Zwicker

W.E.B. Du Bois edited by Shamoon Zamir

George Eliot edited by George Levine

T.S. Eliot edited by A. David Moody

Ralph Ellison edited by Ross Posnock

Ralph Waldo Emerson edited by Joel Porte and Saundra Morris

William Faulkner edited by Philip M. Weinstein

Henry Fielding edited by Claude Rawson

F. Scott Fitzgerald edited by Ruth Prigozy

Flaubert edited by Timothy Unwin

E.M. Forster edited by David Bradshaw

Benjamin Franklin edited by Carla Mulford

Brian Friel edited by Anthony Roche

Robert Frost edited by Robert Faggen

Elizabeth Gaskell edited by Jill L. Matus

Goethe edited by Lesley Sharpe

Thomas Hardy edited by Dale Kramer

David Hare edited by Richard Boon

Nathaniel Hawthorne edited by Richard Millington

Ernest Hemingway edited by Scott Donaldson

Homer edited by Robert Fowler

Ibsen edited by James McFarlane

Henry James edited by Jonathan Freedman

Samuel Johnson edited by Greg Clingham

Ben Jonson edited by Richard Harp and Stanley Stewart

James Joyce edited by Derek Attridge (second edition)

Kafka edited by Julian Preece

Keats edited by Susan J. Wolfson

Lacan edited by Jean-Michel Rabaté

D.H. Lawrence edited by Anne Fernihough

Primo Levi edited by Robert Gordon

Lucretius edited by Stuart Gillespie and Philip Hardie

David Mamet edited by Christopher Bigsby

Thomas Mann edited by Ritchie Robertson

Christopher Marlowe edited by Patrick Cheney

Herman Melville edited by Robert S. Levine

Arthur Miller edited by Christopher Bigsby

Milton edited by Dennis Danielson (second edition)

Molière edited by David Bradby and Andrew Calder

Toni Morrison edited by Justine Tally

Nabokov edited by Julian W. Connolly

Eugene O'Neill edited by Michael Manheim

George Orwell edited by John Rodden

Ovid edited by Philip Hardie

Harold Pinter edited by Peter Raby

Sylvia Plath edited by Jo Gill

Edgar Allan Poe edited by Kevin J. Hayes

Alexander Pope edited by Pat Rogers